. . . I woke, ate, did the task assigned me, and had but one thought: "Why?" For the first of many times, I considered walking into the air-tight brick room with the next group of people. Why didn't I? The only answer I've been able to think of is that some inner, divine spark of life would not allow it. I sincerely felt that by living, I would one day bear witness. . . .

ABIDING HOPE

Bearing Witness to the Holocaust

BY

Benjamin A. Samuelson

AS TOLD TO

Jeff Shevlowitz

Published by Ulyssian Publications, an imprint of Pine Orchard Inc.

Produced for the Greta Savage Memorial Foundation.
9601 Wilshire Blvd. Suite 620
Beverly Hills, CA 90210

The Greta Savage Memorial Foundation (GSMF) is a charitable foundation
dedicated to educational programs, promoting tolerance between all ethnic,
religious, and gender groups.

Book design by Pine Orchard. Visit us on the internet at www.pineorchard.com

Printed in Canada.

9 8 7 6 5 4 3 2 1

ISBN 1-930580-49-5

Library of Congress Control Number: 2002116002

IN MEMORY
of those close to me
who were murdered by the Nazis:
My mother Rachel, my father Samuel,
and little sister Gitel Marim.

My sister Frieda who survived the horrors of the Holocaust
and went on to build a life for herself in Israel.

My sister Chana who went to Palestine at age 16
and helped build the State of Israel.

Also, the six million other Jewish victims of the Holocaust,
a million and half of them young children,
many of whom have no one left
except us to say *Kaddish* for them.

Finally, in grateful memory of Uncle Lou and Aunt Esther,
who continually helped my family when I was a child
and provided me with a home and parents
when all of that had been taken from me.

—Benjamin A. Samuelson

IN MEMORY
of my aunt, Lily Machicoff,
who introduced me to Mr. Samuelson.
Her warmth, love, and support
helped make this work possible.

—Jeff Shevlowitz

CONTENTS

ACKNOWLEDGMENTS

I wish to thank:

Aunt Tillie Szabo (of blessed memory), mother of Michael Savage for introducing me to my wife.

I wish to thank my wife Toby, without whose understanding, love, encouragement, and support, this book could not have been written.

Thanks also to my three children and their spouses, who offered support, understanding, and help whenever it was needed, and to my six grandchildren who were the inspiration for this undertaking.

Many thanks to Michael Savage, the Greta Savage Memorial Foundation and Cheryl Kane, Executive Director, for their dedication to, and support for, this project.

Lou Lenart, who was instrumental in bringing the first planes to Israel for use in the Israeli Air Force. With this support, I could be transported to a hospital from the battle zone during the War of Independence.

Marlene Bronkhorst, who read the manuscript and was immediately enthusiastic and determined to expedite its publication.

My deepest appreciation goes to the Eagle family. Norman and his wife Betty helped with constructive analysis and made suggestions that were invaluable. They also spent an enormous amount of time in preparing the manuscript for submission to the publishing industry. David and his wife Nancy contributed their knowledge, advice, and time on the legal paperwork needed before the book could be considered for publishing.

A special thanks to Dr. Carolyn Gravelle of Pine Orchard, a publishing consultant, who was a great help in getting this book published. Thanks, also, to Mary Pennomon, assistant to Rabbi Steven B. Jacobs.

And last but not least, I wish to thank Jeff Shevlowitz, whose support, patience, and time helped me bring my memories to the written page.

FOREWORD

In December of 1925, Benjamin A. Samuelson was born in Rumania. *Abiding Hope: Bearing Witness to the Holocaust* is the story of birth, death, and the journey of a man who lived to witness the Holocaust. It took Benjamin 50 years before he could begin to relate his story to Jeff Shevlowitz.

In the year 2000, I buried one of the survivors and witnesses of the Shoah. Leopold Page lived to tell the story of Oskar Shindler. Leopold defined the immortality of influence. For several years, I was captive to the miracles of the Holocaust as told to me by my dear friend Leopold. I have known many survivors who lived to witness and share their miracle of life.

As I read *Abiding Hope: Bearing Witness to the Holocaust*, I sat mesmerized. As much as I have read, Benjamin's telling of his narrow escape from death so many times leaves one limp. His narrative leaves your heart beating as his words and journey become so real. You become aware that you are Benjamin, buried beneath the clothes of the dead as he attempts to escape Auschwitz.

"After the earthquake and the fire comes the still small voice." That still small voice of a child and a young horrified man who watches as his 11-year-old sister is led into the gas chamber becomes the haunting voice that his generation and every generation, hereafter, must read. Listen to Benjamin's heartbeat from one concentration camp to another and then into freedom.

How many times have each of us wondered about some bitter aspect of our life that left us numb and distraught? Benjamin's journey into freedom is not just for him—but for humanity's sake. Through him, we have the opportunity to remake our own destiny.

Benjamin A. Samuelson answers the writer Graham Greene's observation that "we are all resigned to death; it's life we aren't resigned to."

L'chaim, Benjamin! Your journey was through fear and death. With each chapter, with each journey, you bring the reader to appreciation and life.

Rabbi Steven B. Jacobs
Woodland Hills, California
Hanukkah 2002

PROLOGUE

Why, after more than fifty years of silence, have I now chosen to speak of my experiences during the Nazi era? The question is a very good one. I ask it of myself often as I walk through the dark halls of my home in Southern California during the middle of the night, unable to sleep, afraid to dream, tormented by visions of events I managed to convince myself I had forgotten decades ago.

After my liberation and continuing until very recently, I consciously chose to say nothing. I felt guilty and ashamed for surviving when so many others perished. I was never one to shirk hard work, but I went out of my way to seek it out. For decades, no matter what job I did, I worked ten to fourteen hours a day, six or seven days a week. It was easy to explain that I did it to ensure prosperity for my family. I never admitted that I also did it in large part so that I would not have the time and energy to remember.

Retired now, my children grown with families of their own, I don't have the luxury of working the majority of my waking hours, keeping the memories at bay. One of the promises I made to myself during my incarceration by the Nazis was that I would someday bear witness, tell the world what I had seen. While remembering my experiences, I also recall that promise and feel ashamed that for over fifty years I never spoke out when so many other voices have been silenced.

There will come a time, not too many years from now, when no one who suffered at the hands of the Nazis will be here to be able to proclaim: *"I was there. This happened to me. I saw this."* In order to keep the promise I made more than half a century ago, I feel I must now tell my story, while I am still able to, in memory of those who can no longer bear witness for themselves.

Prior to my liberation, I was in four different concentration camps. I was there. This is what happened to me. This is what I saw.

PART ONE

Life

Rozavlea

I survived.

This simple, two-word statement sounds plain enough. It's the reason I'm here now. I often think about those words. Their meaning is easy to understand. What is more difficult is asking questions about how and why. There has never been any one answer to those kinds of questions. There has never been any good answer.

For many years, for my entire life, I ask how I was able to do this thing, to survive. I do not think only about my time in the Nazi concentration camps, though that may seem obvious. Recently, I was told that I was one of only six known survivors, worldwide, who had worked the crematoria at Auschwitz. For almost fifty years, I thought I was the only one. I would try not to think about it. I was rarely successful.

I think about my childhood as well as the times after liberation. I was in Sweden for a time, and then went to Palestine, where I fought the Arabs in order to help establish a Jewish homeland. I was there when Israel became a sovereign nation and needed soldiers. Fighting in the Israeli Army, I was almost killed on more than one occasion.

No matter how many times I review things that happened, I cannot really answer the question of my survival. I ask myself why is it that I have survived while so many others did not. I do not know the answer to this, though the question is never far from my mind. I think there should be some kind of answer, like on a test, right or wrong. It's not like that. I often ask myself how God could open the Red Sea to save the Jewish people and open the doors to gas chambers to kill them.

It is possible that it has been merely luck, capricious at best, that has been operating all of these years. This would explain, in part, why there has been no rhyme or reason to who lives, who dies. But, if that were true, where has God been? Would God allow a man's fate to be decided, with no thought or care? Or, even worse to think of, would God allow a good man to be murdered while an evil man enjoys life, health, and freedom? This is not the God of whom I was taught.

There were many times when I was angry at God, so angry I could think of nothing else. I realize now this anger was a validation of God's existence. One cannot be angry at something that never existed. Anger, even hatred, and love are closely related. They speak of a passionate depth of feeling and commitment. The opposite of love is not hate. The opposite of love is indifference. Only by looking back, do I understand that it was my anger that kept alive my faith in God.

If a person's survival depends on divine intervention, then it should be possible to understand why one lives and another dies. One's actions may have been pleasing to God, his soul righteous. But I have known many good, righteous people who are no longer here for me to speak to. It would seem God favors some over others. Why did God favor me above innocent babies? Thinking this way, I know this cannot be the answer either.

Perhaps there is no one answer, or no answer conceived within the soul of God that is comprehensible to an individual human being. Only now can I begin to grasp the idea that it was my enduring faith that was at least partially responsible for keeping me alive. In my time in the camps, I never witnessed the deeply faithful or religious take their own lives. It was certainly easy to do, a quick release from unimaginable torment. I witnessed many who chose this option for themselves. Doctors, lawyers, engineers—men who were highly regarded in their communities prior to the war. To a person, those who chose death were those who had their fundamental belief in God taken from them along with everything else.

Survival is not an isolated instance, a single event to be studied and dissected without considering what else is happening at the same time. It does not happen once, never to be repeated in a person's experience. It can be charted throughout the course of a person's life. It occurs in subtle ways that are easily ignored at the time. Thinking back, I can see it happening in some way, at some time, in every stage of my life.

I learned this early in life by listening to stories my father told about his own experiences when he was a young man. More importantly, I learned how one incident may have impact on another unrelated incident in the future.

When my father was a young man, he fought in the Hungarian Army in World War I. Most of the fighting he was involved in would now be called "hand-to-hand" combat. The weapons in wide use at the time were swords, mostly sabers. My father was skilled, but skill and luck are needed in nearly equal proportions when in combat. His lucky moment came about in a most unexpected way.

During a battle in which many men died from both sides of the conflict, my father accidentally fell into a large hole, a pit. Whether it was a natural crevice or dug out on purpose, I don't know. Four or five soldiers were already there. They were dead. My father tried to get out, but the pit was too deep for him to climb out of. He called out for help. Because of the noise of the battle going on, no one heard him. After the fighting ceased, he called again. A passing soldier heard his cries and pulled him out with a rope. By then, the fighting had moved on. He was one of the few to survive from his unit.

Years later, when he worked as a secretary for a rabbi in Bucovina, another state from where we lived, he was riding on a train for a visit home. Anti-Semitism was never far from the surface in Eastern Europe. Somehow, it became known to the other travelers on the train that he was Jewish. Some of the passengers thought it would be a good idea to tie up my father, attach the rope to the back of the train and drag him along.

Naturally, my father protested; but this only made them more intent on carrying out their plan. Only when he mentioned his record as an Hungarian Army veteran from the Great War, did sentiment change in his favor. Several old soldiers also happened to be on the train. They intervened on my father's behalf because at that time, their shared experience in the army was of greater value than my father's Judaism. There was still a bond of honor among veterans. He survived.

For me, survival began on the day I was born.

I was born in mid-December of the year 1925, in Rumania, in a small town called Rozavlea, 22 miles southeast of Sighet. Really more of a large village, it was home to approximately 3,500 people. The population included over 700 Jews.

I was the fourth child of five and the only son. The day of my birth came far earlier than was expected. I was almost two months premature. Nowadays, a child born so early, entering the world small and frail, would be in a hospital, in an incubator to keep the baby warm and healthy. No such things existed for me.

My parents were concerned, fearing their newborn son would not live. With no doctors or hospitals in our town, they had no one to turn to for help. Our house didn't even have electricity. In the entire town, there was only one telephone; and that was in the post office. They would have had to take me to the big city to get the kind of assistance they needed for me. I was too little. And even if it were possible for me to make such a journey, there was still little or nothing the doctor would be able to do for me.

My parents were intelligent people. They knew I must be kept warm and not simply the kind of warmth you find within the folds of a blanket. It needed to be the kind of warmth that I left too early.

My parents went into town and went to the slaughtering house. There, they explained the situation to the butcher. They arranged for the butcher to give them the stomach from a cow, cleaned and washed, and that is what they put me in. At least once a week, they would go to the slaughtering house and get a new, fresh, warm cow stomach. That was how I spent the first six or seven weeks of my life—warm and safe. Gradually, steadily, I gained weight and grew to the point where I was like a normal-sized baby, and my parents no longer feared for my life.

And so that day, born two months premature, and for the next several weeks, I was able to survive because of the efforts of my parents and the help of several cows I would never meet.

My own family was Orthodox Jewish, as were all of the other Jews in the town. At that time, we had no Conservative, Reform, or Reconstructionist. My parents owned a farm, a legacy from my mother's parents. The farm had been handed down through my mother's family for hundreds of years. In fact, my grandparents still lived in the house and we lived with them. The farm itself was huge, hundreds of acres. It went as far as you could see, all the way to the river. Then you would cross the river, and that would also be our farm. We grew crops; had a variety of fruit trees; and also had cows, chickens, sheep, horses, geese, turkeys, and ducks.

Of course, I don't remember the story about my being born. To me, it's simply a story my family would tell me. My earliest memory is quite different. So often now, as I reflect on my life, I cannot help but be amazed at the wealth contained within a person's life. There are so many incidents, which at the time seem trivial but taken together, give life texture and meaning. The things I've forgotten could easily fill volumes. Then there are the things I've experienced which I want to forget. There are even times when it's possible to pretend those memories have dimmed beyond recognition, or are gone altogether. Then, there are the things that, pray as I might, can never be forgotten.

That first memory of my own is one of joy, an affirmation of life. At its center is Moishe, my grandfather, *Zade* I called him in Yiddish, my mother's father. I was very attached to him, and he to me. He was like a father to me. I adored him. Minga Leah, my mother's mother, *Bubbe* in my native Yiddish, passed away when I was about six. She, too, was very special to me, and I to her.

My grandparents' house was really little more than one large room off a long main hall. It had no electricity or indoor running water. It was originally built next to the river for convenience; but as the river gradually swelled with spring runoff or winter floods and inevitably changed course, the house was moved.

It was made of logs, mud, and straw filling the cracks, resting on a flattened mound of hard-packed dirt, protected from rain and floods by close-set rocks around the perimeter. A few steps led up to the front porch which was itself made of hard-packed dirt. The hall and main room had wood floors while the walls were covered with a material similar to plasterboard that we whitewashed to give the rooms a clean, finished appearance. A couple of smaller rooms across the hall from the main room had only dirt floors because we couldn't afford the wood. We used the smaller rooms mainly for storage.

At the end of the hall was a large oven. In the storage rooms, we also kept chickens and geese. In the large main room, there were the stove, a table and chairs for our meals, and the beds we slept in arranged around the room. Naturally, the beds closest to the stove remained the warmest during the freezing cold winters. For added warmth, several family members shared beds. My four sisters slept together. My mother slept with Bubbe.

When the geese needed to be fattened up before being slaughtered, Mother would feed them twice a day, forcing corn down their throats, using a little oil to ease it, until she could fit in no more. The geese became so fat, their bellies dragged on the ground.

The chickens liked to sleep up off the ground, and would perch on the ladder leading up to the attic.

The chimneys from the stove and oven opened into the attic, which we used as a smokehouse. I often would sneak up to the attic, a small knife in hand to trim a little smoked meat for a snack. We also kept onions there to prevent them from freezing in winter.

I shared a bed with my Zade, even when Bubbe was still alive. He called me his little stove. I was young, and so naturally kept the bed warm. For an older person like Zade, this must have seemed to be a gift from heaven. With no such thing as central heating, the house was often cold, especially in winter. Had Zade been alone, he would not have been as warm. This way, fulfilling the need for physical comfort, led to an emotional closeness with Zade Moishe I would not have had otherwise.

When I was three, I started *cheder*, Hebrew school where I would study the Torah, the Hebrew bible. Zade made certain that it would be a happy, memorable day for me. He went with me, that first day. For Zade, it was not enough to merely walk with me, side by side. Instead, he lifted me up and carried me on his back. He also covered me with a tallis, the large prayer shawl.

Before we left, he had draped the tallis over me. I thought it great fun to be covered like that. He brought the tallis down around my shoulders, and looking at me, very serious, explained why he did it: "Today, your eyes will begin to view the beauty of Torah, the wonders of God as you learn to read His words for yourself. Today, you will see no bad things. Today, you will see only good things." He kissed me gently on the head, brought the tallis up over my head, and carried me to school.

Once we arrived at school, Zade set me down inside the door, taking the tallis from over me. A little piece of candy fell near me. It seemed to appear from heaven. Zade and the Rabbi smiled as I ran to get that bit of candy. Even at that age, I vaguely suspected that the Rabbi tossed it up in the air, when I wasn't looking, to make it seem as though it came from beyond the ceiling.

It was much more fun, though, to play along with the Rabbi when he told me an angel threw it down for me from the gates of heaven. "The angels," he told me, "want you to know that study is sweet." I smiled back at him, Zade at my side, the bit of candy already in my mouth. It was easy to agree with him. So far, study had indeed been sweet.

After that, my older sisters Frieda and Chana walked with me to school. Our town had many dogs used by the farmers to ward off wolves; but at times, the dogs themselves became aggressive. Chana was almost eight when I began cheder, and she felt it her responsibility to make certain her little three-year-old brother made it to school and back safely. As I walked between my big sisters Chana and Frieda, no dog dared to come near me.

Raised in a loving, supportive, extended family, I always felt safe and protected. Perhaps that is why, even at an early age, I took risks. Sometimes it was too much, the risks being dangerous for a child. For example, there was the time when I was very young, perhaps about four years old. Of the different fruit trees we had, I loved the apples the most. Without using all the modern farming techniques available now like pesticides and chemicals, our apples still managed to grow huge, sometimes to the size of small cantaloupes. I decided that the apples at the top of the tree were very important. I knew they must be much better than the apples near the bottom of the tree. I can't tell you now why I thought this. Maybe because they were closer to the sun. Maybe because they were closer to God. In any case, there was a large, beautiful apple at the top of one of our trees. That one was the apple I decided I had to have.

The tree with this apple was a very tall tree. I climbed to the top and was within reach of the particular apple I wanted, but a branch that can support an apple is not strong enough to support even a little boy of four years old. The branch gave way and I fell to the ground. I was in a coma for a couple of days. I know this because my mother told me I didn't respond to her, or anyone, for that time. I have a clear memory of reaching for the apple and falling, but all I remember of the days following the fall was hearing my mother cry and my being unable to speak or react in any way.

To this day, I can remember the sound of my mother's voice, soft, good-natured, rarely raised in anger or annoyance. She could not have stood taller than 5'7" and was slender, yet she possessed more than enough energy and stamina to take care of a farm, her aging parents, and five children. She and Father both had dark hair and eyes, something we all inherited, except Frieda, whose blue eyes resembled those of Bubbe Tzirl, and of course, little Gitel Marim, whose blonde hair and blue eyes made her appear angelic.

Later, I found a much better, safer, way to eat the apples. On Shabbes, the religious day of rest, we are not allowed to work in any way—not even pick fruit from a tree. I considered it enjoyment to pick a nice apple and bite into it. To do such a thing, though, was prohibited. Some of the apples grew to be so large that they weighted the branches, especially the lower ones. The fruit would hang low, sometimes near the ground. I would lie on the ground with those big, ripe apples hanging low above my head. All I had to do was sit up a little, and I could take a bite from the apple without having to raise a hand. True, it wasn't those nice apples from the top of the tree, but I didn't have to pick these. I guess now you would call it "bobbing" for apples. I just saw it as a way to have apples on Shabbes without working.

Zade Moishe would tell me stories about how, when he was a little boy, the same apple tree was there and old even then. He taught me to drink fresh apple juice by pounding the apple enough to soften it without breaking the skin. Then, you make a small hole in the top. You squeeze the apple and drink the juice as it comes out.

Growing up on a farm, I developed a deep love of animals. I can't recall a time when I didn't enjoy being around our animals, taking care of them, at times coming to regard them as cherished pets rather than mindless beasts. Of all of them, two stand out in my memory. One was a female buffalo and the other was a rooster.

As far as I know, that buffalo was on the farm before I was born. She was the only buffalo among all our cows. I have no idea how my family came into possession of her because a buffalo was a rare animal in Eastern Europe.

She gave milk, but not as much as a cow would. What she did give was extremely rich, from which we made excellent cheese and butter. In fact, it was of such a rich, high quality that we sold dairy products from her milk for a higher price.

I loved that buffalo. As young as five years old, I loved to ride her around the farm, holding on to her horns for balance. She was not nearly as pleased about my riding her as I was. Since I was always rather small for my age, I was at best a tolerable annoyance to her. I chose to ignore whatever discomfort I might be to her because I enjoyed the ride so much. She had her own methods of making her displeasure known. I will never forget the ride when I wanted to get from one side of the river near our house to the other. At about the mid-point of the river, she stopped. No amount of begging and pleading on my part could entice her to move. She simply stood, water up to her shoulders, which meant I was sitting in water up to my waist. I finally resigned myself to waiting in the cold river water until she felt like moving again.

The rooster, though, was an entirely different thing. I was only about five years old when I was playing in the front yard and heard the sounds of loud cawing and the unmistakable screams of terror from a young chick. I looked up to see a large, black bird, one of the biggest crows I had ever seen, carrying a chick in its claws. The chick might have been only a day or so old. The crow was flying low enough for me to see it and the chick clearly. I took my hat and threw it as hard as I could at the crow. The crow was startled enough to veer away sharply, opening its claws as it did so.

The chick fell to the ground, still screaming, running madly as soon as it felt solid earth under it. For the next few minutes, I ran around as madly as the chick, trying to catch it. I finally took my coat and threw it over the chick. Wrapped in the warmth and comfort of my coat, listening to me as I spoke quietly and soothingly to it, the chick finally calmed down. I fed it and brought it into the house. To keep it warm, I put it into the warmer we had built next to the oven for exactly that purpose. Since I knew the chick had to be kept warm, I felt there was no better place to put it. I had decided I would take care of it from then on.

The chick grew into a fine, and very large, rooster. I fed it by hand, every day. It followed me all over the farm as I did my chores. My mother went so far as to allow me to have the rooster come into the house with me. It became so much a part of my life, it ate off the table with me. That rooster was a part of my life for almost two years.

As much as I loved that huge, gorgeous rooster, to my mother, it was something to be tolerated for only a while. To her, no matter what my feelings were for it, it was still just a farm animal. By the time it was two, my mother felt it was getting old enough that the meat might start getting tough. Like other farm animals before it, it became Friday night dinner, which that particular night I refused to eat. To this day, it pains me to think about the fate of that beautiful rooster.

Because of the variety of crops and animals on our farm, we were never hungry. From the chickens, we had fresh eggs every morning and chicken dinner on Shabbes. From the cows and sheep and, of course, our prized buffalo, we had milk and cheese. When the time came that the cows no longer provided their share of the milk needed for dairy products, we sold them to one of the butchers in town. We also sold our lambs, steers, and goats.

The butcher skinned and deveined the animal, after it had been slaughtered according to the laws of *kashrut*, the various rules governing what can be eaten and when. A *Shochet*, a man specifically trained to kill animals in accordance with Jewish religious laws, actually killed the animals. Part of the ritual required making certain the animal was clean. Even if it passed, the butcher could not sell the whole thing. Only the front part of the animal could be sold as kosher meat because to be kosher, the veins had to be removed and the butchers did not have the knowledge to completely remove the intricately complex veins from the hind part. The butchers sold the back half to the Gentiles in town, but for much less money than the kosher meat. And just because the butcher bought an animal, that didn't mean he could sell the front half as kosher. It had to be checked first. This was done by blowing up the animal's lungs. If they were clean, the animal could then be sold as kosher. The butcher worried throughout that test. He couldn't afford to sell an entire animal at half price.

It may sound like we had more than enough, with the farm and all our animals, but we were far from rich in terms of how much cash money we would have. Many of the crops we would labor so hard to plant, grow, and harvest would sell for pennies. We had no tractors, no trucks. We had horse and wagon, our own legs and muscles. We fertilized the soil with what we had, usually cow dung. We had no modern irrigation system, no timed sprinklers watering the plants for us. When the plants needed to be watered, we carried pails of water from the river, making many trips, or from the well near the house. Once the crops were harvested, we would often take them to the city, where we could get a slightly higher price for them.

My sister Frieda found a job in town, working with a dressmaker, planning to learn the trade. She was paid nothing and helped clean the dressmaker's house, but she hoped to learn enough to begin her own business and help the family out with some extra cash. The reason my father worked away from home was that the little extra cash he was able to send us was more helpful than the extra hand would have been on the farm.

When a few pennies are counted as precious, a few dollars can seem like a fortune. My mother was one of eight children, five of whom had already left to live in America. Two brothers, Shimen and Mordechai, remained in Rozavlea. We all tried to help each other when we could, but all of us living in Rozavlea were poor. Uncle Shimen had nine children, while Uncle Mordechai was the father of ten. Both lived in houses smaller than ours. Of the two sisters and three brothers in America, we heard most from Uncle Lou and his wife Esther, who lived in New York.

Uncle Lou was not a wealthy man, raising his own family and making a living running a bakery; but sometimes in his letters to us, he sent five, ten, or even twenty dollars. The money might not have seemed like a lot to him; but to us, once converted to Rumanian currency, it was an enormous windfall.

We took his American money with us to the big city when we sold our crops and with it we could afford many of the things that would otherwise have been impossible for us to obtain. I'm not even referring to luxuries, but some staples we often did without. With Uncle Lou's money, we could afford many items we could not provide for ourselves, among other things, the precious artificial sugar we used in place of the more expensive real sugar, oil for cooking, kerosene for lamps, and white flour for *challah*, as well as wine and candles for Shabbes. We could afford to repair, or even purchase, new shoes along with other clothing. If I was good and behaved myself on that particular trip, Mother might even indulge in the luxury of buying me a penny candy.

Uncle Lou sometimes sent us an old, used suit of his. To him, it was something old to give away. To us, it was a wonderful, helpful gift. We took the suit, tore out all of the seams, resized it, and made a suit for me out of the material. Whenever that happened, I felt special and proud because for me, I had a brand new suit from America, something not everyone in town could boast of.

We always wrote back to Uncle Lou, expressing our thanks for his thoughtful gifts. I don't know if he ever realized how very helpful and how much those things meant to us.

Many other families from the town had farms. Some farms were larger than ours, some smaller. We all grew basically the same crops. With so much food available, no one family could make much money. Sometimes, it was the case where we had to throw things away. Since we had no electricity, no refrigeration, milk and cheese would spoil quickly. Often, we would give these things away.

Cows must be milked every day, as often as three times each day. They can get sick if they aren't. With no place to sell the milk and no where to store it, we still had a choice of what to do with it. While we could get a few pennies by selling the food, Mother had other plans. I clearly remember getting up early, well before the sun rose, to begin my chores. As early as I rose in the morning, I would see my mother, already up, dressed, working. She would have a milk can, filled with fresh milk. Or sometimes she would have cheese, sometimes fruits or vegetables. Whether it was a can filled with milk or food, she would take it to the home of one of the poor families in the town who could not afford even the few pennies to buy it. There, in the darkness before the morning sun, she would leave the milk for them. If it were fruits and vegetables, the food was wrapped up and left near the front door. She would never tell them who left the food. Somehow, we always managed to have the milk cans returned. We certainly couldn't afford to give away an expensive item like that, yet I don't recall anything ever being said about who had them or why, or who returned them.

It was a practical lesson in charity, what is called *tzadakeh*. Of course, I learned of tzadakeh in Hebrew school, ever since I started at the age of three. But to put it into practice is something else. Many people can easily tell you what they should do, but can never actually do it. The Talmud, the book of ancient Rabbinic commentary on the Torah, teaches the importance for people to maintain their dignity, that they aren't seen as needing or accepting charity. Also, that when one gives, it is best done anonymously, without the recipient knowing the giver. Thus, I learned the concept of tzadakeh from words at school, while I learned how to practice it through my mother's actions.

Rozavlea was in the state of Translyvania in the country of Rumania. It was common in that time and place—in fact, expected—for people to speak more than one language. I was no different. The language of my family, what we spoke at home, was Yiddish. From that day, when Zade took me to cheder at the age of three, I went to Hebrew school, where I learned the Hebrew language as well as studying the Hebrew bible. At the age of six, I started going to the public school. I already knew how to speak Rumanian, having learned it from the other people in town. When children are young, they naturally learn the languages around them. In school, I learned to read and write Rumanian.

The Rumanian public school we went to was only for four years. After that, if we wanted to continue to go to high school, we had to go to a town about forty or fifty miles away. There was no way I could go to that school. It was too far. We didn't have the money to send me there. We certainly didn't have the money for me to stay there. We were happy, though, with the four years I had.

The school's standards were high, their implementation very strict. If you didn't pass the tests they had at the end of each year, you had to take the classes again, until you did pass. I passed my tests, no problem. By the age of ten, public school was over for me.

At public school, we were taught all of the normal school subjects: mathematics, history, geography, reading, and writing. All of this study, of course, in Rumanian. As Jews, we were treated differently than the Rumanian students. The most obvious way was being forced to sit apart from other kids, at the back of the room. I usually sat with my cousin Hertz, whose father Mordechai was my mother's brother. We really mixed with the Gentile kids only at recess, when we played, and sometimes fought, with each other. It was simply the way things were.

Life was very much a routine. There were certain things that needed to be done. There were things we were expected to do.

We would get up early in the morning to help on the farm. There's a lot to do on a farm. We had to take care of the animals as well as the crops. We had lots of fruit trees. In addition to the wonderful apple trees, we grew pears, plums, cherries, and more.

After helping out with the animals, I would go to Hebrew school for an hour, sometimes a little longer. Then I would go to the public school. I would be there until about 3 p.m., sitting with the other Jewish students in the last rows. The teacher treated us little differently from the other Rumanian students. Even so, we were different from them, always seen as being other than Rumanian.

We knew how the Gentile students felt about us. Aside from usually dressing differently from the Gentiles, we looked different. Obeying the biblical instruction not to cut the *peyes* (the hair growing in front of the ears that become sideburns in grown men) the Jewish boys had long ringlets of hair in front of their ears. After public school was done for the day, I would go back to the Hebrew school, staying until late in the evening, sometimes until seven or eight at night, learning the Torah, the Hebrew bible.

When I got home, I would eat dinner and then do my homework for the next day's classes. I enjoyed school; but at times, it was a struggle. I was a fairly good student because I worked hard at it. At times, it was a challenge for me, and I enjoyed that, too. I'm glad I did because, like it or not, it was something we had to do. It was our routine. Five days a week, I would go to the public school. Six days a week, I would go to the Hebrew school. There was no school on Saturday. It was Shabbes, a day to rest.

For my mother, most of the Shabbes preparations began at four or five in the morning on Friday. Some things she prepared beforehand, on Thursday, like baking the challah, the bread made especially for Shabbes. Naturally, we tried to help any way we could, though mostly it was my four sisters who helped with Shabbes preparations. The meal generally consisted of wine for *Kiddush*, the point in the evening ceremony when we drink the "fruit of the vine" in recognition of God's bounty. This was an absolute must. Even if we couldn't afford meat, we had to have the wine. Fish was also a must. There was chicken soup and often meat or chicken, sometimes both, with a side dish of horseradish made red by mixing it with beets. There were stuffed cabbage, sweet carrots called *tzimmis*, and stewed or cooked compote made of apple or prunes. During and after the meal, as essential as the food, was the *zmirot*, the prayers thanking God for life, family, and food.

I would try to eat as much of the rich, fatty food as I could. It tasted so good and, not having it everyday, was very much a treat. My mother, without having to raise her voice, would sternly warn me about the hazards of eating too much, especially on an empty stomach. "Be careful, Benjamin," she would admonish. "Eating too much on an empty stomach can make you sick." I learned to be careful about what I ate.

Several years later, I saw the same scene enacted with Gitel Marim, wanting to overeat on the wonderfully tasting, but fatty, food. "But I'm hungry, Mama," Gitel would plead.

"All the more reason to eat only a little at a time," Mother replied. I had already learned my lesson well.

"If you eat too much, too fast, you'll get sick," I told Gitel, joining my warning to Mother's. Even then, though I followed Mother's instructions, I'm not entirely certain I believed her. Years later, though, my mother was proven correct. Refusing to eat rich food on an empty stomach probably saved my life.

Synagogue, or Shul, was the most important thing on Friday night. On Friday evenings, after the women had spent the day preparing the house and food for the Sabbath, we dressed in our best clothes. Mother lit the Shabbes candles, then only the men went to shul, the women staying home. After services, we came home to the meal my mother and sisters had prepared. Friday night was always nice with the whole family together.

The Shul I went to was, as I said, Orthodox. The men and women worshipped separately. Even as a child, I was with the men. My sisters stayed with my mother and the women, upstairs, able to look down at what we, the men, were doing. But they remained separate from us during the service. The Shul was always full. It had fine wood floors, the brick walls plastered over to give it a clean, finished appearance. The Ark, against the western wall, held the priceless legacy of the Synagogue: five or six Torah scrolls. The *Bima*, the table where the Torah rested, was in the center of the room, the men forming an eternal circle around it.

No one who was physically capable of attending services would ever consider not going. Actually, our town had two Shuls, one on each side of the town. On one side of town was the bigger one. On the other side was a smaller one. People decided which one to go to based simply on which was more convenient for them. Even so, there was only one rabbi in the entire town. The town was too poor to afford to have two rabbis. I happened to go to the larger Shul, the one that had the rabbi.

Neither Shul had a cantor. Instead, we had what is called a *baltfilla*. He's like a cantor, but isn't a professional cantor. He doesn't have quite the same voice; it's more for just religious singing.

The next morning, Saturday, is when the whole family went to Shul. This was from about eight o'clock in the morning until close to one in the afternoon. After that, we have a regular Shabbes meal, mostly food left over from Friday night, since no one is to work in any way on Shabbes, plus some previously prepared chopped liver and onions, eggs, and *chulint* (a wonderfully filling dish made with barley, beans, and beef). After the meal and a short nap, the men returned to the Shul until the first three stars appeared in the sky. Whenever my father was home, he would join us as well. Upon returning home, we had *havdalah*, the ceremony conducted at home, requiring a special braided candle, spice box, and wine. Havdalah separates the Sabbath from the rest of the week, marking the difference between the sacred and the secular.

Simply because the women did not spend as much time in Shul does not mean they felt less deeply than we did. For example, Bubbe Minga Leah was a very intelligent woman. It was unusual for a woman of her generation to read and write, but she did both. Even though I was very young, I clearly remember her leading her own study group, consisting of anywhere from ten to fifteen women, on Saturday afternoon. When the weather permitted, they would all sit under the apple tree near the house. There, Bubbe would read the bible to the other women, discussing and studying with them. It was a tradition the women looked forward to each week.

Saturday night, after Shabbes was over and we had havdalah, we returned to our regular routine. We took care of the animals on the farm, tended the crops, and took care of whatever else needed to be done. There was always something to do. Since none of us were allowed to perform work of any kind during Shabbes, we had to make provision for the animals. They still had to be fed and cared for. We did that by hiring one of the Gentiles from town to do the work that day.

My father traveled a lot when I was young. He was the secretary for a rabbi in another state, known as Bucovina. For most of my young age, I was raised, naturally by my mother, my Zade Moishe and my Bubbe Minga Leah. At that time, there was no such thing as an old-age home. Adult children took care of their parents at home.

We really only saw my father when he would come home for the High Holidays. At that time, he would come home for four weeks. He would also come home for the week of *Pesach*, Passover. Then he would go back to work.

About every three or four weeks, we would visit my father's parents. They lived in Cūhėa, about five miles away in the town next to ours. Much smaller than Rozavlea, it was home to only about fifty Jewish families out of the entire population. My father's parents were one of those families. I would look forward to these trips, with the chance to see my other Zade, Abraham, as well as Bubbe Tzirl, my grandmother, and tell them everything that was happening. This Zade was a salesman, dealing in religious books. He traveled all over the country, selling those books.

We would simply walk over there, because transportation wasn't the best. We didn't have cars. Just a horse and wagon to get from place to place. If the horse and wagon were busy working in the field, the only way to get anywhere was to walk. So if we didn't walk, we wouldn't have been able to see them as much as we did. In order to help make our shoes last as long as possible, we took them off as soon as we left town, walking barefoot until we approached my grandparents' town. Then, we stopped by a river at the outskirts of the town, washed our feet, and relaxed as our feet dried before putting our shoes back on. It simply wouldn't do for other people to see us walking without shoes, thinking we might be too poor to afford them.

By the age of six, my risk-taking had not diminished. At that age, I got hurt by a horse. To be honest, I didn't think of that particular instance as taking a risk. To keep the horses from going into the field and eating the corn, we kept them tied up. We hobbled their feet, tying rope securely around their back feet so they shouldn't wander around, or get into the fields tramping on or eating the crops. I felt sorry for one of the horses. Here I was, free to run around and play, and the horse had trouble moving and walking. So I untied him.

To thank me for my efforts, the horse kicked me. His foot, with all of a horse's power and speed behind it, caught me in the head. I was hurt very badly. My head was cracked almost in half. Some other children were with me at the time. They ran to get my mother, calling, yelling for her to come to me.

As you know, head wounds bleed more than any other. This was no different. They tried to stop the flow of blood from my head. It wasn't easy. With no doctor in the town and no time to take me to the city with our horse and wagon, my mother tried using old-fashioned ways. One of the neighbors suggested that we should use fresh, unsalted, pork fat on the wound, the fat helping the flesh to heal. It may sound unusual to you that this would work, but it did. After three or four weeks, my head started healing nicely. Naturally, I was bandaged up as well for that time. After a relatively short time, though, I was fine and back to my normal routine.

It only took about a year for me to get in trouble again. I never saw these things as looking for ways to hurt myself. Each time I felt there was a very good reason why I would do the things I would do. At this time, I was playing catch with some of the other children.

I was throwing a ball to some other kids, seeing who could catch it. I thought it would be a much greater challenge for the other kids if I could throw it harder or faster. A seven-year-old can only throw a ball just so fast. I knew I was going to need some help.

On our farm, we had a barn; it was a large structure. I decided that from the top of the barn's roof, I would be able to throw the ball down so it would be more of a challenge for the other kids to catch it. The easiest way up was by climbing the ladder. So far, I thought, so good. Everything went just as I had thought it would, until I slipped. I don't remember if I actually slipped on something, or if I just lost my footing. All I really remember was that one moment I was on top of the roof, throwing that ball as hard as I could; the next moment, I was on my way down from the roof.

There are many things around a barn that can kill a person under the right circumstances. One of the many things we had next to the barn was a millstone. I never actually hit the ground on my way down because, instead, I hit that millstone. There went my head again. I suppose I was lucky in that I could have easily been killed by falling on something sharp, or falling differently and breaking my neck—any one of a number of things.

I guess I have a pretty hard head because this time wasn't even as bad as the last time. I didn't even need the pork fat to help it heal. It was bad enough, though. We created a poultice, of a sort, from what we had available from things you would find in the hills—leaves, plants, roots, and things like that. They were applied to my head. It worked, healing up pretty good.

When I was seven, my little sister Gitel Marim was born. I had hoped for a little brother, but I was much happier with Gitel. I was still the only son, which I understood allowed me more freedom than my sisters enjoyed.

As usual, I was at Hebrew school most of the day. That evening, I arrived home about seven. Like me, Gitel Marim was born in our house. I walked in the door, greeted by more activity than I had seen in a long time. The midwife was there, along with my three older sisters.

Chana, the eldest, was still with Mother. My middle sister, Frieda, was taking care of chores that Mother was unable to do. Sippora, just about a year older than me, seemed that she could not stop smiling. It was she who finally told me. "We have a new little sister. She's beautiful and healthy." Unlike me, Gitel Marim was not born premature.

I put my books on the table. But before I could make my first move to see her, Sippora took me by the hand. "Come with me, Benjamin. We've been waiting for you."

When I saw that tiny baby for the first time, I began smiling like everyone else in the house. She was everything Sippora said and more. She was sound asleep, so I didn't get to see her eyes; but I saw her hair was very fine, light blonde. Over the years, her hair would thicken and darken only slightly. I touched her hand very gently, afraid to waken her. Her skin was softer than anything I had ever felt.

Zade came up behind me and put his hands on my shoulders, leaning over to whisper in my ear. "We're the men of the house," he said quietly. "It's our responsibility to take care of her."

I took Zade's words very seriously. Still looking down at that new baby, I knew I would do anything for her. I would never allow anything to harm her. As her big brother, as one of the men of the house, I fully accepted my responsibility.

A couple of years later, I was maybe ten or eleven, there was another accident. Not me, this time. My older sister, Sippora, who was about twelve at the time, was running home from town. She was coming across the river on our property that I told you about. She knew that river as well as any of us. Maybe because she felt she knew it so well, she was not as careful as she should have been. She lost her footing on one of the wet rocks. She fell, hitting her head very badly.

By the time we found her, she had already lost a lot of blood. The blood was coming, not from a head wound like mine had, but from her nose. We tried everything we could. Nothing worked. The blood continued to flow from her nose. She lost blood at an alarming rate. We found ourselves unable to help her. She passed away from her fall.

Like my own family, some of the Jewish families had lived in this same town for generations. It didn't matter. To the Gentiles, we were seen as trespassers, transients—despite the fact that we all lived, worked, and did business together. This sense of the Jewish residents as being interlopers was passed from parents to their children. This fact was impressed upon me in a scene I will never forget.

During recess at the public school one day, there was an argument between the Gentile kids and the Jewish kids. Confrontations such as these were not uncommon. They often escalated into fights. Everyone knew it. The priest who came to the school to teach religion to the Gentile kids was watching us and knew it, too. He moved close enough to hear everything, ready to intervene should it prove necessary.

One of the Gentile kids was glaring at us, taunting. "Why are you Jews sitting in our school? Why are you even here?"

Another, emboldened by the first, continued. "You should be in Palestine. Go there!"

The situation was steadily worsening. Some of us countered that we had been here longer than they had. They insisted we go away. They wanted us all to go to Palestine, "where we belonged."

Before things degraded any further, the priest came over. Everyone became quiet, but the anger and resentment were still there. He addressed the Gentile kids with stern authority. "Why are you sending them to Palestine? That's not their land either. They have no homeland. They are lost dogs."

I hoped, I prayed that one day we would be able to show the world that we *do* have a homeland. Who could have imagined, that day during recess, that I would, in fact, be in Palestine one day? Not only that I would be in Palestine, but that it would become the State of Israel and that I would be in the army, fighting for, being a part of its creation.

Fortunately for us, the public school was not the most important thing for the Jewish youngsters. It was far more important for us to attend the Jewish school. There, we learned

Hebrew and studied the bible. There, we studied six days a week. Saturday was not an official day of school, but we would still study and discuss the Jewish bible as a part of the service.

After services on Saturday, during the biblical discussions with the other youngsters, the Rabbi would often join us for a while. He would listen to us, to see how we were doing. Naturally, everything was according to the bible. We didn't do anything that went against Jewish religious law.

If there were ever any question, we would consult the *shelchenurach*. It's a book expounding on each of the Hebraic laws. It's like a law book that a lawyer uses for reference. This way, we were guided as to what was the Jewish religious way of doing things. As a matter of fact, this book was in every Jewish house. Each person should know what to do, what not to do, what was expected of him. We would study this book at home, as well as in the Synagogue.

At the time I left public school, around the age of ten, I began a new course of study. My father knew firsthand the importance of learning German. In his work as the assistant for another town's rabbi, it was essential for him. It was the language of commerce, education, the arts, and politics. To understand German was a distinct advantage in dealing with anyone. Even better educated and well-traveled Jews spoke German. My father decided I should be one of them.

About the age of ten, I began to learn my fourth language. I enjoyed learning German. It was similar in some respects to Yiddish, my first language, so I didn't feel as though I was now learning something completely new. It was easier for me to pick it up than it would have been to learn a totally new, foreign language like English would have been.

By learning German, I was now able to read and understand some of the greatest works of philosophy and literature. I admired the Germans for being able to think of and talk about such things. I tried to read whatever I could in German. I learned how the German mind worked, what thought processes they used.

Thinking back, perhaps this was one of the many things that helped me to survive when I was in the camps. I was able to understand what was important to the Germans and to use that knowledge to my own advantage on occasion.

By the time I began to learn German, my beloved Zade Moishe, my mother's father, had passed away. Not long after that, my father's mother Tzirl also passed away. It was then that Zade Abraham, who had made a living selling religious books, came to live with us. He had been living with us for two years or so by the time I began my German studies. My father had three sisters and two brothers. Two of the sisters were already living in America. One of the brothers was killed in an accident. Of all of the children, Zade Abraham and Bubbe Tzirl were closest with my parents. When Bubbe passed away, it simply made the most sense for Zade to come live with us.

For me, it was wonderful. My father was still gone most of the time, working in Bucovina. His father gradually became like a second father to me, filling the void left by Zade Moishe.

Zade was with us for almost four years when he passed away. He and Bubbe Tzirl had already bought cemetery plots in their hometown, many years before. That's where Bubbe was buried. That's where Zade would be buried, too.

There was just one problem: According to Rumanian law, at that time, you were not supposed to transport a dead body from one city to another, one town to another. In order to bring Zade home, we had to use a little ingenuity and the tools at hand. We had sleds, horses, and hay. We laid his body on a sled and covered it with hay. My father was gone, my mother and sisters unable to leave the farm. I was, maybe, twelve years old at the time. With Zade gone, I was now the man of the house. I took Zade back to his hometown, by myself.

The daughter who did not go to America still lived in his hometown. My aunt Malka and my uncle David and I made the funeral arrangements. Basically, we made certain that the arrangements he had made so many years earlier with Bubbe were carried

out. A special group of people put him in his *tachrichim*, the white
burial shroud specified by Jewish religious law, and then followed
the laws for burial. His stone, casket, and plot next to Bubbe were
all taken care of. None of us would ever have imagined that in spite
of all the deaths in the next several years, Zade would be the last
one to be buried according to Jewish law.

I would have liked the chance to visit with Aunt Malka
and Uncle David under happier circumstances. Except for family
gatherings, I did not have the opportunity to see them very often.
Uncle David owned a bar in his town, so he and Aunt Malka kept
very busy running his business and could not easily leave, even to
visit relatives.

In fact, I had always looked forward to these family gatherings. Usually, the entire extended family would make the trip to
our house, out of respect for my mother's parents, who would
have found traveling elsewhere to be difficult. In the fall, during
the traditional harvest festival of Sukkot, Mother and my sisters
would cook for what seemed like days. I was always delegated
some task which forced me outdoors, most probably as a means of
keeping me from getting in the way.

Fresh bread, baked pies, strudel, lamb, geese slaughtered and
the meat hung in the attic to smoke and cure, the house cleaned—
activity seemingly without end. But I would always find an
opportunity to sneak into the attic and trim a slice of goose meat
as a snack, forcing my mother to worry that I wasn't eating enough
because by dinnertime, I was already full.

From early morning, we greeted the arrival of aunts, uncles,
and cousins. Uncle Mordechai, with his large family, usually
arrived first, since they lived in town. Just in case there may not
be enough to eat, he always made certain to bring more food,
which his wife and daughters had prepared. I'd wait on the porch
for his son Hertz. We'd take off together, sometimes before the last
of his family made it into the house, to play Tag or Hide-and-Seek
among the fruit trees. The day before, we had picked the choicest
fruits we could, fresh off the tree so that those arriving from out

of town might have the best, ripest food which Rozavlea, and by extension ourselves, had to offer.

Somehow, Aunt Malka and Uncle David managed to find a way to leave their bar and bring their family to join the rest of us by coming to town the day before and spending the night with Uncle David's parents, then walking to our house for the Holiday. Uncle David always wore a smile as he walked into the house, inhaling the wonderful aromas wafting from the kitchen. I know Aunt Malka, especially, loved the chance to come, relax, and visit her brother (my father). She would immediately do whatever she could to help Mother. I suppose that working in the kitchen is not work if it is in your brother's house.

Late morning usually saw the arrival of my father's cousin Abraham and his family. His daughters, Peri and Miriam, were close in age to Hertz and myself. If we had not yet returned to the house, Peri and Miriam always seemed to know where to find us. I still remember them, very close even for sisters, Miriam quieter than the more outgoing Peri.

Early afternoon was when food was served. Everyone had arrived by then. Hertz and I, often with the assistance of Peri and Miriam, had handfuls of fresh fruit. We need not have bothered. There was always far more food than even a gathering of so many people could eat. Most of the afternoon, we ate, talked, caught up with those relatives we had not had the chance to see for a while. We children played together, games of tag, races, anything we might think of. The adults talked about business, or sometimes who had gone to find their fortune far away from our hometowns. Sometimes, the other children and I would listen to the stories our grandparents told us of times, so very long ago, when, as children themselves, they played in the same groves of trees and fished in the same streams. Without realizing it, these stories gave us a profound sense of continuity, of belonging to a people and a place.

All of the women automatically began cleaning up as the day came to a close. With so much extra food, everyone took some home with them. Those who lived in other towns had to leave before nightfall. Aunt Malka, Uncle David, and their children usually left first, always with the promise to visit more often. Uncle Mordechai's family, the first to arrive, was the last to leave, having only to walk back to their own home in town. Knowing I would see Hertz and my other cousins the next day at school, I didn't waste time on long goodbyes.

I always slept soundly on those nights, exhausted from playing with my cousins and so full I could hardly climb into bed. I sometimes felt sorry for my cousins because the stories that our grandparents told which we all loved so much to listen to, I was able to hear every night while they could only hear them once in a while, on special occasions. It made me feel that every night I had with my grandparents, hearing their stories, was therefore a special occasion.

By the age of twelve, I was already enthralled by the attraction of the big city. Even at that age, the farm was, for me, a dead end. I felt there was no future for me as a farmer. The work was extremely difficult and the rewards were, at best, minimal. For someone of my background, the only alternative to being a farmer was to be a rabbi. I had even less inclination toward that than I did to farming.

That did not mean that I stopped my studies. Such a thing would have been unheard of. While my formal, public education ended at age ten, I continued my Hebrew studies six days a week. Sometimes, getting home at seven or eight in the evening, my little sister would still be awake, doing her own homework for school, Mother helping her with anything she had difficulty with. What always impressed me was that Mother never had to help her very much. Gitel Marim was very intelligent. I watched as she did her studies and remembered, not that many years earlier, doing the same lessons. She never seemed to have to study as hard or put as much effort into it as I had to do. I suppose I could have been envious at how easy she made it all look; but instead, I was very proud that such a smart little girl was my sister.

At the age of thirteen, I had my Bar Mitzvah. Today, such occasions are huge events accompanied by extravagant banquets. The day was very different for me. It was certainly important, marking the time when, according to Jewish religious law, I would be counted among the men. For ten years, I studied Hebrew and Torah, but this was the first time I was allowed the honor and privilege of standing on the *bima*, reading from one of the Shul's Torah scrolls during a regular service.

My mother, sisters, and cousins Peri and Miriam watched and listened from the women's area upstairs, while my male relatives watched me from their seats. Uncle David and Aunt Malka couldn't make it from their town, but I saw cousin Abraham and Uncle Mordechai solemnly nodding their approval. Hertz, Joseph, and other male cousins remained serious, perhaps recalling their Bar Mitzvah and their own first time being on the bima.

After the service, my family gathered around me, full of congratulations, treating me, it seemed, with a little more respect because I was no longer a child, but a man. I received a bottle of wine and a honey cake. Even after ten years, study was still sweet; but as a man, I could have something a little stronger to help carry that sweetness throughout my body.

I was not the only member of my family to have little inclination to remain on the farm in Rozavlea. My older sister Chana wanted desperately to go to Palestine. It was a dream of mine as well, but I was only ten. My sister was fifteen. The lure of Palestine, of the Holy Land, was instilled in us from our earliest memories.

Chana belonged to a Zionist youth organization. They would meet once a week, their goal to establish a Jewish State in Palestine. Chana was an ardent member of this group. I wanted to join as well, but I was too young. You had to be a certain age. She would bring home the group's literature and read it with me. She was very dedicated, devoted, and ever hopeful that one day she would be able to go to Palestine.

At first, it didn't seem promising for her. There was no way she could go by herself. Our family simply did not have the money for something like that. But there was a Jewish organization in Palestine (I think it was funded by the Rothchild family) that would pay the expenses for large families of eight, ten, twelve kids to immigrate. However, there was no way they would take her alone.

Chana never gave up hope. Perhaps that is a family trait. It was that same tenacious adherence to hope which helped me survive when it would have been so much easier for me to give up. As far as my father was concerned, he wasn't particularly interested in uprooting the family and moving to Palestine. Even if he was, our family was not big enough. My sister found another way.

My uncle Shimen, my mother's brother, was selected from our town to go to Palestine with his family. He sold his house and what little land he had for whatever he could get. The organization paid the rest. Chana went with him, as though she were one of his daughters. With Chana, Uncle Shimen's family now totaled twelve people.

She was very excited when she left home with Uncle Shimen and his family. Things were going well for her. She was happy, until they reached the port of Constansia. There was a checkpoint of sorts that they needed to pass before boarding the ship that would take them to Palestine.

It turned out that her documents were not in order. She was not allowed on the ship. She watched Uncle Shimen, his wife, and children leave for Palestine, living her dream. At least at that point, there was no choice for her. She came home as miserable as she had once been excited.

There was, however, a glimmer of hope. Chana focused on that, never giving up. She was promised that in a short time, she would receive permission to go. The British controlled Palestine at that time. They controlled who entered by imposing quotas. Only so many Jews were allowed to immigrate per month. To those fortunate people, the British issued a particular paper.

It took Chana almost six months, but she got that paper. It was 1935. She was only fifteen when she left, this time to join Uncle

Shimen and his family. We missed her very much and kept in touch by writing each other often.

We told her in detail of Uncle Lou's continuing generosity, like the time he sent money to help pay for the headstones for his parents' gravesites and how, a short time later, he sent some more money to cover the rest of the cost that the family in Rozavlea had trouble saving for. Father wrote to her, expressing how much he would like to be able to see her again. Father sometimes played a version of the lottery. He would write to Chana, telling her that if he won, he would send her a ticket so she could come home to visit. He never won. Chana remained in Palestine.

Frieda would write, telling Chana how much she wanted to join her in Palestine. Frieda wanted to go to the Holy Land every bit as much as Chana did, but we had no money to send her, and Chana had no money to send for her. No other relatives went as Uncle Shimen did, so there was no other family for Frieda to join as Chana had.

Life was hard for Chana, but she loved it there. We read her letters over and over again, stories of working in the orange groves with our cousins, finding work on her own cutting rocks to make roads. To Gitel Marim, the letters seemed more like mystical fairy tales, adventures of a sister who left for a faraway land before she was old enough to really remember her.

Chana even met a nice boy named Abraham. He was also an immigrant, having come from a town not very far from ours. They met while working in the orange grove. He was very intelligent and highly motivated. He learned diamond cutting and became very respected in the field. He and Chana married. They lived in Israel for the rest of their lives, raised two daughters Leah and Shoshana who between them gave my sister six grandchildren and twenty great-grandchildren. Chana and Abraham now lay side by side, beneath Israeli soil.

Between school and working on the farm, it may sound like we had little time for anything else. Sometimes it may have seemed that way, but it was always possible to enjoy the things that had to be done. For example, we went fishing very often. Doing this was not a relief from work, but one of the ways in which we had different food to eat. The fish we caught was our breakfast for the next day, sometimes even dinner for that night.

By the time I was six years old, I was making my own breakfast from the fish we had caught the night before. I would fry them with the butter my mother had made from the milk we got from our cows. She didn't have to help me. I'd make breakfast using the smaller fish that were, maybe, three ounces. Then I would go to school.

Fishing could be done in more than one way. Our breakfast fish, the ones that were only about three or four ounces, were fairly easy to catch. Near our house was a small lake where we did a lot of our fishing. Normally, fish like to sleep around rocks or wood that's under the water. I think it makes them feel secure. While our lake had fish, it lacked a lot of rocks or submerged wood. A stream from the lake came near the house. That stream had the rocks the lake didn't.

Somehow, the fish knew about the rocks in the stream. At night, you could hear them swimming up into the stream from the lake so they could sleep safely among the rocks.

At night, after the fish had fallen asleep, all of my sisters and I would go to the stream with a candle or kerosene lamp. My little sister Gitel Marim, seven years younger than I was, took a special delight in splashing in the water, trying to catch a fish. Usually, she succeeded only in scaring them away; but every once in a while, she would actually catch one, holding it out proudly for us to see. Sometimes even Mother would join us. We never failed to have a wonderful time. We then picked up a rock, and underneath was the fish, waiting to be caught. These are the little fish that I would then fry the next morning for breakfast before leaving for school.

If you wanted a bigger fish, you had to go during the day. Even then, there was an easy way to catch the fish. This kind of fishing was done at the lake. The fish there were bigger, ranging up to a pound. The best way was to take bread with you and feed the fish. That way, they come close to the surface. Once they're used to that, you toss in some bread that you've soaked in alcohol. The fish, near the surface, eat it up immediately. It doesn't take very long for them to get drunk. They just sort of float around, not really paying much attention to anything. At that point, it's an easy matter to pick up whatever fish you want.

Even though we worked hard almost all day, our town was not without professional entertainment. Naturally, there were the *klezmer* players, who provided the music at weddings and special occasions. Mostly, though, it was only the rich who could afford their fees.

One of the traditions I never was able to fully take part in was when a man got married; the adult men gave him a party. I always wanted to be able to be a part of that, but was too young. Sometimes I went anyway, but was always made to return home.

Our town also had a Jewish family who performed around the country. There were about a dozen people in the family, all very talented. They played all kind of instruments as well as sang. They traveled all over, putting on concerts. They would be gone sometimes six months at a time. Whenever they came back, it was a big event in town.

There was something else very interesting about the family. They were midgets. Of the entire family, only two were what would be considered normal size. They were all very nice, respected people in our town.

They were also one of the very few families in town to own a very large, custom-built car. They used it to travel from one concert to another. How they all fit in that car, I have no idea. They probably did not all travel at the same time. Being able to be even close to a car was so rare, it was like a privilege. They used to wash their car in the river near our house.

When I was about seven years old, a few friends and I felt that luck had smiled down upon us. That river was actually on my parents' property. My friends and I had every right to sit nearby on the riverbank and actually be close enough to touch that almost magical machine. Then we had the stroke of luck. They allowed us to wash their car. This was an unbelievable experience, an honor we didn't expect but took full advantage of. We were being asked, even encouraged to touch that car. This state of grace lasted for a few years. Whenever they came back to town, the car would be taken to my river where my friends and I would wash it for them.

After a couple of years, when I was older, I also got a little smarter. I was able to enjoy the car just as much without working. I let them wash their own car.

You never know what connections will turn up later. There was no way any of us would guess that less than ten years later, the Nazis would come into our town. They didn't kill this talented family. Instead, the entire family was taken to Auschwitz. They were part of the group of musicians who would be used by the Germans to play in concerts and confuse the new arrivals.

When my family and I arrived in Auschwitz on the transport, we recognized the family of midgets from our hometown, playing in the band the Nazis used to greet new prisoners. Bright, upbeat music playing loudly conflicted with harsh orders being shouted in German, all played out under intense, bright lights that were almost painful after spending days in the dark confines of the boxcars. Hearing the music and recognizing the musicians, it was almost possible to think that, for a moment, things would not be too bad.

There were other incidents that impressed upon us the fact that, though we lived and worked alongside the Gentiles, we did not have the same rights as they did. In 1939, the Gentiles of our town decided that they needed a dancing hall. It was determined that the best place for it would be to simply take our second, smaller Synagogue in the town and make it into their dancing hall. We were not asked if this would be acceptable to us. It was simply done.

The only decent thing they did about it was to allow us to remove the religious objects, Torahs and so on, before they took over the building. We were powerless to do anything. This created a great deal of anger and resentment among the Jews of the town. There was no way we could know that what appeared to us to be such a terrible thing at that time would, in retrospect, become almost nothing.

Anti-Semitism was not only something felt on a personal level by many of the Gentiles of Eastern Europe towards Jews in general, it was also something which, at times, was sanctified by law. The Rumanian government was never very stable in the best of circumstances. Depending upon who happened to be in power at any given moment, laws would be passed that were more or less punitive towards Jews.

Sometimes the anti-Jewish laws validated robbery of Jewish businesses or open murder of Jews, often called *pogroms* in Eastern Europe. Sometimes, without legal sanctions, organized hate groups would carry out acts of destruction or murder. By doing nothing, the government showed approval of the acts. I can clearly remember hearing stories of such groups of men going through a neighboring town, killing a Jew or two at random. They then took the bodies to one of the butcher shops. There, they hung the bodies on the meat hooks used for sides of beef, hanging a sign on the murdered man reading "Kosher Meat." That murderous level of hatred and violence was not a part of Rozavlea while I was young. We were fortunate in that respect.

Around 1940, politicians came to power who had definite sympathies to the Nazi Party.

That year—1940—was a year of immense change for me. The passage of time and subsequent events have a way of changing one's perspective. At the time, the changes seemed drastic, vast. That was all made relative less than four years later when the Nazis arrived, bringing with them their own peculiar brand of drastic upheaval.

Budapest

As the year 1940 began with the Hungarian invasion of our state, it was impossible for us to imagine what the future would mean for us. Instead, we adjusted, adapted to situations as they arose, each person to his own talents and abilities. When the Hungarian Army invaded my home state of Transylvania, my family and I automatically became Hungarian citizens. The invasion crystallized my growing desire to leave my hometown into determined action.

By that time, I had already decided what I wanted to do for a career, and it wasn't farming. My parents' idea was that if I didn't want to continue on the farm, then I should continue my religious studies and become a rabbi. I didn't agree with this. There is nothing wrong with farming. There is nothing wrong with studying the sacred texts and being a rabbi. It was just that neither of those things was right for me. Since it was my life, I felt it was my decision as to what I wanted to do with it.

As my inspiration and role model for my career choice, I looked not to my father, but to my cousins. Joseph and his older brothers Chanan and Avram Yonkiv had moved to the big city of Budapest and worked in the jewelry line. They manufactured and sold bracelets, rings, and things like that. This intrigued me for a couple of reasons. First of all, I had always been interested in the business world. Secondly, when Joseph, or one of his brothers, came back home to visit, he would be dressed nicely, wearing fancy rings and so forth. As a young boy only beginning to enter his teenage years, I couldn't help but be impressed.

I decided that I, too, wanted to become a jeweler. It wasn't out of some jealousy of my cousins. I simply felt that if they could do it, then so could I. That was why, in early 1940, I left home for Budapest, planning to learn the jewelry line and go into business for myself.

I chose Budapest because it was the largest city in the area. I passed a lot of smaller cities closer to home, reasoning that a city the size of Budapest would provide me with far more opportunities. We had heard stories of there being "gold on the streets." I can tell you, for a fact, that was not true.

Arriving in Budapest would have been a shock for me had I not gone with my mother on some of the occasions when she went to a larger city to go shopping. She could only go when we had the precious American money from Uncle Lou, allowing us to purchase items we could never afford otherwise. Budapest differed from Rozavlea in every way it is possible for two cities in the same part of the world to do so. Aside from the magnitude of the city itself that never ceased to impress me, I walked on sidewalks which lined well-paved streets. Cars, almost commonplace, commanded no special attention. Streetcars vied with the automobiles for possession of the road while pedestrians dodged them all. I felt invigorated to be in the midst of so much activity, everything around me so exciting in comparison to studying for hours on end, or sitting to milk a cow for the third time during the day.

Unfortunately, things did not happen as I had planned. My idea was to get a job as an apprentice to a jeweler or goldsmith. What I had not expected was that so many other people, close in age to me, would have plans similar to my own. Naturally, I went first to see my cousins. They wanted to help me; but working for someone else, they couldn't. If they owned their own shop, things might have worked out differently for me; but while they asked their employer about a position for me, the shop they worked at had no apprenticeships available.

I couldn't find a job. It certainly wasn't for lack of trying. To survive, I went to the local Synagogue. There, out in front, a bunch of kids, close to my age, would beg for money. The lucky ones would have a few pennies at the end of the day. That wasn't going to buy enough food to keep from feeling your stomach tighten with hunger. I wasn't always among the lucky ones. I used to starve. I was always hungry.

An easy solution would have been to write to my parents, asking for them to help me. I didn't, couldn't. It may have been pride, a desperate desire to prove to them that my choice was the correct one. It may have been fear that they would demand that I return home. They couldn't have helped me with money, even if they had been so inclined. They didn't have any extra to give me. They had begged me not to go, to become a rabbi if farming wasn't my calling.

I had made my decision and I was determined to see it through to the end. The price I paid for that was high. At first, I would sleep wherever I could find some shelter. For a short time, I slept underneath some stairs. Eventually, about ten of us kids found an apartment, a room really, in a building. With all of us contributing, we would have enough money to pay the rent. At least, we had a roof over our heads at night. I would sleep on the floor with the other kids. The cockroaches would come out at night and have a feast on us.

When Passover came, I was able to make a little bit of money. Behind the Synagogue, matzohs, the unleavened bread that traditionally was the only bread allowed in the house during Passover, were made for the holiday. I would stay just outside. There, I would wait for the women buying the matzohs. There was no convenient means of transportation like here in Southern California near the end of the century. I rented myself out as a pack mule. For whatever they would give me—ten, fifteen, sometimes twenty cents—I would carry their entire order for them on my back, walking to their house or apartment. By collecting those precious pennies, I was able to afford a little food and maybe a shower.

Even then, the shower wasn't like here. It was a public shower. There was a charge of ten or fifteen cents, for which you would be lent a towel and the right to use the shower. Most of the time, I didn't have enough money for a shower. One of my biggest treats was, with my carefully saved money, to have a shower once every week or two. The rest of the time, I tried to keep as clean as possible by washing over a sink. It wasn't the same. I could never get really clean that way. I felt I was continuously dirty, my body covered with grime and cockroach bites. It was the best I could do.

For the week or two before Passover, every day I would carry matzohs to people's homes. At night, I would return to the little room where all of us kids slept. On Saturday, I would go to the Synagogue to pray.

To escape the cold, some of the other kids and myself would stay in the Synagogue, sitting over the heat vents in the floor. One Saturday night, while we were trying to keep warm, a man came in, an Orthodox Jew, but of a more modern type. He was tall, husky, with a thick black moustache but no beard or peyes. I couldn't tell his exact age, but he must have been close to sixty. His name was Joseph Katz. I will never forget his name. He came over to us, evaluating us as we watched him.

He stopped in front of us and announced, "Would any one of you like to be a tailor?"

Without taking the time to hear more or to weigh the pros and cons, I immediately decided what Mr. Katz was offering was better than freezing in a room with a bunch of other kids, no way to get and stay clean, and being a dinner buffet for thousands of cockroaches. I raised my hand, saying, "Yes. I'd like to be a tailor."

I knew I wasn't being completely honest with him. In the back of my mind, I still wanted to be a jeweler. In hindsight, it's easy for me to appreciate the irony of fate. Like my father before me, this incident would have repercussions years later. In reality, it was only a few years later, in the concentration camp of Dora, when being able to say "I was a tailor" saved my life. That Saturday night in Budapest, though, all I knew was that being an apprentice tailor meant that I would have food to eat and a clean place to sleep. At the time, it was enough.

He studied me for a moment in silence, like King Solomon weighing evidence before rendering a judgment. "How old are you?" he finally asked me.

At that moment, the opportunity to become his apprentice was the most important thing in the world to me. I lied to him again. I told him I was seventeen. I wanted to appear older, thinking he'd be more likely to take me on. I didn't have any documents to verify my claim, no IDs. I really didn't look older, the way some kids do. None of it mattered. He took me at my word.

"Okay," he said. "I'll take you on. Come with me to my house."

There were electrical trains at that time in Budapest. "Streetcars" is the more common term. I had yet to ride any of them. I never had the money for it. It seemed that my life had forever changed for the better. We rode the streetcar to his house.

When we arrived at his house, he introduced me to his wife. I must have looked as hungry as I felt because, almost right away, she asked me if I wanted something to eat.

By that time, I had been in Budapest for about three months. There had not been one day during that time that I really had enough to eat. I was constantly hungry, almost starving at times. I told her, "Yes, I would like to have something to eat." It was the absolute truth.

She gave me a big bowl of chulint. She had added potatoes to the barley mix, something we sometimes did at home. The aroma reminded me of home and how we'd put the chulint in a ceramic pot and place the pot in the oven on Friday night. Naturally, the oven is heated up first with lots of wood. In our town, a lot of families couldn't afford so much wood. Other families, sometimes as many as ten, would bring their pots of chulint to our house. Once all of the pots were in the oven, it was sealed up with animal dirt so that the heat wouldn't escape. It would then cook for almost twenty hours. After Shul on Saturday, the oven would be opened, each family getting their own pot of chulint. It was always worth waiting for.

The chulint that Mrs. Katz gave me that Saturday night in Budapest was exactly what a hungry fourteen-year-old needed. The best prime rib in the world would not have tasted better to me.

While I ate, Mr. Katz began asking me questions. We spoke in Yiddish because, after only three months in Budapest, I didn't speak enough Hungarian to be able to converse with anyone. Among the many questions he asked me were how long I'd been in the city, where I came from, how many were in my family, why I wanted to become a tailor.

I was determined not to give him any reason to reject me. "I always wanted to be a tailor," I told him with as much conviction as I could. I prayed that he would find that reason to be acceptable.

To my relief, he did. As he announced his decision, I could feel myself begin to breath normally again. I hadn't realized how anxious I was until I relaxed at his words. "Okay," he said. "I'm going to teach you to be a tailor. To become my apprentice, you have to sign on for three and a half years." He didn't own a factory, but a shop, employing several tailors. They made custom-made ladies' clothing. Beautiful work came from that shop and it enjoyed a fine reputation throughout the city.

I didn't want to do anything that might destroy my chances of having a warm place to sleep and enough food to eat. "Yes, yes. Of course. I'll sign anything you want me to."

"Before we can sign the contract, you have to bring your birth certificate from your hometown."

"Of course. I'll write to my parents."

Naturally, I never seriously considered being a tailor. Even at the age of fourteen, I knew that signing a contract committing myself to something I didn't want was not a good idea. I purposely delayed sending home for my birth certificate.

I soon discovered we had different definitions of the word "apprentice." To me, it meant someone who learns a line or trade from another who is experienced and established in that line. To Mr. Katz, "apprentice" was a synonym for "slave." In fact, I often thought that Pharaoh treated the slaves in Egypt better than the Katzes treated me.

They had no children. Perhaps that's why, having no idea how to treat me, they wound up treating me more as a trained animal than a human being.

I was given a little room to stay in and food to eat. Nothing else. I slept on the floor like a dog. My chores began at five in the morning, so I had to be up before that. Each morning, my bones would ache, my muscles stiff from the discomfort during the night. I had no money to spend since I was not paid. One of the only good things was that with so much work to do during the day, sleep came quickly at night, despite the discomfort.

Until I could learn the Hungarian language better, I knew I had little choice but to do the best I could under the circumstances. At five in the morning, my job was to dust and clean the house and mop the floors, doing the work of a maid. When that was finished, usually around mid-morning, I would go to the shop. There, for an hour or so, I would help out as much as I could. That was where and when my education as a tailor occurred. Sometimes, it was possible to glean information from observing the tailors. Sometimes, Mr. Katz would teach me a little bit. This schooling never lasted very long because I was then sent to do the deliveries. After that, while I was out, I would also pick up merchandise to bring back to the shop.

Since Mr. Katz wasn't willing to spend the few pennies for the streetcar, all of the deliveries and pickups took much longer than they would have otherwise. I had to walk everywhere, carrying the merchandise on my back. When I returned to the shop, my job was to make certain the area was clean for the next day.

In order to make it through the days and weeks, I never gave up the hope of one day becoming a jeweler. I kept telling myself that things would be better one day, holding on to the thought that this current state of affairs was not going to last forever.

During the week, there was no free time to work toward making these hopes into reality. On Shabbat, everything was different. Being Orthodox, neither Mr. Katz, nor any of his employees, including me, worked on Saturday. That became my day to look for someone in the jewelry line who would be willing to take me on as an apprentice. I was determined to knock on the door of every jeweler in Budapest if I had to.

As my Hungarian improved, communication became easier. I was able to talk with more people, learn more, make my desires known more effectively. Unfortunately, ease of communication does not automatically result in employment. I continued trying, but still could not find work as a jewelry apprentice. As the weeks became months, Mr. Katz kept pressing me to get my birth certificate. I continued to delay and postpone. There was never an end to the reasons why it didn't arrive and there would be no contract until it did. After working in the tailor shop for about eight months, my fortune changed.

One Saturday, I went to a large, nice jewelry shop. The owner was a young, Gentile man named Bondy. He was in his mid-30s, single, tall and well built with light brown hair, a thick blonde moustache. He even had his father working for him, though the elder Bondy did little more than watch the other workers. By then, my Hungarian was good enough so that I was able to clearly explain that I was seeking an apprenticeship. I told him, honestly and sincerely, that I wanted to be a jeweler, emphasizing that I was a hard worker and a quick learner. "You're not going to be sorry," I assured him. "I'm going to do anything I can."

He must have been impressed because he said, "Okay. I'll hire you. You can start on Monday."

I was so happy. I wasn't certain what to do first. I hadn't even left his shop, and I was already looking forward to Monday and the new job, when I would start learning the jewelry trade. Before I left, I made certain that Bondy knew how excited I was and that I would never give him any reason to regret his decision. I'm certain it was easy for him to see how I felt.

By the time I got back on Saturday night, the Katzes had already gone to sleep. I went to my own little room, curled up and went to sleep myself. I'd looked around my room at my meager belongings. It wouldn't take long to get everything ready to leave.

The next morning, instead of getting up to dust the house and clean the floors like I was supposed to, I prepared to go to my new job. Mr. Katz came to my room and asked why I was not working yet.

Standing, as tall as possible, I said simply, "Mr. Katz. I'm quitting."

"What?!" He was as furious as I was happy.

This was my chance to tell him how I felt. "I'm quitting. I don't want this job. For the past eight months, ever since I've worked for you, you've treated me like a slave. Worse than a slave. I don't want to be a tailor anymore."

I expected him to be angry. I didn't expect him to come over and hit me. Between the surprise and the force of the blow, I fell to the floor. I was very hurt by that. The physical pain was only a small part of it.

I ran outside and went directly to the first Hungarian policeman I saw. As I explained the circumstances to him, that I was hit simply for quitting, the policeman became angry. After all, as far as he was concerned, I was just a little kid.

"Did you have a contract with him?" the policeman asked me.

"No," I told him honestly. "I never signed a contract."

"Come with me," he ordered. He took me by the hand and had me take him to Mr. Katz. I was not sure what I expected as I went with him to confront Mr. Katz. The policeman went directly to Mr. Katz as I stood by the wall nearby.

"Why did you hit the boy?" the policeman demanded.

Mr. Katz evidently felt justified in his treatment of me because he showed no sign of fear or remorse. "I trained him for almost an entire year," Katz told him. "He agreed to work for me for three years, but he suddenly quit."

As Katz spoke in self-righteous indignation, I could see the policeman becoming increasingly angry. Katz didn't seem to notice, even as he was asked if I signed a contract.

"No, he didn't." Katz was becoming angry himself, which only served to exacerbate the policeman's ire. "The boy promised, but did nothing except delay."

I never expected what happened next. The policeman beat Mr. Katz, inflicting far more harm than I had received from the old tailor. I know I should have said something, but a small part of me felt Katz deserved it. A much larger part feared what would happen should the policeman's anger be turned upon me.

Starting on Monday, I worked at Bondy's shop, a nice establishment across the street from the Orthodox Shul on Cozince Street. I did my best to keep every promise I had made to him. I worked very hard, learning everything I could. I spent close to a year doing that, asking questions, acquiring new skills and then honing and mastering those skills. Bondy not only taught me, but paid me as well for the work I did. I was finally able to afford a small apartment.

By the time I had been with Bondy a year, it was early 1942. Through hard work, I had the skill and experience to work independently. During the day, I was an employee for Bondy. In the evening, I worked seriously to establish myself as an independent contractor. It was very difficult at first. I had to prove to jewelers who knew nothing about me that I could be trusted with their gold and my work was good.

It started out very slowly. One jeweler would give me a bracelet to make. Another would give me a ring—just to try me out. To help motivate them, I charged very little for my work. It was cheaper for them to give me the work than to have their own employees do it. I would work at my regular job with Bondy for ten, twelve hours a day. Then I would go to my apartment, where I had been able to set up my own little shop. There, I would work making the jewelry that I was doing on my own.

I made certain that everything was done well and delivered on time. I would then be paid so much for the bracelet, so much for the ring. The jewelers appreciated the quality of my work. It didn't take very long before they were confident I was not a thief who'd steal their gold. Gradually, they gave me more and more work. Four bracelets from this one, two bracelets from that one, some rings from another. Even Bondy gave me work to do.

In a short time, it became obvious that I was actually getting too much work. That was when I quit my job with Bondy's blessing and opened up my own shop in a very nice, upscale area of town called Belvarosh. I had been able to make enough from all the extra work I had been doing to rent a location. Starting there, I had some of the customers who were already pleased with my work. The shop was not very large, but I had enough business that I soon had to hire people to work for me. Not only did I have a shop, but a small store for retail customers as well in the front of the shop. I began making a lot of money. I was doing very well for a sixteen-year-old kid.

It didn't take very long before I learned that being the sixteen-year-old owner of a jewelry store had some difficulties. Many times, customers would come into the store and tell me they wanted to speak with the owner.

"I'm the owner," I would tell them.

Nobody believed me. They thought I was just some kid hanging around or maybe the owner's son. Their most common response would be, "Little boy, why don't you go call the owner? I'd like to speak with him about placing an order."

"I *am* the owner," I would repeat firmly, trying to sound very owner-like without being rude.

It rarely worked. The customers thought I was making some joke at their expense. They would become offended, frustrated, or angry. They'd simply walk out. Naturally, no store owner wants to see a customer, upset, walking out of his shop. I was no different. Finally, I came up with a way I thought would be able to make everyone happy. I went to one of my workers, Miklosh. A nondescript man of medium height, Miklosh was a good, honest man who looked like he was old enough to have a shop and several employees. At about 35 years old, he was the oldest employee I had.

Like all of my employees, he already knew of the problem. I explained the solution to him. "From now on," I told him, "when someone comes in asking to speak with the owner, they'll talk to you. I'll help you out, tell you what to say, what to buy, what not to buy."

He wasn't as happy as I thought he'd be. "I don't know anything about that part of the business. I'm a worker. That's it." He was concerned he'd make a mistake, do the wrong thing.

"Miklosh, my friend, don't worry about that," I assured him. "I'm not going to let you down. I can't afford that. It would be as bad for business as people walking out."

Miklosh reluctantly agreed. I made a small hole in the door from my office to the factory. When a customer came to speak with the owner, I sent him out. He would be dressed very nicely. The people would be impressed by the "owner." In the meantime, I would guide him concerning prices and so forth. It actually worked out quite successfully.

Not only was that plan successful, but, as I mentioned, the business as a whole was very successful. I was able to send money home for my family. With all the extra money coming in, my father no longer needed to work in another state. He quit his job and stayed at home to manage the farm.

With my father home again, I felt that all of the maneuvering and struggle I went through in my first few months living in Budapest was worth it and had paid off. For the first time in a long time, my family was together, able to relax and enjoy life. Perhaps it's best we cannot foresee the future because we had no idea how short-lived our time together would wind up being.

In addition to money, I would send packages home as often as I could. In the packages were all kinds of items that would be difficult, if not impossible, for them to find in their small town. Food which was either very expensive at home, or simply not available, would be easy to find and inexpensive to buy in Budapest. I'd send home salami of the best quality, at least half a meter in length; sugar; cooking oil; and so forth. I always made certain there were a lot of cigarettes along with the food. My father was a heavy smoker, and I saw no reason why he shouldn't be able to enjoy himself.

I would come home for the High Holidays and Passover, spending three or four weeks at that time. On those occasions, I was able to bring home treats and surprises for the family that otherwise wouldn't travel well, like the time I brought home a huge fish.

While preparing to visit my family, I was shopping, looking for a surprise for them. I happened to pass by a fish store where they had fresh fish swimming around in tanks. People picked out what they wanted by pointing to a particular fish. Swimming idly in the tank, oblivious to its own ultimate fate, was a huge carp. I had never seen a fish that big. I fell in love with it on the spot. I knew that I had to bring it home for my family. We were used to the three-ounce fish from our stream. This carp could feed the family for a week.

I bought it, explaining to the man that I wanted to take it home with me. I was afraid that it would spoil by the time I got home, at the end of an eight-hour train ride. The man helped me a lot, giving me the advice I needed to keep it fresh. As a matter of fact, using his advice, the fish not only remained fresh, it was still alive when I presented it to my family.

He instructed me to get a sturdy suitcase, made of wood with holes cut into it. The fish was carefully packed inside and kept wet and moist. I also fed it some bread soaked in alcohol. The fish got drunk in no time. All the way home, I kept it wet and drunk. When I got home, I emptied the water trough near the house and refilled it with fresh water. I dumped that huge fish into the trough. By then, word had already gotten out around town about the unbelievable size of the fish. People from all over town came to view it as it relaxed in the water trough. That fish did wind up providing meals for close to a week. It also provided entertainment and stories for the townspeople to tell each other for months.

Each time I came home, I would bring gold back with me to bury in the ground near the house or in the orchards. I fashioned the gold into rods approximately 10 inches long with a diameter slightly more than an American nickel. We put these rods into gallon glass jars, sealed them, then picked a spot to bury which we would remember because of a certain tree or landmark. I knew that, if times ever got very bad, gold was the best, most reliable currency and would help us survive.

There was a problem in obtaining enough gold for the business. By Hungarian law at that time, the government would sell each jeweler a specific, fixed amount of gold per month. Jewelers could not, legally, have more gold than what the government sold them. My business was doing so well that my amount would last less than a week. Other, more plentiful gold supplies had to be found. The equivalent of what might be called a "black market" was the answer. I bought foreign gold coins, all kinds, wherever and whatever I could. A lot of American gold coins came into my shop.

Since all of the coins were 24-carat gold, we melted them down, adding silver and copper to make 14-carat; 14-carat was the best amount to work with. More than that, and the jewelry was too soft and wouldn't last. Less than that, and it didn't contain enough gold to be of value to the average customer. An added benefit for me was that it helped the gold last longer and the people didn't care. We were honest about exactly what we were selling. They wanted anything we could provide. It was 1942. War and uncertainty had begun to be felt in Budapest. People became increasingly concerned as political and economic stability waned. Hungarian money began to lose value, slowly but steadily. Throughout history, people rely on gold in such times, knowing it will always retain its value no matter what the national currency is doing. Naturally, this is still true to a certain degree.

At the time, I never questioned the success of my business. In retrospect, I have to admit that if there had not been a war going on at the time, I would still have made a living, but never the small fortune I had so quickly accumulated.

As public anxiety increased, the demand for gold jewelry increased in direct proportion. My clientele was mixed, including both Jews and Gentiles. Rings, bracelets, necklaces. They bought whatever they could put their hands on. I could hardly keep up with the demand for bracelets alone. Many times, they were so anxious to take possession of the merchandise that they didn't want us to bother polishing it. There was an almost desperate need to have the gold in hand.

This led to another legal problem. According to Hungarian law, a gold bracelet could be no more than twenty grams. Neither the public nor I was happy with this restriction. For me, I was paid by the gram. The labor on a twenty-gram bracelet was essentially the same for a hundred-gram bracelet. Naturally, the profit margin on a hundred-gram item was far greater than the twenty-gram item. For the customers, who wanted gold they could carry with them, wearing a hundred-gram bracelet made far more sense than wearing five twenty-gram bracelets. I made the larger items. By doing so, I risked government sanctions, if not imprisonment. I also had to deal with the black market in order to keep up with the demand my business made for gold.

Delivering the product was not always easy, either. With the exception of the streetcar and some taxis, transportation meant walking. There was always the concern of being robbed by hoodlums or caught by the police. Neither alternative was pleasant. It was best to be as inconspicuous as possible. Dressed in dirty work clothes, I'd carry the merchandise in a toolbox. The jewelry would be carefully wrapped at the bottom of the box. On top, I'd have all kinds of tools. It was a system that seemed to work.

One day, I was on my way to a meeting with some people dealing in black-market gold. I was carrying my toolbox, the bottom filled with jewelry and foreign currency. Even then, foreign currency was gaining value over Hungarian currency. As I got closer to the street I wanted, I noticed the police were conducting an investigation, evidently searching for black-market contraband. Periodically, they would cordon off three or four streets. Uniformed police and plainclothes detectives checked each person who came and went, as well as each house in that zone.

My first instinct was to run back, putting as much distance as possible between the police and me. Ironically, it was fear that kept me from running. I was afraid that running away would only arouse their suspicions. If they chased me, I knew they would eventually catch me.

Instead, I continued walking and went directly to the first policeman I saw. "Excuse me, Officer. I need to go through. I have some repair work to do."

"You can't go through now. You'd be better off just going back."

"Are you sure? I'd really like to go do my work."

"You heard me. Now get out of here, kid. Stop bothering me."

Doing as he said, I just turned around and went back. Maybe it was luck. Maybe it's like I've often said, you have no time to think, but you must make a decision—fast. Had he allowed me to go on through, they would have checked my toolbox. That would have been the end. I wouldn't be here now.

As the political and economic situation gradually began to deteriorate, life for me remained busy and constant. I actually got busier, making more and more money and having less time to spend it. I had little social life. I was far too busy working. Even so, one can't be completely isolated from society. One form of contact came once a week by way of the Hungarian Army.

We were required to serve the civilian branch of the army one day a week, doing whatever work needed to be done. It might involve building roads or digging ditches or repairing drains— anything. I felt it was punishment enough to lose a day's work. I didn't want to have to work hard as well.

After the first few weeks, I showed up as ordered, but I had my arm wrapped up as though it were bandaged. While I was still required to remain with the work detail, I didn't have to do any of the hard, manual labor. The ruse worked very well for several weeks. Then the officer in charge questioned me.

"That's a long time for your arm to be hurt. You should be able to work by now." He expected me to do my share of the work. He insisted that my arm must be well. He wanted me to take off the bandages and begin working immediately.

"If that's what you want," I agreed with him. "But it'll be your responsibility if it gets worse."

He thought about that for a moment, ultimately deciding not to press the matter. I still had to show up once a week, at which time I was given the task of watching the food or clothes of the men who took off shirts and jackets in the heat of the day. I nursed that "injured arm" as long as possible.

By this time, my cousins had opened their own jewelry shop, Hertz having come from Rozavlea to work with them. I had the chance to become close with my cousins professionally as colleagues and also as friends. Hertz and I had purchased bicycles; and when we could, we enjoyed riding around the city. First, you have to understand that it was really two cities, Buda and Pest. We lived and worked in Pest. One of our favorite destinations was the public swimming pool, located in Buda.

This swimming pool was immense, easily the size of two city blocks, enclosed so that it could be enjoyed throughout the year. Hertz and I would ride our bicycles furiously up the steep hill to the pool, then relax in the water or race each other to see which one of us could swim the farthest or the fastest.

After a few hours, we would ride back down the hill, coasting, the wind helping to dry our hair from the pool. Usually, this was a very easy ride; but one day, as we came down the hill, Hertz lost control of his bicycle. I didn't even see why. Only that one moment he seemed to be fine, riding easily near me; the next, he was on the ground, rolling, his arms becoming tangled in the bicycle. He soon skidded to a halt, and I stopped next to him.

His bicycle was mangled beyond repair, but it was Hertz I was concerned about. I tried to help him, but he yelled in pain. The fall had broken his arm. Slowly, carefully, I helped him to stand. We managed to take him to a hospital where his arm was set. Hertz, always a young man of good humor, made light of his accident; but as long as we remained in the city, he always afterward walked down that hill.

I had never forgotten Mr. Katz, and it was important to me to prove to him that not only had I become successful, but I was actually making more money than he was. I did this by buying a seat in the Synagogue. At that time, you paid for your seats and if you paid enough money, you could request a particular seat. I made certain that my seat was next to Mr. Katz's. I didn't have to say anything. Simply sitting next to him, my clothes of the best quality, was enough to get my point across. In fact, I made a point of saying nothing to him, simply sitting and worshipping in the Synagogue.

Finally, one day he turned to me and demanded to know what I was doing there. I calmly told him that I was making more than enough money to purchase a good seat for services, and saw no reason why I shouldn't. I could tell that he was furious, his face flushed with anger, but there was nothing he could do.

Aside from becoming closer to my cousins, I counted, among my friends, several other young jewelers. We all worked long hours, but we also made time to see each other. Usually on Friday night, we would meet for dinner at a mutually agreed-upon restaurant. We made a point of going to expensive, fancy places. There, we relaxed for several hours, taking our time to eat. Since we did little else besides work, the conversation inevitably returned to the subject of the jewelry trade, techniques we used or recently learned, designs that we found popular in rings or bracelets.

Once in a while, the lure of society overcame the need to work. One thing I always wanted was to see what the inside of a nightclub was like. At seventeen, I was too young by several years to be allowed in. I still wanted to see what the inside was like, what happened in there. I decided I was going to go, too young or not. All I had to do was find a way. Borrowing the ID from an older friend easily solved that problem. I bought a nice tuxedo for the evening. With three older friends, I went to the nightclub. One of them had a car. He picked us up at my apartment and we went to the nightclub in fine style.

The main concern at the nightclub seemed to be if we could pay the tab. Money was no problem at that time. We were given a nice, fancy table. That night, I would witness an event that, small in and of itself, illustrated a lesson that has stayed with me to this day.

Sitting at the table next to ours was a very important, wealthy man. He was wearing an immaculate, expensive tuxedo. Well known in the nightclub, service for him was especially attentive. He appeared to be, at most, fifty years old. Sitting so close to his table, we couldn't help overhearing him. He called the waiter over and his request seemed so strange, we paused in our own conversation to listen.

"I want you to bring me a big pot of coffee," he instructed the waiter.

"Excuse me, sir?" The waiter was clearly confused. "A pot of *coffee*?"

"Yes, that's exactly what I want." He then proceeded to give specifics as to how big the pot should be, what kind and how much coffee to put in it. Everyone was looking at him like he was crazy. He ignored the stares. Crazy or not, he *was* very rich. He was paying for a particular service and he received it.

The waiter brought the pot to his table. Actually a large tureen, it was placed in the middle of his table. He then rose, taking off his bowtie and jacket. With something approaching ceremony, he immersed the jacket and tie in the coffee. Everyone began laughing. He paused for a moment, waiting for the commotion to subside.

"I'm sick and tired of people groveling for me because of what I have. A fancy tuxedo commands your attention and respect—not me, the person wearing the clothes. You confuse me with this fancy jacket and tie. So, as far as I'm concerned, let the clothing have the coffee."

The waiters were aghast. The rest of the customers continued laughing at the unexpected show. What he said stayed with me, though. He was right. You're judged by the suit you wear, the car you drive, the home you own. People glance at these surface things and by them, decide your worth as a human being. That's how it was in Budapest in 1943. That's how it is in the late '90s in Los Angeles where I live now. It's that way anywhere people gather. I don't think it's ever going to change.

In the latter part of 1943, my mother came to Budapest. She was diabetic. At home, there weren't any doctors, let alone a hospital where she could receive decent care. She went into the hospital. My sister Frieda and I made certain that she had excellent care.

Frieda had been living in Budapest for over a year by then. She also worked in the jewelry line, doing the polishing, but not for me. She would tell me how the other company did their work. It sounds like she was some kind of a spy for me, but it's not true. I have always felt that no matter how much I know, I can still learn something. I knew the jewelry line very well by then; but if there was a newer, better way of doing something, I wanted to learn about it. I really had only four years of public school. It was my only general education. Most of what I know, I learned from observing people, taking the time to absorb what they were willing to teach me.

My mother was quite ill. Frieda and I visited often. She was in the hospital for three or four months. Also in the hospital, there happened to be a lot of Polish Jews. They had left Poland, coming from the ghettos and villages. Some had been forced from their homes. Some harbored fears of what might happen to them if the Nazis did force them from their homes. They came to Hungary in the hopes of finding some stability.

Since the Hungarians signed a pact with Germany joining the Axis powers in 1940, our position, while precarious, appeared tolerable to us. It was understandable why the Jews from Poland would come to Budapest to find a safer place. Even so, the Nazi presence became increasingly apparent. Jewish people found the streets increasingly dangerous. Nazi sympathizers or Nazi youth groups began to regularly attack Jews in the streets.

The youth groups, more like gangs or packs of wolves, initially preyed on the weak or defenseless. As they did not suffer any legal ramifications from their assaults, the attacks gradually increased in frequency and violence. If anything, they found police and government turning a blind eye, at times even encouraging them. With their greater confidence, they began to look to other victims.

One night, a few friends and I went out for a walk. A gang of Nazi youth, equal in number to our group, felt we represented a threat to their superiority. They attacked us, convinced we would not fight back or prove a challenge if we did. Neither my friends nor myself intended to cave in to their threats. We fought back, delivering blows better than we received. To the surprise of the Nazi youth, my friends and I beat *them* up.

Bruised and somewhat the worse for the encounter ourselves, we couldn't help laughing at their expense as we finally continued on our way. We saw them as pathetic and cowardly. In the months to come, I would meet many more exactly like them. I had no idea to what murderous lengths a coward will go to prove himself brave.

People no longer trusted Hungarian money, preferring the universal appeal and perceived liquidity of gold. While this was good for business, particularly my business, it didn't instill feelings of confidence or security.

At the beginning of 1944, the world changed yet again. Life would never be the same for me or anyone I knew. The Germans occupied Hungary.

In Transit

The German occupation of Hungary impacted everyone immediately. Even those who did not consider themselves political in any way could not distance themselves from it. It was the only news we heard of. If you read a newspaper or listened to a radio, you got little information about anything else in the world. For the people living in Hungary, there was nothing else of importance in the world.

The situation only made people feel more compelled to buy and carry gold rather than currency. If I could have worked 24 hours a day, I would have been busy the entire time. My sister Frieda and I tried to maintain a semblance of normality to our lives. Neither of us would ever work so many hours that we could not visit our mother, who was still in a hospital to help treat her diabetes.

One day, not very long after the occupation, I got a call from my mother. "I want to go home," she said to me.

"What does the doctor say? Are you all right?"

"I'm scared. Please, I want to go home."

That was all she had to say. Frieda and I went to the hospital to get her. Mother was very anxious. Even with Frieda and I trying to calm her, it took some time before we were able to understand what had frightened and upset her so much.

The story was one neither of us expected to hear. Sharing my mother's room had been a Jewish woman from Poland. Like many Polish Jews before her, the woman had left her native country to try to find safety in a foreign land. When the woman heard the news on the radio about the German army invading Hungary and occupying Budapest, she had become hysterical.

My mother, in the bed next to hers, was finally able to help her calm down a little bit. She confided to my mother that she had come to Budapest to run away from the Nazi threat. "I don't want to be in their hands again," she told my mother. "Not another time." She told some stories of what the Nazis were doing to the Polish Jews.

My mother tried to reassure her that things would be different in Budapest. After all, it was a large, modern city. What had happened in Poland was the work of individual thugs and gangs, made possible by the strong undercurrent of anti-Semitism in Poland at the time.

Inconsolable, the woman jumped from the window of their fourth floor room. I still don't know which scared my mother more: the image of the woman's suicide, or the fact that she obviously felt death was preferable to being in the hands of the Nazis. It was so easy at the time to think the woman had over-reacted, that it was an isolated incident. It couldn't possibly be as bad as she said or perhaps even imagined. It was easy to see her stories as, at best, exaggerations of actual incidents. Human beings simply did not behave as she described. I would meet many other people over the next eighteen months who felt the same way as that woman who had shared a hospital room with my mother. I would experience for myself how human beings can behave.

With my mother so adamantly demanding to return home, I felt responsible for making certain my mother got back to Rozavlea.

Becoming frightened for Frieda and me as only a mother can, she insisted we return with her. Of course, we agreed. In an attempt to learn everything I could, I became a voracious consumer of all news and information.

On the radio, the newscasts continually updated the new laws, new restrictions. It was how we learned that the railroad station had been closed down. The train was still running, people still arriving. Our freedom of movement had just become abruptly limited. Public access to the station was now severely restricted. Essentially, no one could leave Budapest by rail.

It seemed reasonable that if the train arrived, it also left. If it arrived with people, it didn't make sense that it would depart empty. I went to the train station myself to see what was going on. When the Germans made a rule, they were very strict about carrying it out. The station was sealed off. I couldn't get in.

I watched carefully to determine what kind of access there was, if any. At one point, an ambulance went into the station. It was not stopped or checked by the guards at the gate. Seeing this, I reasoned this would be the best way to get into the station and from there, get out of Budapest.

I have always found that when something needs to be done, it is best to go directly to the person who has the authority to do something. To implement my idea, I went to the doctor who was the head of the hospital where my mother had been, explaining to him the situation up to that point. My sister and I simply wanted to take our mother back to our hometown. I was careful not to mention Rumania. Since the Hungarian Army invaded in 1940, my hometown was officially a part of Hungary.

He listened patiently as I explained what I planned to do. Through the hospital, he would order an ambulance, its destination being the railroad station. My mother, sister, and I would be traveling in the ambulance as patients. Skeptical, he did not believe such an idea would be successful. Despite his reservations, he was willing to try. As I was paying all of the expenses, he felt he had nothing to lose.

There was little time to prepare. I took all the available currency. More importantly, I stopped by my shop. Like the majority of my customers, confidence in the universal negotiating power of gold was deeper than in paper. I took as much as I could. Everything else I left. Getting into the ambulance for the trip to the station was the end of many things. I never went back to my shop. Perhaps the landlord took it over. Perhaps Miklosh, the employee who had so often pretended for me to be the owner, actually became one.

Thankfully, the doctor misjudged our chance for success. When our ambulance reached the station, we were allowed through, without any question or problem. We bought our tickets, boarded the train, and dared to hope the worst was over. The fear that had propelled us was diminishing. We were on our way home. We were safe and secure.

A couple of miles out from the city, there was a lake that the train crossed by bridge. We felt that once we had the physical barrier of the lake between the train and Budapest, we could begin to relax. That thought was premature and short-lived. The train had not yet reached the bridge when the engineer got a red light, signaling him to return to the station. The anxiety, that had only begun to dissipate, returned full force.

Upon arriving back at the station, all passengers were made to disembark. No one was allowed to leave. Everyone was sitting around the station. Some were perturbed, some angry, some frustrated. None were happy.

My mother was sick. Frieda and I were concerned about her. All three of us were uncertain about what to do next. Feeling they would be safe for the time being at the station among the other passengers, I left Mother in Frieda's care while I set out to assess the situation.

In the middle of the night, I sneaked out of the station by following along the tracks. There was a small city nearby. Going from house to house, I began knocking on doors in the hope of finding shelter. It was frustrating. People were understandably reluctant to open their homes to an unknown teenager. That didn't mean to stop trying.

Finally, a young bachelor opened the door to a small home. He was willing to listen to me. I briefly outlined the situation at the station. I needed to rent a room for my mother, sister, and myself for a short period of time. I thought it might be for only a couple of days. It wasn't charity. He would be paid for the time we spent there. He agreed.

Returning to the station, by the route I left, posed no problem. Guarding the tracks, at that time, was evidently a low priority. Using that same route, Mother and Frieda went with me to the house where I had rented the room. I felt better knowing they had a proper place to stay.

Every day for the next two or three days, I went back to the station. It was the only way to learn what was happening. Although rumors were common, one caught my attention by its very persistence. Word was out that women and children would be allowed to go through. It wasn't everything we had hoped for, but it was enough at the time for me.

I was very happy to hear it. Not wanting to take the chance of missing the opportunity in case the rumor was true, I had Mother and Frieda return with me to the station. I bought them tickets again. They didn't want to leave me there, but I couldn't go with them. Though still only a teenager, I was too old to qualify as a child. Only my sincere assurances of joining them soon placated their protests. They got on the train. It left, with them, on schedule. It did not receive a red light, forcing it back. I was left alone at the station.

Now I was faced with the dilemma of how to keep my promise. With the next train that came in, I took the initiative. The engineer was the one who could help the most, I reasoned, if he chose to. There was also the fear that he would choose not to. He had little to gain by the former and nothing to lose by the latter. I approached him, telling him simply that I wanted to go home with the rest of my family. Even with the promise of a sizeable cash payment, he was reluctant to agree.

The final plan was one with which he could feel comfortable. I was to follow the tracks out for a mile or so, then wait nearby. If the train then goes by me at full speed, it means the SS are on board, likely up front with the engineer. If it slows down, then I was to jump on the train in front with the engineer. Once the train gets back up to speed, it was only a matter of, at most, ten miles before reaching the bridge. To get to the far side of the bridge was the goal. On that side, there was no problem.

When the train left the station, I was waiting a mile away, near the tracks as we'd agreed. Waiting, not knowing what to expect, I could only hope things would work out. To my surprise and relief, the train slowed as it neared me. I was as happy as I could be. I jumped up on the train and rode with the engineer.

Again, happiness was short-lived. After traveling only another mile or so, the engineer got a red light, the signal for him to return to the station. There was no choice. He started back to the station.

Fearing that he might be caught, terrified of what might happen to him if he was, he yelled at me to jump off the train. It was not open to discussion or argument. I jumped into the river as we passed by.

Not willing to take extraordinary chances, I waited in the water several hours past the time when the train disappeared from my sight. It was dark by the time I went into the woods, cold and wet. With nowhere else to go that I would feel safe, I returned to the home where I had rented a room for the past few days.

I was very fortunate. Once again, he helped me out with a place to stay for the night. By the next day, my clothes were dry. I went back to the railroad station.

There was a definite risk in returning. I knew that, but I had never been one to negate a course of action because of it. The risk came in the form of the SS, who were patrolling the forest. If they would catch me, they would not hesitate in killing me. No appeal on my part would stay the execution. For whatever reason, I was lucky. I made it back to the railroad station without encountering any SS.

This time, I tried a different option. Again, I spent some time observing what was going on, what was being done, and how it was being done. The railroad workers had no problem going through. They had their official IDs: the Nazi swastika on one side; their photograph on the other.

I went to the same conductor. I suggested to him that he allow me to use his ID. He was understandably dubious, knowing what would happen to him if he didn't have the proper identification if and when he might need it. To allay his fears, I agreed to say, in the event I was caught, that I found the ID in the station. He would say he had lost it. We both hoped we would not have to tell the story.

Getting on the train was no problem. The SS boarded the train as well. While avoiding contact with any of them for as long as possible, I watched carefully as the other rail workers presented their IDs. When requested, they held the picture, showing the swastika to the officer. Eventually, I could avoid it no longer. An SS officer came to me, requesting my ID. In compliance, I held out the conductor's ID, my thumb causally covering his photograph.

There was no internal lighting on the train. The officer used a hand-held flashlight to check the IDs. He was obviously bored with his job. He glanced perfunctorily at the ID I held out for his inspection. I held my breath without meaning to. It sounded so loud to me, I was certain he could hear the rhythm of my heart beating.

"Very good," he pronounced. Without another glance at me, he continued on his rounds.

Shortly after that, the train crossed the bridge. With relief, I watched, as the physical barrier of the lake grew more formidable. The SS were on the other side. I changed trains at that station, without any of the obstacles I experienced on the other side of the bridge. Before I left, I returned the railworker's ID to the conductor. He was happy both with having his document returned and with the large monetary payment I had made to him in Budapest.

I was going home. I could allow myself to believe that the worst was over. I couldn't have been more mistaken.

The train came to a stop in the city of Sighet, a city not far from Rozavlea. The Germans were already there. My heart sank. Everything I had done to put the Germans behind me had been useless.

I made my way home as quickly as I could. When I got there, I immediately began to prepare for the worst. We felt that no matter what may happen, in exchange for gold, you can always get something to eat. With that thought in mind, Frieda and I began to fashion as much of the gold as I had been bringing home during the past year or so into items we could easily carry with us. I made belts for my father and myself. On my mother's fur coat, we removed the heavy, original buttons. We replaced them with buttons made of 24-carat gold. We sewed gold into all kinds of clothing. We didn't know what was going to happen, what to expect. We could only hope that our precautions would be enough.

The gold Frieda and I worked into clothing and accessories represented only a small portion of the amount of gold I had been bringing home with me over the previous few years. We never had the opportunity to exhume most of the jars from their burial places in the orchards of our farm. Over the years, I sometimes wondered what ever happened to it all. I imagine some farmer may have accidentally dug it up, or perhaps some of it was washed away as the river changed course over the years. The only thing I know for certain is that no one in my family ever saw any of it again.

Restrictive orders were being announced and summarily enforced on a daily basis. All Jews were required to wear armbands displaying the Star of David. A strict curfew was imposed. Jews had to remain indoors at night. Minor infractions could carry a swiftly meted-out death penalty.

Each morning, a drummer went through the town. He was a Rumanian Gentile who was a village employee. Every few blocks, he would stop, loudly beating the drum to command attention. He then proceeded to announce the new orders for the day. His voice carried. He repeated the proclamations. No excuse for disobedience was accepted.

Living with the uncertainty of what the next day would bring, Frieda and I worked tirelessly to fashion gold buckles, buttons, and so forth. We replaced whatever we could as quickly as possible.

On the morning of April 15, 1944, the drummer made the announcement that all Jews were ordered to gather at the Shul. We were to bring with us whatever we could carry. Everything else was to be left behind. It would all be cared for and returned to us after the war was over.

At the Shul, they had complete control over our movements and actions. In the Shul, around the Shul, in the backyard of the Shul, the local *gendares*, the Hungarian police, augmented the number of German Nazi guards.

From the beginning, we were told that we were being taken to a camp, far from the fighting of the war, which would have everything we needed. It was to be only a temporary situation until the end of the war. It was a measure undertaken for our own safety, to keep us away from the deadly advance of foreign troops. At the end of the war, we would be allowed to go home. Everything—our farms, property, business—would be protected for us until then, returned to us at that time.

We had very little contact with the outside world. Even though my mother had heard the stories from the Polish woman in Budapest, it was easy to believe what we were being told.

Waiting for us at the Shul were long lines of horses and wagons. The omnipresent guards ensured nonconfrontational compliance. While nobody likes having someone point a rifle at his back, we still didn't feel a deep-seated reason to disbelieve what they told us. No one could possibly have imagined what was actually awaiting us. Whatever suspicions we may have had were easily rationalized and dispelled.

We had always been taught not to fight. This situation seemed to be no different. With no choice but to leave behind everything we'd worked for all of our lives, there was a certain level of comfort in accepting their word.

Under the watchful eyes of the Hungarian gendares, who were themselves watched by the German Nazis, we cooperated, complying by doing exactly what we were told. We got into the waiting wagons with almost no protest, my family making a concerted effort to remain together. When all of the Jews were in the wagons, we were taken to another town, Dragomiresti, approximately twelve kilometers away, where the Nazis created a ghetto by combining the local populations of Jews from about ten other towns and villages. The Nazi control seemed complete.

Approximately 4,000 people from throughout the area crowded into Dragomiresti, putting living space at a premium. Forty people or more would share a single house and barn. Most of the houses being used had not belonged to Jewish families. A Gentile family would be forced by the gendares to house a number of Jewish families. Naturally, this served only to exacerbate any animosity between Jews and Gentiles, who now saw us as, at best, unwanted intruders. Latent irritations easily surfaced. We were then charged an inflated rent for our accommodations.

And still the lies from the Nazis continued, the lies we chose to accept as truth. This inconvenience was only temporary. For our own protection, we were being taken to a safe camp until the war was over. Everything would return to normal then.

Again, we had no idea how long the current situation would last. Food was scarce. I was reminded of my first days in Budapest, when I was constantly hungry.

Young and healthy, I took it upon myself to look for food for my family. One night, in defiance of the curfew, I went out looking for something we could eat. Two SS guards stopped me. One of them wanted to shoot me immediately. For the first of many times, my fluency in German was a benefit to me.

Fortunately for me, the second guard was not as quick to mete out capital punishment as was the first one was. Taking advantage of their disagreement, I simply explained to them, in German, that I was out looking for food.

It was my good luck that the more lenient of the two guards took over. "Just don't do it anymore," he told me sternly. "Next time, you *will* be shot."

Thanking them both for their understanding, I ran back to the house I was sharing with my family and several other families. Though I brought back no food, as I had told them I would, my mother was glad to see me. I never told her how close I came to not returning.

While in the ghetto of Dragomiresti, we had even less awareness of the outside world than we had back home in Rozavlea. Even so, there were rumors and speculations. There were those who chose to believe the rumors and not the Nazis. Many of those wanted to resist, fight back. Some advocated escaping from the ghetto, hiding in the surrounding forest and fighting from there.

I was approached by some of those who planned to try escape. I must admit that I found the offer very tempting. If I managed to escape with them, I would have the chance to fight back, to regain control of my own life. I seriously considered the option. When I mentioned the possibility to my family, my parents became very upset.

"Where will you go?" my mother asked me. "How will you survive in the forest, living like an animal?" I know she also feared losing contact with me. How could any of us have ever imagined that soon, I would, in fact, be living as less than an animal.

The whole family could not have left in the best of circumstances. Gitel Marim could not survive in the forest and my mother would never leave her behind. My father and Frieda both had the strength to go with me, but my father would not leave my mother and little sister alone. Frieda preferred to stay with the family.

The chance to leave and fight back was all I could think of for most of the next couple of days. For a while, I thought that if I left,

I might be able to find a safe place for the rest of my family. The more grandiose my ideas became, the more I realized the futility of them. I finally told them, "No."

Even at that time, I had a difficult time believing that things would get very much worse for us. I even believed that after the war, we would go home. The determining factor for me, though, was my family. They were the most important thing to me. I didn't want to leave them. In my own way, I had always tried to take care of them, provide for them however I could. If our trust in the Nazis should prove misplaced, I could not abandon them. I simply could not leave them to unknown whims of fate. If it should be that they would somehow suffer, then I would be there with them, sharing their fate.

I have often thought back to that chance to leave Dragomiresti. At the same time, though, I remember my parents, my sisters. I especially remember my little sister, eleven-year-old Gitel Marim. I have no regrets about what may appear to others to be a lack of action. Even in hindsight, I feel I made the right decision.

During our time in the ghetto, the house we stayed at was home to almost forty people. There was no such luxury as one family per room. It was more like each family having its own corner. There were no beds. You slept on the floor, close to each other for comfort. For warmth, as well as emotional comfort, we held each other, covering ourselves with whatever coats or heavy clothing we may have brought with us as blankets.

We had been in Dragomiresti for only four weeks when the orders came that forced us to move out again. We had to meet the train that would take us to the promised camp where we were to wait out the war. The ghetto was in a town only about ten miles from Rozavlea. It was still too small for a train station. This time, the Nazis provided no wagons for us.

On May 15, came orders to leave the homes we had temporarily occupied, orders to leave the ghetto. We would be marching to meet the train. Once again, we made choices as to what to bring with us, what to leave behind. Carrying belongings to the Shul in Rozavlea was different from carrying things on a march of unknown length to an unknown destination.

By being forced out of the ghetto in late spring, we avoided the harsh winter conditions. Instead, ice and snow had recently melted, soaking into the winter-hardened earth. The ground was really just thick mud, greedily holding onto our shoes as we tried to keep up with the pace set by those in front, who kept a pace set by the Nazis. The march was, at best, difficult and arduous.

Not everyone had the strength or stamina to keep pace on the march. We tried to help each other, however possible. We encouraged each other verbally, held each other for physical support. For some people, it was simply not possible to continue. They couldn't keep the pace, trudging through the mud. Those individuals would just stop walking, moving away from our makeshift column, letting the rest of us pass them by.

The pace set by the Nazis never slackened, never giving us the chance to stop. We never even paused to allow those who had moved out of the column the opportunity to catch up with us. To do so would have invited a beating, or death. Those who were unable to continue walking simply stood, or sat in place, their few remaining possessions at their feet or held in their arms. Left behind on the road, we soon lost sight of them. Behind us, the sharp report of pistol fire reached us, diffused by distance.

We still did not stop.

Finally, we reached our destination. The march had lasted most of the day. We had walked close to 25 kilometers, over the Carpathian Mountains and through the energy-sapping mud. We had not been allowed to pause or rest. When the order came for us to stop, we were almost too tired to be relieved.

In any other circumstances, the image we encountered might have appeared humorous. There was no city, no town, and no village to be seen. We found ourselves at a standstill in a huge, open field near the town of Vishveh. There, in the middle of the field, was a train with hundreds of empty boxcars. No station, just tracks and train. It appeared completely out of place, like some mythic sea creature stranded on land.

With no station, there were no porters, ticket booths or rail workers. Instead, there were SS—hundreds and hundreds of them. Each SS man held a machine gun as though it were an integral part of his physical body.

Orders shouted in German accompanied sharp prods and blows when people who had no knowledge of the language didn't respond quickly enough. Few of us had much in the way of personal belongings left. Some of what little we had of our former lives was to be left on the field. Once again, the decision of what to leave, what to take, had to be made. My family and I felt ourselves fortunate because we still wore the clothing with the concealed gold that gave us the sense that we might still be able to purchase any necessity. Between all of us, we also carried some extra bags containing personal belongings. Many other people had only the clothing they wore.

Decisions had to be made quickly. The SS were impatient with our lack of speed. Dissatisfied with how long the boarding was taking, we were hit, thrown into the waiting boxcars like animals. Not really like animals as I'm certain that animals would have been shown greater compassion.

There was no dissension. If someone had been inclined to protest, the inclination was efficiently beaten out of him. We were forced into the boxcars with less concern for comfort or accommodation than is given to cows or goats. No space inside was left unoccupied. Maybe a hundred people were forced into an area where fifty might have felt ill at ease and cramped.

When a car was loaded to capacity, the doors were shut and bolted from the outside. Hearing the metallic sound of the bolt sliding shut to lock us inside did more than anything else up to that point to fill me with a sense of foreboding. The interior of the sealed boxcar was dark, claustrophobic. The very air soon became thin, stale. I wanted nothing more than to take a deep breath, but found that short, shallow breaths came easier. Someone began to cry.

Another demanded the crying stop. It did no good. Entreaties that the complaints might anger the Germans fell on uncomprehending ears. We talked, everyone full of questions.

Where were we going? Most were willing to voice their uncertainty. Others were willing to share their knowledge: "To the camp, of course. The nice camp the Germans had promised us."

Where was this camp? Of that, no one was certain. The train moved steadily to a place no one imagined. Even then, trapped like animals in the dark, we chose to believe the Nazi lies. We had no choice. Not believing did not change our situation. No one could remotely imagine what actually awaited us. The Germans were intelligent, civilized people. Things might be bad for a time, but that would only be temporary.

The more a person loses, the more desperately he may try to hold on to what remains. Space was at a premium. We sat in each other's laps. Each boxcar was allotted one pail for all of the people to use for waste. With up to a hundred people in a car, the pail filled quickly. The doors locked from the outside, there was no way to empty it. It soon overflowed. The stench was choking, stulifying.

No food was given to us. A few in the car had a little food they had carried with them since leaving the ghetto. It was soon gone.

Once every 24 hours or so, the train stopped. At that time, the doors were opened. We would gasp, desperate to fill our lungs with fresh air, coughing out the stale, rancid air we'd been forced to breathe. It was also our opportunity to empty the pail.

From each car, one or two people were designated to fill a few pails with water. That water was to be shared by all in the car until the next stop. I was one of those chosen from our car to get the water.

It was hot in the enclosed boxcar, so I had taken off my shirt to make myself more comfortable. The train had stopped at an open field. There was an old-fashioned hand pump for water. We were allowed only a specific amount of time to accomplish the task. When the designated water carrier placed the bucket under the spigot, another deportee quickly pumped the water. All this was done under the watchful eyes of the SS.

In reality, we were prisoners and had been for some time. No one, neither German nor Jew, had yet been willing to state the truth of the situation. No one was willing to pierce the façade the Germans had labored so hard to create. No one was willing to expose the truth of what the Germans had set in motion and no Jew had the ability to stop.

When my turn came to place my bucket under the water pump, I wasn't fast enough. The Germans, an almost obsessively punctual people, had a strict schedule that was to be followed. My perceived incompetence imperiled the fulfillment of their timeline. Punishment was swift and painful. The SS guard near the pump beat me across my back with a stick until I could barely stand. To this day, I'm surprised he didn't break any of my bones. I got the bucket of water filled and returned to the boxcar.

By the time I got there, my back was black and blue. The pain was unlike anything I had experienced up to that time, stinging and throbbing simultaneously. My mother wanted to comfort me, help ease my pain. To even touch my back brought renewed pain at the point of contact. Mother could do little more for me than to hold my hand.

Gently, she held my hand and stroked my face. Her voice soft, she said to me, "I just hope it will never be worse than this." She had an instinct, a growing feeling shared by us all that this was not the worst, but merely the beginning.

A few buckets of water does little to quench the thirst of only a handful people for an entire day. For close to a hundred people in a hot boxcar, it was little better than nothing. Even trying to make certain that everyone got a little, inevitably some people received nothing at all. The heat of the car made us feel our thirst even more keenly. Any water, any moisture was coveted. We would lick the walls of the car in the hope that some residual morning dew might take an edge off our dry tongues.

The trains stopped once more for water. I often wondered why they bothered giving us water at all. The only reason I can think of is that they needed workers, slave labor. There was a war going on. Roads needed to be graded, pipes laid in the ground, factories built, and so on. The younger people, the healthy ones, the strong ones were kept alive—barely, only enough to be able to perform the required tasks. When they could no longer do the job, they were killed or gassed, along with all the others who had not been among the lucky ones chosen as slaves. It was as simple as that.

After traveling for almost three days, the trains slowed to a stop. We heard the sound of the doors being unbolted, a sound heard only twice since we boarded the train after the march from the ghetto. We had no idea where we were. I thought perhaps it was another stop for water. Someone else thought we had finally arrived at our promised destination. We had no time to speculate.

Everyone in our car blinked in automatic response to the bright light flooding into the boxcar as the doors slid open. It was impossible to determine, at first, if it was night or day.

Nobody had died in our car. I learned later that was unusual. Most of the other cars contained at least some corpses, people who would never again be bothered by the light.

With the light came the harsh, shouted orders for everyone to get up, leave the boxcar. Sore and stiff from the cramped quarters of three days in the boxcar, it was difficult to disembark swiftly. Those who didn't move quickly enough received beatings for their disobedience.

There was no longer any decision to be made about which possessions to take, which to leave. All personal belongings had to be left in the boxcar.

None of the shouts or orders gave us the name of the camp. It would not have mattered. I doubt if any of us had ever heard of it before. Only later would I learn the name of the camp, a name now synonymous with misery and death.

We had arrived at Auschwitz.

PART TWO

Death

Auschwitz

As we disembarked from the boxcars, dragged out if we did not move quickly enough, the assault began immediately. It was physical, mental, emotional, visual, aural. Glaring, bright lights seared our vision. It was physically painful after so long in the darkness of the boxcar. Like many others, I held my arm up in front of my eyes as they adjusted to the intensity of the lights. The artificial light gave the view a surreal, garish quality. Day and night, the lights blazed. We couldn't tell right away if it was morning or evening.

Before we had the chance to clear up that confusion, we were shouted at in German to get out of the boxcars: "Fast, fast!" If you moved slower than it was thought you should, you were beaten. If one of the guards didn't like your looks or clothes, you were beaten. If one of the SS simply felt like hitting a prisoner at that moment and you happened to be in front of him, you were beaten. The slightest infraction of instructions elicited a beating, the sound of gunfire attesting to the common administration of capital punishment.

Families became separated easily and quickly in the mass of humanity. My family was no different. No amount of shouting drew their attention back to me. They may have been shouting for me, but their voices were lost in the confusion of sound. We never had the chance to say goodbye to each other.

Upon my arrival in Auschwitz, I saw flames in the distance, providing a surreal backdrop to the bright lights and music. I didn't know what the fire was from. I felt there was only one way for me to find out.

Aside from beatings and killings, there was no physical contact between prisoners and guards. To them, we were beneath animals. Whereas an animal, like a dog, might actually become a cherished pet, in their eyes, we were fit only for work and death. Human contact came in the form of other prisoners. They pulled us out of the boxcars, pressed us to move more quickly, collected our personal property, which had to be left and was now property of the Reich. The SS watched, making certain everything ran on schedule, ready to mete out corporal or capital punishment as they deemed expedient.

A number of disparately different things commanded complete attention at the same time: blinding lights, making vision difficult, shouted German imperatives, cries of anguish from prisoners, barking of guard dogs, sounds of distant and not-so-distant gunshots, a full orchestra playing loudly over the din. It was impossible to think, to concentrate on any one thing. Every sense was overwhelmed, the cacophony adding to the confusion.

Because of that, I can't describe any one thing in great detail. And yet, to this day, over fifty years later, I can close my eyes and my senses are attacked once again. The sights, sounds, smells are so distinct; I fear, if I open my eyes, I will find myself stepping off the train, about to be pummeled by an SS guard for taking too long.

In a setting where nothing made sense, the most incongruous element was the orchestra. Made up of any and all instruments, it contained forty or fifty musicians. The family of midgets who had not so many years before traveled all over the country to perform were now playing in the orchestra which greeted us as we left the train. The rest of the orchestra was made up of internees from all over Europe. They played loud enough to draw attention. Perhaps they played loud enough, with enough single-minded dedication, to be able to forget where they played and for whom.

Before our arrival, thousands upon thousands of Jews representing virtually every country of Eastern Europe had been brought to Auschwitz. Some of those were accomplished musicians who, by some unbelievable miracle, still had their instruments in their possession. If a musician arrived without an instrument, it really didn't matter. The Nazis would simply provide the new member of the orchestra with any one of hundreds of professional instruments that they had recently acquired.

Even as we heard the shouts and screams to move, move quickly, other German shouts could be heard asking if anyone from our transport played an instrument of any kind. To pause long enough to isolate the request from the general melee of sound was to risk receiving a beating.

We were tired, hungry, thirsty, dirty, confused. We didn't know what was going on. We didn't know where we were going, even as the SS forced us to move away from the trains. We didn't know it was Auschwitz and certainly not what that meant for us. Only by seeing the name on a sign was I able to associate the name with the current location. Part of the sign had the inscription *"Arbeit Macht Frei,"* German for the statement "Work Will Make You Free." Even that told me nothing. I had no idea where this place was. It seemed even then to exist in its own reality, outside of anything from my own experience.

It was no longer surprising to us to be treated as less than animals by the SS. They herded us to a large, open, lighted staging area under a barrage of blows from sticks and rifle butts. At the end of the area was the now infamous Dr. Mengele, playing God, pointing his cane slightly to the left or right as he decreed a person's life or death after the most fleeting of glances. Naturally,

I had no idea that the well-dressed man who arbitrarily separated loved ones, untouched by any plea, was Mengele; or even that at that moment, he condemned people to death with a calm tilt of his cane. Only later, did some of the other prisoners tell me who he was. I soon saw for myself the destination he sent thousands of human beings to. Years later, I read of medical experiments he conducted on inmates, torture proclaimed necessary in the name of scientific advancement.

Women and children formed one group, lining up by fives, men in a separate group. The shouts and screams, which had never ceased, included new directions. We were instructed to line up in front of Dr. Mengele, each line to contain no more than five people. As usual, a person not following directions precisely was beaten into obedience. Those around him might just as easily be beaten for allowing the transgression. If the offense was deemed too egregious, the offending individual was simply executed on the spot. With that as an incentive, lines of five people formed in front of Mengele, stretching across the staging area for perhaps a quarter of a mile or more.

Mengele's cane had a gentle curve for a handle. It had a graceful elegance, which usurped by Mengele became soulless precision. If someone dared hesitating after receiving the pronouncement of death or life, right or left, Mengele would use the curved handle to pull that person in the intended direction. On his slightest whim, the curved handle pulled someone by the neck, forcing them out of line. He never touched someone with his own hands. Jews were too far beneath him. The cane provided him with a buffer of distance that made contact tolerable for him.

I no longer had the luxury of calling or looking for my family. It happened that I wound up in one of the lines of five near the front. I could see Mengele as he glanced at the five people in front of him. He had very dark eyes. What struck me was that dark eyes normally seem warm and caring. His were devoid of sentiment or human emotion. He'd send human beings to death with less concern than stepping on an ant.

Our line of five drew closer. Even then, watching him point right, point left, had no real meaning. I had no idea that one meant death, the other slave labor's temporary reprieve from death. I did know the price of not following instructions to their satisfaction. My back had not yet had time to heal. I had no intention of doing anything that might possibly incur another beating.

As our line slowly moved forward, another man came to stand in line beside me. Now our line contained six people.

"You can't stay here," I told him. "The line can only have five people in it."

He ignored me. I quickly looked around, trying to find out where the guards stood, afraid the man's presence would earn us all beatings. They stood far enough away not to notice our transgression. I tried again to reason with him. "There can't be six in a line. If you stay, we'll all get hit."

It didn't matter. He refused to leave the line. Unwilling to risk a beating for someone else's disobedience, I left the line. Now, I had to find somewhere to go, a line which contained only four people that I could join as the fifth. I ran along the column, heading to the back of the staging area. I checked line after line, counting, searching.

Every line was full. From my original position near the front, I was now almost at the back. It felt like I had traveled more than a mile. In reality, I had gone no more than perhaps a quarter of a mile. Even while seeking a line to join, glancing at hundreds, if not thousands of faces, I did not see my parents or sisters. I felt very alone.

At the rear of the staging area, the last line contained less than five. In fact, there was only a single man, silently following the people in front of him. To my amazement, I recognized my Uncle David.

He was very happy to see me, no less surprised than I to find a relative. His experience so far had been similar to mine. He had quickly lost contact with Aunt Malka and his children. I was the first relative he had seen since being separated from them when they had come off the transport.

He grabbed my hand, determined not to lose sight of me along with the rest of his family. "Hold my hand," he said. "We need to stay together."

I held my uncle's hand, but didn't respond. Slowly, inexorably, we walked forward to face Mengele. I can't really explain what I was feeling then. Certainly, I was overwhelmed by sight, sound, the ache I still felt from my beating only two days before. Holding my uncle's hand, knowing that a relative, even one only by marriage, was beside me was reassuring to a certain extent. Yet, I felt anxious.

In response to my uncle's vows to stay together, I said nothing. I did not want to make a promise to him that I might not be able to keep.

We approached Mengele. We could see his cane as he moved it gracefully from side to side, indicating to the prisoners in front of him the direction to move. Left. Right. Life. Death. We had no way of knowing which was which. For that matter, we had no way of knowing that death was waiting in one of the directions pointed out by the cane.

Finally, no more lines of prisoners separated us from Mengele. My uncle and I stood facing him. He glanced at us as at all those before us. When I expected his cane to move, telling me the direction to take . . . nothing. He gave us no indication, no instruction of any kind. The inaction numbed me. I didn't know what to do or think.

My uncle, still holding my hand, made the decision. "Come with me," he instructed, as he started to the left.

To this day, I have no idea what impelled me to disobey him. It might have been a feral instinct. It was certainly not a considered, rational decision. I pulled my hand away from his. "No," I said. "I'm not going with you. I'm going my own way."

He called to me, even as he continued walking to the left. I ran from him, ran in the opposite direction as fast as I could. I don't know why I ran or what I was running toward, but I ran. The people from our transport were already gone. No one stopped me. No one told me anything. I continued running like a crazy person.

Finally, I found a large group of deportees. I became a part of the crowd, mixing myself up with the rest. It happened to be a group designated as workers. Only much later, did I learn that Uncle David had gone in the direction of those to be gassed. Whether he died that day, the next day, or in two days, I never knew. That is because I also learned later that not everyone selected to be gassed was killed right away. They didn't have the capacity to gas so many people at once. Some people were kept alive for a day or so until room in the gas chamber could be made for them. All I know for certain is that I never saw Uncle David again.

No time was wasted in putting us to work. After all, the Reich had already incurred a great deal of expense in time and money on our behalf. The use of a train for three days, the personnel to run it, not to mention the guards, dogs, and bullets. The money for these things had been spent. They expected a return on that investment. I was assigned to a work detail almost immediately. I wasn't even given the chance to change my clothes.

There were only a few people assigned with me. The work we were given was simple and not strenuous. The guards led us to another building. Already, I was getting used to their presence. Always, everything was under the watchful eyes of the guards. The building they led us to was the place where the women prisoners were brought. The male prisoners went through the same treatment in a separate building.

The Nazis called it a "barbershop." It was actually a large barracks, like a warehouse. People stood in line, waiting for their hair to be shaved off, more like a factory than anything else.

Shaving the hair off of the prisoner was the first part of the process of being completely integrated into the camp. This applied to any prisoner who was not immediately gassed. It may have been an attempt to control the ever-present lice infestation. I think that happened to be just a fortunate by-product. I believe it was done as a form of humiliation, especially for the women.

The hair was not cut very short, but shaved completely off. And it was not just the hair from the head, but from every part of the body. To accomplish this, people were made to strip naked prior to entering the barracks. Kept in line by the guards, they waited, nude, for the barbers. Using electric razors, the barbers shaved the women. Head, arms, legs, and pubis. The shaving was done as quickly as possible to make room for the next person.

The women were then led out of the barracks, led into a steam shower. On the opposite side of the shower was the exit. Led out, they were issued prisoner clothing, then assigned to their own work units or *kommandos*. Some never had more than a few days reprieve before being led to the gas chambers, immediate execution awaiting anyone who made a move toward stepping out of the line of five. This went on every day, seven days a week, twenty-four hours a day.

My first assigned task was to pick up the hair. It accumulated quickly—mounds of it. There seemed to be tons of it, a never-ending supply. After every two or three people were shorn, I collected the hair from the floor and put it into bags. When the bags were filled to capacity, other prisoners took them away. Many years later, I read somewhere that the hair was used as insulating material on the German U-boats or made into cloth and sold to German firms for 50 pfennings per kilo.

That first day, as I picked up hair, only women had been lined up, stripped, waiting to have their hair shaved. Hundreds of them had come from my hometown. Girls I knew, nice-looking girls—there they stood, naked, cold. They recognized me. I was embarrassed, but not nearly as much as they were. I went about my business, concentrating on the hair, cleaning the floor as best I could. Sometimes, glancing up and catching their frightened look was unavoidable.

I never spoke with any of them. There was nothing to say. The girls looked away from me. Some turned or tried to hide behind someone else. Some hunched their shoulders, attempting to cover as much of themselves as possible with their arms and hands, trying to make themselves as small and inconspicuous as possible. I felt sorry for them and tried to focus on something else, anything else.

This went on hour after hour. I can't even remember how long I was there. Finally, I was taken to another barracks. It was a long building, containing rows of bunks stretching from one end to the other, three tiers high. The bunks themselves were little more than long planks of wood. It seemed as though hundreds of prisoners had to crowd into the one barracks. We slept as close as possible to each other, not for comfort, but out of necessity.

At mealtime, our treatment was no better than how we had fed the animals on our farm. One plate of food was shared among three or four people. We had no utensils. We either grabbed whatever food we could and ate with our hands or went hungry. Amazingly, I saw some people who refused to share a plate of food under those conditions. They chose not to eat. The others, sharing that person's plate, were happy because that meant they had more food for themselves. We were unable to wash, so we ate with dirty hands, unlike home where washing hands before eating was an essential preparation for the meal. I knew that I had to eat to stay alive. I was able to manage by closing my eyes, trying not to see things as they were. I hated to be forced to behave like an animal. Even so, I grabbed my portion from the plate.

More trains like the one I arrived on came in. Like the parade through the makeshift barbershop, the trains arrived seven days a week, twenty-four hours a day. Nothing stopped. The electric razors removed hair from new arrivals without pause. Only the barber holding the razor changed. Sometimes, he returned to shave more of the new arrivals. Sometimes, he didn't. The concept of time held little meaning anymore for many prisoners in any practical way. Some of the prisoners clung to the days and weeks as the only constant in our new life, something that was the same in the camp as it was out of it.

In the distance, in another part of the camp, we could see constant fire, the flames I had seen upon my arrival in the camp. One of the first things I did was to approach one of the other prisoners, a young man, perhaps only a few years older than myself, who had already been in the camp for a while. Considering him a knowledgeable old-timer, I asked him what was going on. He looked at me gravely and said, "It's a bakery."

Within a few days, I learned the truth. He must have thought it was some macabre joke to tell me that; or perhaps he honestly wanted to believe that himself.

At night, the glow of the flames dominated the horizon. I didn't believe it was a bakery even as he told me, but didn't know what, in fact, it was. When I asked some other prisoners, no one had an answer. Like me, they didn't know or else they wouldn't say.

After ten days working in the barbershop, I was given a new job. They took me to the far end of the camp, where the fire was. On the way, I saw a group of children, waiting outside, surrounded by a wire enclosure. It vaguely reminded me of how we sometimes kept animals on the farm in enclosures when we wanted them close at hand before slaughtering them for dinner. I had no idea at the time that the kommando I was being assigned to was the *sonderkommando,* or "special unit," and my work would be in the gas chamber and crematoria. I suppose I should have been afraid— that I wasn't, I have never thought of as being brave. I had already developed a level of numbness. I simply didn't know enough about where I was taken to understand how frightened I should have been.

There, the workers were under constant supervision. Each one had a number tattooed onto his forearm. I never received that particular identifying mark. To be perfectly honest, I have no idea why not. Perhaps I missed it when I ran from my uncle and mixed myself up with the other workers. I was even wearing my own clothing for the first few days. When I was finally issued the prisoner clothes, my head shaved like those of everyone else, my number 98,576* was on the patch sewn into place on the uniform.

---

*This number has been changed to protect my identity.

Not once did a guard ever ask to see my arm. If I was required to be somewhere or to do something, I was merely pointed at and given instructions. If they needed to know my number, they had only to look at the patch on my uniform.

At the time, it didn't strike me as unusual not to have the tattoo since not everyone had them. Again, it was years later that I read that only some groups of prisoners received the identifying tattoo, and then only in Auschwitz.

Perhaps they didn't feel the need for any further identification. No one left this area unless the guards or SS knew about it. Most likely, they simply never knew I did not have the tattoo. Somehow, number 98,576 slipped through a very small crack in the machinery of Auschwitz.

They had complete control over us. Working the crematoria was itself a death sentence, a fact that the Nazis and guards made every effort to conceal. One of the prisoners, who had been there longer, in response to my question, told me that, at most, a person was allowed to live, to work for ninety days. Most never made it that long. If someone was lucky enough to survive for ninety days, the person was then executed, replaced by one of the thousands of constant arrivals who would, in turn, be executed in three months. The perpetual turnover was a considered part of the Nazi plan to have no living eye witnesses among the prison population.

As part of the sonderkommando assigned to the gas chamber and crematoria, I was separated out from the general camp population. This was called Auschwitz I, the original camp of the Auschwitz-Birkenau complex. It had been built, then its use discontinued in favor of the much larger, more efficient killing structures at Birkenau. With the huge influx of Hungarian Jews, it was put back into service, designated specifically for the "treatment" of children.

The crematorium was right next to the gas chamber. The children were taken out of the chamber, stripped, their clothing put in piles to be sorted and shipped out of the camp. No child, as far as I saw, ever had a number. I suppose they were meant only for death, and the time and effort needed to tattoo their arms were considered unnecessary.

Four or five barracks made up the shelter for our kommando, the barracks themselves much smaller than those at others camps. Somewhat over 100 of us assigned to this particular kommando, we had no contact with the prisoners outside our area or anyone else in the camp. We were isolated, under the constant eye of SS, guards, and Kapos. I seemed to be one of the youngest workers, most of the others appearing to be in their thirties. For me, witnessing the constant murder of children, many not much younger than myself, left me numb, my sanity dependent on that insulation, that need to not feel anything. For the others, it was just as bad in a different way. For them, the children represented their own sons and daughters. I'm certain they survived much as I did, by thinking and feeling as little as possible.

The Kapos, themselves prisoners, got a little more food for being in charge of the rest of us. They were the foremen, the prisoners directly responsible for those prisoners under their supervision. Because of the additional privileges, however slight, there was always someone to volunteer to be a Kapo. Any prisoner—Pole, German, Jew—could be a Kapo. Other than that, they died the same as the rest of us. As far as the SS were concerned, they never introduced themselves to us. They simply watched us as well as watching the Kapos who, in turn, watched us.

Work with the sonderkommando was varied. There were many different things to do. I did whatever was required of me. To refuse, to shirk the job in any way was immediately punishable by death. I had no desire to die.

One day, I would lead the children, ranging in age from as young as two to as old as fourteen, into the gas chamber. We formed them into the standard lines of five across, a means of making counting easy and efficient.

Another day, I was assigned to a group that dug ditches or pits into which would go the ashes of those cremated. At home on the farm or working in Budapest, it never occurred to me how little a person can be reduced to, once he is cremated. A human being, particularly a child, will wind up comprising only a couple handfuls of ashes. In order to fill the deep, wide pits we dug, required the cremation of hundreds, thousands of children.

We put the bodies in the ovens on a grate, so that when the burning was complete, usually about ten to fifteen minutes, depending upon the size of the child, the ashes fell to the floor of the oven. Four or five children could fit at one time in the oven. The ashes were then removed by shovel or even by hand, put into wheelbarrows, which we then pushed to the pits we had previously dug, and buried them there.

The next day, I might be putting the bodies into the crematoria. The most frightening thing is how quickly the mind becomes numb and accepts things that only a few weeks earlier would have been inconceivable.

I was there only a couple of days when I learned the truth and accepted the obvious. Like the people I led to the gas chamber, I, too, would be gassed and cremated in turn. I knew I had to get out. I simply had no idea how to accomplish it.

I knew that if I had any chance to survive, I had to remain strong somehow. On my first or second day there, the Kapo in charge of my barracks announced a need for volunteers to bring food to the rest of those in the barracks. The reward for getting up earlier than everyone else and beginning to work during the precious few hours we might possibly sleep and hopefully be too exhausted to dream, was to receive an extra helping of the thin soup made of vegetable remains that a few weeks earlier I would not have fed to our animals. I immediately volunteered. With the promise of extra food, more men volunteered than the Kapo needed. I felt myself extraordinarily fortunate to be among the four men chosen from my barracks.

This part of the camp was run in two slightly overlapping "shifts" with one group working the approximately twelve hours of daylight, the second group working the corresponding time at night. My typical day began at 4 a.m. when the three other men from my barracks and I would go to the kitchen set up not far from the barracks. There, we got two large drums, much like trash cans, filled with soup. Each one, when filled, required two men to carry it. By the time we returned to our barracks, the rest of the men had gotten up and waited with their tins for us to arrive. The soup was ladled out, everyone pushing, wanting to make certain he received his fair share, each hoping to have the prize of a piece of vegetable. The trick to getting a bit of vegetable, meager and rotting though it was, was to wait until near the end. The vegetables would naturally sink to the bottom, so whoever got the last bowlfuls sometimes also got a bit of potato peel. The problem, of course, was timing. If you waited even a minute or so too long, you risked missing out and getting nothing. This sometimes even happened to those of us who woke early to get the food. Instead of receiving extra, on occasion, I got nothing.

Next was the *apel plotz* which was, for my barracks, the first of the two times during the day when every person in the kommando was assembled, keeping in neat lines of five so the Nazis could count us, making certain none had escaped or determining how many had died since the previous count only twelve hours earlier. If any discrepancy arose, we waited, at attention, silent, until the count was done again . . . and again, if necessary. Finally satisfied, the Kapos were given the task of filling the day's assignments. They did this by merely pointing to someone and saying, "You! Do this. You! Do that."

Once given the day's task by the Kapo, along with whatever basic instructions you needed to carry it out, you went and began work. After about twelve hours, you gathered for another count. After that count, the three other men and I again got the food. Sometimes, the soup was accompanied by a few ounces of bread. By the time I returned from the kitchen, some of the other men had already fallen asleep. Not everyone ate all of their bread at once. Some saved small pieces for later, hiding them near them, usually in their clothing. When a man died during the night, and we moved the body out of the way, the first thing we did was search his clothing. If we happened to be lucky, we might find an ounce or two of bread. I did not take food from those who were still alive, but I needed the food more than someone who had died and had no problem eating whatever I was fortunate enough to find.

We talked little among ourselves. When you are insensate, even if out of self-defense, the desire to form friendships or even strike up conversation is simply not there. Having already lost so much, I did not want to face someone as a friend, knowing that person might be dead the next day. When we did talk with each other, we would make jokes out of our desperation. "How many more days do you have to live?" was a common way to begin a conversation. We were, in many ways, little more than walking dead.

Each night, I prayed only not to dream. Dreams of the camp made sleep as horrific as being awake. It was worse, though, to dream of home, for it reminded me of how very much I had lost and might never have again. I missed my family, but was afraid to even think of what might have happened to them.

At 4 a.m. I rose to begin the process all over again.

Within a week of my arrival, I was given one of the jobs whose images haunt me to this day. Near the gas chamber was an open field. It was to this field that the Nazis brought the children. When the transports arrived and the selections made, the children were automatically separated from the adults. Babies were taken from their mothers' arms. Toddlers and school-age children were herded away from parents powerless to do anything but watch. No plea, no entreaty kept families together. It was all given the façade of normality.

The children stayed at the open field—hundreds and hundreds of them, perhaps thousands. Sometimes, they merely passed the field on their way to the gas chamber, marched in orderly rows, each line containing five children. Sometimes, they stayed at the field for a few days before being selected to fill the ever-present lines and rows of the procession to the gas chamber.

The field was open, empty, except for the children, barbed wire strung to act as a barrier, keeping the children in place. No tents, no structures or shelters, no protection of any kind were provided for them. The guards, perhaps going on the knowledge that the children would be dead in a day or so, didn't bother to give them food.

Cries of pain, fear, and confusion never ceased to be heard from that field. Young voices calling out for comfort from mothers and fathers, who were probably dead, filled the air. While it was impossible to discern a single voice from the sounds, I was able to recognize individual words spoken in German, Yiddish, Hungarian and Rumanian. These added to other East European languages with which I wasn't familiar to create a multi-lingual cacophony.

That particular day, my job was to make certain the children maintained proper lines and rows as we walked them into the gas chamber. Some cried, begging for their mothers. When families of siblings or cousins had been able to remain together, they tried to reassure each other, hugging each other, holding each other. Some were silent, all tears and emotion already beaten out of them. Looking into the vacant eyes of those children, it was far too easy to imagine them as already dead, their souls prematurely fleeing their brutalized bodies.

At least fifty children at a time could fit into the gas chamber— usually more because they were small. That day, within the mass of children, I saw my little sister Gitel Marim. She was only eleven years old at the time, her eyes still red and swollen from crying but dry, all tears used up days earlier. It was the first time I had seen her since our separation after getting off the train, perhaps only a week before. I know she must have seen me. We were so close to each other, yet unable to speak. For that, I'm thankful. Knowing what was going to happen, I would have had no words of comfort for her.

I walked with the group of children to the gas chamber. Without having to watch her, I still knew, at any given moment, exactly where Gitel Marim was. Without being told, the children sensed what was about to happen to them. I didn't want to, but I watched as Gitel Marim entered the chamber. I wanted my last memory of her to be seeing her alive. Never in my life have I felt more powerless, useless, to do anything to help my family.

The chamber itself was a square, brick room. It was large, like a barracks. The only things inside were showerheads along the walls. A small, air-tight window allowed visual access so the guard would know when the children were dead. Depending on the number of children inside, the time required to pass from life to death varied from between a half hour to an hour. Occasionally, it might take a little longer. Sometimes, the guards were anxious to put the next group in. When that happened, there might sometimes be a child who was still breathing. That never mattered. Everyone, dead or still barely alive, was taken out, piled onto racks and put into the crematoria. When the crematoria could not handle the volume of bodies, they would be piled liked cordwood at the side of the building, then loaded onto wheelbarrows and taken out to open pits to be burned. This happened quite often as many more children can be gassed in an hour than can be cremated in an hour. The ashes were then buried, some at Auschwitz, some taken elsewhere by truck.

Watching Gitel Marim step inside that room, becoming part of the process, I wanted to yell, scream, strike out at those who would indiscriminately kill young children, kill my sister. Instead, I stood, knowing any such move or outburst on my part would justify my own immediate execution. An hour after Gitel Marim walked inside, her body was pulled out along with the other children by another member of the kommando and put into the crematorium. By then, I was leading another group of children from the field.

During that hour, an important part of me withered into virtual nonexistence. I don't even remember if I cried as her body was disposed of. I don't remember having any tears left.

In fact, I recall very little of the next few days. I do recall that evening, in the barracks, I mentioned to some of the other men that I saw my little sister put into the gas chamber. As I had no words for Gitel Marim, no one had any words of comfort for me. I don't even believe any such words exist.

I woke, ate, did the task assigned me, and had but one thought: "Why?" For the first of many times, I considered walking into the air-tight brick room with the next group of people. Why didn't I? The only answer I've been able to think of is that some inner, divine spark of life would not allow it. I sincerely felt that by living, I would one day bear witness.

Several days later, when I felt nothing else could touch or affect me, I was proven wrong. Again, my task was to make certain the children formed and stayed in neat, orderly lines. A group of young, very Orthodox boys, maybe twenty in all, stayed together for comfort and reassurance. Despite our telling them nothing, they seemed to know and understand what was about to happen. The boys remained calm and polite. They followed our directions, standing patiently in their lines of five. Not one of them questioned or argued as we began our walk from the open field.

Spontaneously, one of the little boys started singing. The other boys joined him. The song *"Ani Mamim"* was one that I had also learned in Hebrew school. "I firmly believe in the coming of the Messiah; and although he may tarry, I daily wait for his coming," they sang in Hebrew. Their voices strong and confident, they walked into the gas chamber. They continued singing as we closed the doors. The words from their song remained strong, clear. As Zyklon-B gas gradually replaced breathable air, their voices grew weaker, softer. Within an hour, where once Hebrew words rose to God in devout voice, there was only silence.

The gas itself had little, if any odor to it, or perhaps it had dissipated enough not to notice by the time we began pulling bodies from the room.

The unique, unbelievably revolting stench of burning human flesh was so prevalent, such an integral component of the very air we breathed, it almost immediately became simply one more thing to not think about. It is only in retrospect that I find myself amazed at how quickly I no longer noticed any unusual smell.

Once in a while, something would not go exactly as the SS planned or intended. A pipe might become blocked, or they might run out of the Zyklon-B gas. When such an instance occurred, the children in the gas chamber remained locked inside while our work did not stop. The ovens continued burning, ashes removed to provide room for more to drift down through the grate. The bodies piled in the room would continue to be fed into the flames.

For the children locked in the gas chamber, their brief respite gave them no hope or comfort. Until whatever obstacle was dealt with, the children remained in the chamber, their pleas and cries audible as we walked by in the course of our assignments.

In order to survive, to retain even a semblance of sanity, you automatically shut out any normal human impulse bordering on compassion or empathy. You concentrate completely upon the job at hand, giving undivided attention to pulling ashes out of an oven while not allowing yourself to remember or think about what went into the formation of those piles of ashes; or making neat piles of the clothes removed from the recently murdered, thinking only of matching different clothing items, pants, shirts, shoes and then stacking them neatly—not whose sister or little brother may have worn them only an hour earlier.

Try as I might to force myself into a private existence where sights, sounds, smells, and even my own actions held no meaning for me, the muffled sounds emanating from the chamber pierced my illusion of noninvolvement, striking deep into my soul. I could not hear any voice distinctly, yet each voice reached me.

Whatever the problem was that caused the delay in the system, it was quickly solved and within an hour or two, the process would begin anew, as though no delay had ever occurred, slowly, inexorably silencing the voices from inside the locked room. The work continued, in spite of the slight interruption not worth taking the time to think about, let alone expending the effort to comment upon.

Of everything I had seen and done, nothing had greater impact than the sight of innocent children—babies—being led into that room. Decades later, after marrying and having children of my own, the images remain with me.

The song the group of boys sang touched me, bringing back some sense of life. I began to consider anew what action I needed to take to survive. I knew that in only a few months, at most, I would be executed. There seemed to be only one alternative to death: I had to escape. I did not have any idea how I was going to accomplish this. I only knew that it had to be done. I reasoned that whatever I tried, I had nothing to lose. The end result of staying was obvious. I paid attention to everything and to everyone, especially Kapos and guards. I just needed to find the right opportunity, the right time and place.

Days became weeks. The time of my execution grew nearer. I said nothing of my plans. Perhaps others had the same thoughts as I did. I have no way of knowing for certain. No one spoke of such things to anyone else.

I remained alert to any situation that I could use to my advantage. Under what I knew to be an ever increasing time pressure, I had no choice but to be patient. When I had been there about six weeks, I knew that, at best, I had only five or six weeks left.

At every step, at every job, was the ever-present watchful guard of the Kapos and the SS. They had complete control over every aspect of our lives. They had complete confidence that no one could do anything without their knowledge. It was their supreme confidence in themselves that provided me with my opportunity.

I carefully studied the guards, what they did and how they did it. Those of us working at the crematoria constituted our own miniature camp within the greater Auschwitz complex. We remained under constant, heavy guard as we carried out each of the tasks necessary to running a small camp. Constantly being rotated from one task to another, I was able to study the behavior of the guards as they watched us performing each of the tasks our unit was charged with carrying out.

At this time, I was rotated into the task of processing the clothing. Having done this before, I was familiar with the required routine. A group of us, consisting of twelve to fifteen men, took the piles of clothing left behind by the people who had been killed. We sorted the clothes and loaded them onto trucks. All this was carried out in an enclosed area. As usual, the guards knew they had full control of everything and everyone.

From past observation, I knew the SS had no fear that any of us would so much as attempt to do anything other than our assigned tasks. They knew their mere presence and the threat that presence implied, were effective deterrents. It was that very confidence which allowed them the latitude to feel they could safely relax their vigilance.

That day, my particular assignment was to stand on the truck, piling the clothes as to type and kind. Three or four of us worked together doing this. As the pile steadily increased in size, it was common to momentarily lose sight of one or another of the other prisoners. I reasoned that if I lost sight of the prisoner, then so did the guards. I noticed that the guards never reacted or seemed to think the disappearance strange. They never called out for the person or searched in any way.

I decided this was the best chance I had to try my luck. Actually, at that moment, "luck" was nothing more than the willingness to take an enormous risk and trusting the outcome to God. A major factor in my willingness to take such a risk was the acknowledgment that I had nothing to lose. If I were to be discovered, the SS would kill me on the spot. If I did nothing, then the best possible outcome for me would be execution in less than two months. Death was the conclusion in either case. In the latter, it was a certainty. In the former, it was a very real possibility, predicated on discovery.

I took the chance.

The pile of clothes on the truck had grown to a size where my view of the other prisoners working with me was obscured. The guards and SS were also out of my sight for the moment. With no more conscious thought or planning, I dug myself under the clothing. Burrowing underneath as quickly as I could, I buried myself. Just like that, I disappeared.

At that point, I had done everything I could do. The rest was in God's hands. I kept silent, the suffocating weight of the discarded clothes of hundreds of human beings pressing down upon me. I can only imagine that they did not realize I was gone. I heard no cry of alarm, no strident orders to find me. Despite that, I knew that discovery could happen at any moment. If it did, my death would be immediate.

The task of filling the truck was soon completed by the remaining prisoners. Before the truck was allowed to leave, one of the guards came to inspect the clothing and the work done. I knew what was happening and what was going to happen, having observed the ritual on previous occasions. I instinctively held my breath, irrationally terrified that my slightest sound would alert the guard to my location.

The guard was armed with a bayonet. He took the weapon, randomly stabbing into the piles of clothing. The Nazis who ran the camps were many things, but they were not stupid. Hiding within the clothing was a possible means of escape, one that I certainly hoped to exploit. It was worth it to them to sacrifice a few articles of clothing in order to prevent just such an escape.

As the guard thrust the blade into the clothes, I prayed, my body tensed in anticipation of the pain from impalement.

I clenched my teeth, determined not to cry out, even if struck by the blade. Once, the blade came within an inch of my face. I remained still and silent, but not out of some Herculean effort in self-control; I was too frightened to move or scream.

Satisfied that the truck contained nothing other than the clothes, the guard backed away. The driver was given the okay to proceed. The gate was opened for him. He put the truck into gear and drove through.

As the truck passed the gates, I could feel the difference in the road. A wave of relief washed over me, the immediate danger successfully avoided. Once I relaxed enough to think past the current moment, I knew I was far from safe. I had no idea where the truck was going, certainly not what to expect at the end of the trip. Once again, all I could do was wait and hope. I felt my best chance was to wait until the truck stopped. The weight of the clothing bearing down on me made movement difficult. I hoped that wherever the truck ultimately ended up, would be a better situation than what I left.

The wait did not turn out to be very long. I estimated the trip to be only about a half hour, if that long. Gradually, the weight of the clothes over me began to lessen. I imagined the scene: prisoners unloading the truck, preparing the clothes for further processing. The clothing would be sorted again, recycled, repaired if needed, then shipped to wherever the Third Reich decreed. I read, years later, that much of the clothing was sent to the heart of the Reich, where it was distributed among institutions and needy German civilians.

As the pile of clothing decreased in size, I began to breathe easier, sensing that my plan had succeeded. With only a few layers above me, I pushed my way free, sorting as I did so. I continued working, making my way off the truck, using the actions of the other prisoners as my guides. Immediately, I noticed some differences between this particular place and the one I had just left. Security was far less rigid. The ever-present SS were far fewer in number, and those few much less watchful. I could feel my heart pounding as I dared to hope I had actually escaped.

Dozens of prisoners worked in silence. No one showed surprise at my presence. I finally concluded that with the continual shifting, movement and elimination of individuals, it was difficult, if not dangerous, to get to know people well. As we continued working in silence, I had the opportunity to glance at my surroundings. I stopped, without realizing I had done so. My heartbeat seemed to stop as well as I stared at the buildings, at the barracks that I knew so well. The truck had simply gone from the mini-camp of the crematoria to another area of the main camp. I was still in Auschwitz.

While I was anonymous within the work group, I knew I couldn't stay there. Forcing myself back to work, I focused my mental energy on what to do next. Something had to be done and quickly. Work groups were routinely counted on returning to the barracks. To have one extra, unaccounted-for prisoner could easily prove fatal for the entire group. It was also because of the ritual evening count that I knew I would be missed at my old camp. One prisoner less at the count meant one prisoner to be searched for.

I had to hide. That much was obvious. My mind raced, trying to think of what options I had, trying to find one that would provide me with safety. My only advantage was in knowing how the camp was built, how the barracks within the camp were built. I decided where to go, what I might do. I had no guarantee of success. I knew that to stay where I was would be a guarantee of death.

Work on the clothing continued. I kept busy, mixed in with the other prisoners as I gradually moved away from the immediate work area. Silently, I thanked the guards for not being alert to each prisoner's movements. Unseen, I slipped into the nearest barracks.

Each barracks was a single, long building, perhaps half-block in length. Along each wall were the wooden planks the prisoners used as bunks. In the middle of the room and running close to the full length, was a brick chimney, currently unused since it was summer. With no time to form a more elegant plan, I climbed into the chimney at one end and pulled myself along until I felt I was near the middle of the structure. Exhausted, I fell asleep.

Sometime later, I have no idea how long, I was awakened by the sounds of barking dogs. They were in the barracks, yelping, baying. I could hear voices, shouting to the dogs in German. It was impossible to make out specific words. I was certain they were looking for me. I remained quiet, motionless, breathing as little as possible.

As usual, they were thorough, checking everywhere. Eventually, the sounds faded, then disappeared completely. All that was left was a quiet that I expected at any moment to be broken by the shouts of my discovery. Instead, the sounds were those of prisoners returning to the barracks for the night.

I have no idea why the dogs didn't find me. Maybe they can't smell through bricks. Maybe I was far enough inside that the ashes covered my scent. For whatever reason, I had found myself a safe haven. I knew it was only temporary, that at some point I would have to find a way out of the camp. In the meantime, I slept on a bed of ashes, far softer than a wooden bunk. I did no work, but slept during the day.

Sometimes at night, while those in the barracks slept, I crawled out of the chimney. A small washroom, woefully inadequate for the needs of an entire barracks, was more than sufficient for me. I washed up, drank as much water as I could. Then I filled a small bottle I had stolen somewhere with water for the next day. I also took the luxury of relieving myself. When in the chimney, unable to leave sometimes for more than a day, I had to simply relieve myself where I was.

Once in a while, a prisoner would not eat all of the food he was given. He would keep some, hidden, for a future meal. I felt fortunate to find one or two of those caches. I took what little food there was, crawled back into the chimney and waited. Occasionally, but especially when confinement in the chimney left me no option for personal hygiene, I would also steal extra clothing, both for warmth and in an effort to remain clean.

The next day, the routine repeated itself. The barracks was emptied of inmates as they were forced into labor. Deep in the confines of the chimney, I ate, drank water, and slept. That next night, I might not go out. Each time I left the chimney, I put myself at risk. I would do that only if hunger or thirst made it impossible for me to remain hidden.

Days passed, their exact number blurred into approximations. One night, when I had dared to sneak out for some water, I froze while filling my bottle. Terrified, I felt I had made a horrible mistake. Not all of the other prisoners were asleep. Two men were talking. I remained quiet, still. They spoke softly to each other in Hungarian. Listening carefully, I realized their conversation provided me with the opportunity I was hoping for.

Rumors ran rampant in the camps. Truth and fiction wove together after numerous repetitions, making one indistinct from the other. Sometimes, you just had to believe something. What they discussed, I wanted, needed to believe.

"You know what?" one Hungarian said to the other. "Looks like we're getting out. Being moved from here tomorrow."

"How do you know that?" asked the other.

"I heard one of the SS talking. He said they were taking most of us from here to another camp."

They continued talking, speculating on what it meant, where the new camp was, who would go, who would stay. The progression of their conversation no longer interested me. I stopped paying attention to them and started thinking. I knew I had to get out of Auschwitz. At that point for me, any other camp was preferable to remaining where I was.

Quietly washing up as well as I could, I changed into some of the cleaner clothing I had stolen. I hid myself for the rest of the night, hoping the rumor was true. I was taking an enormous risk, but I also knew that in staying, each passing day increased the chance of my being discovered.

Morning brought confusion because the rumor proved to be true. Disruption of the regular routine brought, at times, conflicting orders. Prisoners had to be moved, but prisoners had to remain and be accounted for.

The confusion worked to my advantage. To the other prisoners, I was just one more face among the hundreds of similar faces they didn't recognize. To the Nazis, I was just another prisoner. In the morning, the barracks was emptied. All prisoners moved outside to be counted. I went out with the rest of the inmates.

The trucks had not yet arrived. As expected, the first thing the Nazis did was to count us. Naturally, at the end of the count, there was one person too many. I was that person. Meticulous by nature, the Nazis could not allow this discrepancy to go unexplained. They counted us again, in case there had been some error.

There was no error. The tally came up the same.

My heart beating like crazy, I forced myself to remain still. I looked around as the other prisoners did, hoping I was conveying the same appearance of curiosity as to what the problem was. Each moment, I expected to be discovered, graphically envisioning my ultimate fate. I would either make it through the next few moments . . . or die.

The Nazis counted again. And again. Each time their total was the same. Standing in front of them was one person more than there was supposed to be. They had no idea who it was or how such a thing could happen.

The trucks to transport us arrived and waited while we underwent yet one more count. Same total. The Nazis yelled at us in growing fury. The SS had a schedule to maintain. The aberrant count was interfering with that schedule.

The SS screamed at the prisoners, ordering us to immediately report anyone who was a stranger. It was a ridiculous order. They knew it, even as they demanded action. With rare exceptions, everyone was a stranger to everyone else. If we actually followed the orders as given, each person would be reporting scores of others. For all of the ranting and threats by the SS, nothing was accomplished.

It seemed as though every German had a deadline that had to be met. The truck drivers were no different. Being forced to wait while the SS counted us yet one more time caused the drivers to run late. They grew angry at what they viewed as a pointless delay. Another officer came, questioning why our transfer had not begun. A short argument ensued, ended by the abrupt order from one of the SS.

"It's no use. Let them go!"

Buchenwald and Transfer to Dora

Immediately following the order to proceed with the prisoner transfer, more orders quickly followed. The Germans loaded us onto the trucks, quickly, efficiently, trying to make up for lost time. I followed directions, went where I was told, and found myself on one of the trucks. I had no idea what to expect, where the final destination would be. Even so, I felt myself relax. I thought, "So far, so good."

The trucks moved out, taking us with them to wherever they decided we needed to be. Conversation was minimal. The ride turned out to be relatively short. In a little less than a day, we arrived at another camp. I saw a sign, proclaiming the name of the new camp. We had been taken to Buchenwald. As when I entered Auschwitz, the name meant nothing to me, never having heard it before.

We didn't do much at Buchenwald. For us, it was merely a transfer camp. We spent, at most, five days there. During that time, we underwent health inspections. It was important for the Germans to know that we possessed enough physical strength to be exploited as slave labor. Otherwise, it would be pointless to waste the effort to transfer us.

Those of us deemed healthy and fit enough to be utilized as slaves made the transfer to another camp. The camp was a new one called Dora. Years later, I read that Dora was a top-secret installation where the Nazis designed and built their V-2 rockets. As had become usual for us, when we arrived, none of us knew where we were. When we arrived, nothing was there, except for a very few barracks. The camp was so new that it did not yet actually exist. We had been brought there to build it.

While we spent ten to twelve hours a day, seven days a week, providing slave labor to construct what amounted to a small city, at night we slept wherever we could, like pigs. We began work on the Jewish holiday of Shavuot, the festival commemorating the harvest. I wouldn't have known what time of year it was except that some of the Orthodox Jews kept track of the calendar. At that point, even acknowledging the day as a Jewish festival required more effort than I was willing to spend on religion.

The first few days, no water was available. Everyone suffered from severe thirst. Water, any moisture, was all I could think about. This preoccupation to obtain even a sip of water temporarily disappeared in shock as I saw, among a group of workers, my father. It was the first time I had seen him since our immediate separation upon disembarking from the train when we had arrived at Auschwitz. He did not see me as I ran to him. He happened to turn in my direction as I neared him. His eyes grew wide when he saw me. His surprise and joy equaled my own. We held on to each other, both of us crying, each promising to help and protect the other as much as possible.

I was the first to notice that some people carried little bottles of water. They came from a distant part of the camp. I stopped one of them, asking where he had gotten the water.

He pointed in the direction he had come from. "Go straight that way. There is a natural well. The water comes up from the ground."

My father and I looked where the man indicated. Already, it seemed that hundreds of people moved toward the hope of obtaining some of the water.

"Wait here," I told my father. "It will be easier and faster if I bring you back a bottle of water."

He agreed. I ran off, determined to make good on my promise and quickly return with a bottle of water for my father.

By the time I neared the well, it was easy to imagine I was one of the last people in the camp to learn of its existence. People converged from every direction, bringing with them anything that they thought might possibly hold water. I saw a small, empty bottle similar to the one the man had been carrying. Without bothering to ask if it belonged to anyone, I picked it up. It became mine. With my new bottle, I joined the press of people.

The natural well was little more than wet dirt—mud. The "water," or what could be seen of it, was black and brown. It didn't matter. It was a miracle to simply be able to make your lips wet. Like the others, I cupped my hands, drinking the dark mud like it was fresh spring water. I filled my bottle with the wet earth, anxious to bring the prize to my father.

Careful not to spill anything from the bottle, I ran back to my father. He wasn't where he had said he would wait for me. I was familiar enough with camp operations to think he may have been arbitrarily conscripted for some work detail or another. By asking other prisoners, it would be relatively easy for me to find someone who had seen where he had been assigned.

It didn't take very long for me to find someone who told me that my father had been taken to another camp. My first reaction was disbelief. Rumors again, merely rumors. Not able to find my father anywhere else, I had to eventually accept that it was not a rumor, but fact. Too many others told me the same thing. In the short time it had taken me to find and return with the water, the Nazis had filled a truck with able men. They had been transferred to another camp, a labor camp. My father was among those in the prisoner transfer.

After that, any time a new arrival came from that camp to Dora, I asked, begged for any news there might be of my father. It was several months before I found someone who knew of him. The man I met was kind, gentle. He gave me all the information he could.

The camp my father had been taken to was a hard labor camp. He was put to work on building a road. He failed to work fast enough or hard enough to satisfy the guards. One of the guards took his stick and began beating my father as punishment for his lack of industry. Other guards felt the punishment was not severe enough, that he was getting off easy. They joined the first guard, all of them beating my father with their sticks and clubs. Within a short time, he was dead, his body summarily disposed of by some other prisoners.

It was a miracle I saw him that last time in Dora, but we couldn't keep our promise to each other. We could do nothing to help or protect each other. I couldn't even return fast enough to give him something to drink, even if it was only wet mud.

The first order of business in Dora was to build barracks. In the best of circumstances, overcrowding of the barracks at any camp was standard. As we built the ones in Dora, there seemed to be even less space than usual.

We slept on the floor, so close to each other that no one had room to turn. You couldn't lie on your back or stomach. You slept on your side, the people on either side of you pressed almost against you for lack of space. If at some point you wanted or needed to turn over and lay on your other side, the move could not be accomplished without disturbing those on either side of you. In most cases, unless they also turned, you couldn't. Naturally, when they turned, they wound up disturbing the people next to them.

Sleep was never peaceful, but it was the only rest allowed us. Having that rest disturbed, even once, elicited abrupt, violent anger. On more than one occasion, I woke to the sounds of a man being murdered for the crime of turning over and disrupting his neighbor's sleep. A quick, hard blow to the head with shoe or fist was enough to forever still the restless offender. The body was then taken to the end of the barracks, where those who died during the night would be stacked up like cords of wood, waiting for the morning when the bodies would be removed and burned. This nightly removal of the recently deceased from the sleeping area of the almost living also had the benefit of providing a little extra room to those still trying to sleep on the floor.

I easily envisioned myself on the receiving end of that form of capital punishment. I desperately tried to think of a way to avoid that fate.

While trying to think of a way to survive the night, I survived the day by feeling nothing. No sight, no sound, no experience moved me to sorrow, remorse, outrage, anything. I thought I was safe in my insensate cocoon where nothing touched me or came near me. It wasn't long before I learned I was not as isolated as I had hoped.

Death, in a wide variety of forms, was a common enough sight that no one, including me, found it worth commenting about. Conversation usually revolved around the most important thing in our lives: Food. No one ever had enough. Every one of us suffered perpetual hunger. With hunger so intense, so constant, we found the motivation to do things we would never have imagined in any other place or time. A son stole a crust of bread from his father. I have seen men killed fighting for possession of a rotting potato peel.

Some had become so numb to death that they felt nothing wrong in using one person's death to their own advantage. Desperate for food, any food, they cut the body of one of the deceased into manageable pieces. Over open fires, the human flesh cooked, a macabre barbecue.

Every one of the different prison populations contained individuals who made such use of their dead compatriots. Whether a prisoner was Russian, Polish, Jewish, German—a political prisoner or prisoner of war—it didn't matter.

I watched as pieces of meat, which only hours before had been living men, became another man's dinner. Hungry as I was, I couldn't bring myself to join in.

"They're going to be burned anyway," I was told. "Why let it go to waste?"

No rationalization swayed me. To me, the bodies remained people, men I had seen, talked with. As much as I wanted to survive, I made the decision to die rather than eat human flesh.

In my own way, I also took advantage of those who had died. I had managed to devise a way to survive at night. I used those who had died to do it. As I mentioned, when someone died, we pulled the body to the side of the barracks. Stacked like wood in the evening, the bodies remained in the barracks at night. In the morning, part of our routine involved removing the bodies from the barracks and taking them to be burned.

At night, I didn't take my place on the floor, but went to lie down on top of the stacked bodies. It was the perfect solution for me. No one bothered me if I wanted to turn over. No one disturbed my sleep by forcing me to wake and move if he turned since my new companions no longer moved at all. The bodies still had some warmth in them, giving me that added comfort. For the first time, probably since my arrival in Auschwitz, I had enough sleep. In the morning, I got up, well rested. I told no one where I was sleeping. It was my secret. I suppose others in the barracks thought I, too, was dead. As far as the bodies went, I decided not to think about them. I was too tired and survival was too important to me to think about the men whose death provided me with a comfortable, warm, safe night's sleep.

With the completion of the barracks, sleeping arrangements improved to the normal overcrowding in the camps. I moved to a bunk, leaving the warm pile of corpses. Once surviving through the night was no longer a problem, I had no need or desire to sleep with the dead.

Two men stand out in my memory of those early days in Dora. One was a doctor named Forkosh. The other was an electrical engineer named Yakov. We all came from different countries and communicated with each other in what had become a universal language: Yiddish. Both men became good friends of mine. Yakov, close to my age, became like a brother. Since I had grown up as the only son in a family with four daughters, to finally have a brother, even under those circumstances, was a welcomed comfort.

With Forkosh, it was a little different. I began to see him almost like a father. He had the bunk next to mine. He was older, perhaps in his fifties or early sixties. It was hard to judge his age. Older men usually didn't survive, while the conditions forced upon us tended to age us far beyond our years. He had a small, husky build, standing maybe only 5'6". Humble and wise, he came from Prague, the capital of Czechoslovakia. During the day, we often worked the same detail. At night, he taught me things, mostly about how to remain strong and healthy under the trying conditions we found ourselves in, continually encouraging me. His breadth and depth of knowledge, as well as the ease with which he shared it, impressed me.

"You know so much," I couldn't help commenting one night soon after I began sleeping on a bunk with the living prisoners. He had already been giving me advice about how to survive.

"I'm a doctor," he said automatically. Then, the tone of his voice changed, became distant, reflective. I was no longer certain if he spoke to me or himself. "At least, I was a doctor, once. Only a couple of years ago. A long time ago. A lifetime ago."

He spoke little more to me about his career as a physician in Prague. He certainly never boasted to any of us about who he was or what he did or how important he was. Maybe because he was afraid he would never do those things again. Other prisoners who came from Prague knew him well, though.

"Didn't he tell you?" one of the prisoners who had known him would ask me.

"No. He told me only that he was a doctor."

"Well," the man continued, his tone implying I was ignorant for not already knowing, "Forkosh is a famous brain surgeon. He's known throughout Europe. To even speak with him, you have to get an appointment and wait. He's booked ahead for three, four months. At least, he was."

Quiet, little Forkosh? An important, famous brain surgeon? He never mentioned anything like that to me. And yet, so many people from Prague told me the same thing. I had no choice but to believe them. I had no reason not to.

"Watch him with the Nazis, sometimes," I was told. I took the advice. What I saw broke my heart. Once in a while, he would go to a guard or even to one of the higher-ranking Nazis. To them, he made clear who he had been in Prague. He asked them, begged them, to allow him to work in a hospital. There, he could prove what kind of surgeon he was. They laughed at him. A man who could barely hold his own digging ditches, a brain surgeon? They made jokes about him making a huge, uneven scar on a scalp as he did on the ground.

All the while, he pleaded with them to give him the chance to work in a hospital. To be a doctor again, he said he would do whatever they needed done. Naturally, he had no papers, no identification except for the number given him by the Nazis. He had no way to prove his claims. The guards laughed louder. They didn't waste time or energy in hitting him. They simply walked away, still laughing, the rebuke more painful to him than a physical blow. After each attempt, Forkosh said less to me about his past. He soon stopped approaching them. He focused on the present. He continued teaching me about how to stay healthy. If not for his help and guidance, I'm certain I would not have survived.

Ours was not the only barracks; and Jews, not the only prisoners. Dora held Russian POWs. One barracks held Italians, who were there as political prisoners or members of the Resistance. Treatment, working assignments, and labor conditions differed for each group. Jews, deemed the most expendable, received the least food and the hardest manual labor assignments. The Russians, kept separate from the rest of the prison population, did most of the mechanical labor. Jews dug miles of ditches through rock. Russians lay down and connected pipes. Some of the Russians had been prisoners for close to three years.

When I had the chance at night, I sneaked out of my own barracks and spent an hour or so with the Italians. Like the Russians, they had their own, separate barracks. In addition to somewhat easier work assignments, the Italians received more and better food than we did.

At first, I went there to perform small services for the Italian prisoners, like shining their shoes. Since none of them spoke Yiddish, communication was difficult, but not impossible. Some of them spoke a little German. They pointed to dirty shoes, and I knew what they wanted. For my efforts, they rewarded me with a slice of bread. Once in a while, they gave me a small potato. I remember the first time they presented me with that rich payment for their clean shoes. My eyes grew wide at the sight of the delicacy, the sheer extravagance of it. The Italians laughed at my reaction. I barely heard them, my entire attention on that potato, an entire potato just for me. In my own barracks, to find a potato peel was considered lucky. An entire potato had taken on the air of something to dream about, an unattainable fantasy.

Very gradually, we could communicate more, though it was never easy. After a short time, I went not only for the extra bit of food I might earn, but because I enjoyed their company. For their part, they came to expect my visits. They began to call me *Piccolo*, which I was told means "little man." They encouraged me to join them, even to relax a little bit. "Piccolo!" one of the Italians would shout to get my attention, "I don't see any Nazis here. You don't have to work so hard."

I found it difficult to follow that advice. I was always a hard worker. After only a few months under Nazi supervision with a swift death being the punishment for any lax in activity, I wanted to make certain that everything I did for the Italians was done quickly, and done right. I wanted to give them no reason to be unhappy with my work. Any one of them could easily inform the guards about my visit. My execution would be immediate, a way of setting an example for any other prisoner whom might imagine leaving their barracks without authorization. I was fortunate. No one ever said anything.

Of the different prisoners, the Italians had perhaps the most freedom. True, they worked, suffered, and died like any other prisoner at the hands of the Nazis. On the other hand, they also had privileges denied the rest of us. Aside from the extra food, which to me was privilege enough, they retained the right to entertain themselves, mostly with music. They had been allowed to keep guitars, accordions, and the like in their barracks, for their personal use.

Sometimes, only the musicians played. More often, though, the music accompanied singing and laughter. At rare times, it was almost possible for me to forget what I had seen and done during the day as I sang with the Italians at night, learning the words by rote, if not necessarily learning the meanings. For me, any escape, even for an hour to hear the music of a guitar or the sound of genuine human laughter, was worth the risk I ran in leaving my barracks.

By the time I arrived at Dora, the camp had already existed as a location where the German war department manufactured munitions. An old salt mine, deep in an excavated mountain, provided concealment and immunity from the destruction of Allied bombs. The Nazis imported us from the other camps to expand the existing work base. Among other things, electricity had to be provided and maintained. Pipes had to be laid to bring in gas used in machinery and equipment. Perhaps a dozen tunnels led into the depths of the mountain.

As an electrician, my friend Yakov found himself responsible for maintaining power for the lights and machinery used for one of the mountain factories and tunnel access routes. Forkosh and I found ourselves among the prisoners responsible for digging ditches. As we completed a section, the Russian POWs lay down and connected pipes that would ultimately provide a steady supply of gas to the builders deep within the mountain.

Many times, I simply had no energy left after a day's work to visit the Italians. Even as Forkosh continued to teach and help me, I worried about him. I was a young man and had no strength left at the end of the day. Forkosh might have been my grandfather. I never heard him complain. Perhaps he realized the futility in wasting energy on complaint.

After a day of digging ditches, the grim and filth felt as though imbedded on our skins. One of the responsibilities of the barracks Kapo included making certain we remained clean. Our Kapo took that responsibility very seriously. He was a German prisoner. Being both a Kapo and a German, he received a lot of extra privileges. He got extra food. The food he got was of a much better quality than ours was. He didn't do much, if any, of the hard manual labor which eroded our bodies and spirits. He had only to make certain that the assigned job was done and done to the Nazi's precise satisfaction.

The shower facility was really just a room with some shower-heads. We had only the illusion of cleanliness. Our Kapo, rather than using his position to try to ease our situation, went out of his way to make our lives worse. He found it fun to take 15 or 20 of us into the shower. To "help" us shower, he brought in a hose and sprayed us with ice cold water. As the freezing water poured over our bodies, he laughed, finding pleasure in our discomfort.

One day, I was among the unfortunate group singled out by the Kapo. In the shower room, I braced myself for the inevitable onslaught of cold water. He began laughing even as he pulled the hose into position and we drew back, trying to put distance between him and us. Some of the men tried to hide behind others, hoping to shield themselves from the worst of the ordeal. The Kapo laughed harder at us, proud of his power to elicit fearful reactions from us without having to do anything.

He continued laughing as the cold water came out of the hose, hitting us full force. I happened to be among the men at the front of the group. We instinctively tried to withdraw, but there was nowhere to go. As my muscles tensed in reaction to the icy water, I realized that much of the Kapo's enjoyment came from having the power to make us cringe and cower. I decided that, even though my suffering was inevitable, I would go out of my way to make certain the Kapo derived no pleasure from it.

Moving away from the other men, I took a step toward the Kapo. I could tell the move surprised him. He retaliated by focusing the stream of water on me. I wanted nothing more than to run away, curl up under a thick blanket, and try to get warm. No such blanket existed for us and I had learned that warmth was relative. I forced myself to stand still.

"That feels good," I said, trying to sound like I actually meant it. "I like it. Give me some more."

Instead of honoring my request, he turned the hose away from me, becoming angry. It was never in a prisoner's best interest to get the Kapo angry with him. Having gone as far as I had, I felt left with no option but to continue.

"Why are you stopping? Please don't. It's refreshing."

His silence lasted only a moment before yelling orders at me, which I had no choice but to obey. "Get out of here!" he screamed. "Get out. Now! I never want you back here."

He kept his word. I was never again among those chosen for his version of a shower. I was never so happy to comply with an order. Later that night, I told Forkosh about what had happened. He laughed out loud at the story. Genuine, warm laughter was seldom heard in our barracks. I drew a great deal of pleasure from bringing Forkosh some good news for a change and hearing the sound of his laughter.

During the day, Forkosh and I continued digging the ditch with the other prisoners. In our wake, the Russian prisoners laid the pipes to be used for gas lines. We knew the Russians toiled behind us, but there was no interaction or communication. Guards watched over us. Guards watched over the Russians. All the guards made certain each person did his specific job and nothing else.

While Forkosh, I and most of the other men in our barracks dug into the hard earth, my friend Yakov received a different assignment. Yakov's job had him working in the tunnel and in the mountain. As an electrician, his responsibilities included making certain no interruption occurred in the electrical feed and that no overload occurred. Like every other work detail, failure was not tolerated and was punishable by death. He didn't have to worry about that. He did his job very well.

It turned out that Yakov did have to worry, though not about his job. He found himself caught in the dilemma of having to obey conflicting orders. Unfortunately for him, there was not any way for him to know it at the time.

One day, while doing his job, one of the Germans came up to him. This particular man was not one of the guards or SS. He was a civilian supervisor. It really didn't matter. Any German giving an order had to be obeyed. Yakov did as the German asked.

The German had Yakov follow him out from the tunnel and brought him to a car. At the front of the car, the German stopped. "Do you know what would look nice here?" he asked Yakov as he tapped the front of the car's hood. Yakov didn't know what to answer, so he said nothing. The German paused, thinking, not noticing Yakov's silence. "A bird," he finally continued. "A little bird to go right here." He tapped the hood again.

Yakov still said nothing. The German finally looked at him, expecting a response. He decided to make his wishes clearer. "I want you to cast a small metal bird for my car."

"I really can't, sir," Yakov replied weakly, trying to protest. "I have to work in the tunnel with the electricity."

"I never asked you about that. I don't care about that. I'm your boss. You follow my orders."

Whether civilian or military, orders from a superior, which meant any German, left no option but obedience. Yakov did exactly as instructed. He made a cast in the form of a little bird. He found some metal, melted it down, and poured it into the cast. Not only was he an electrician, but he proved to be a good artist.

Yakov's little metal bird looked very good as he attached it to the hood of the car. One of the Gestapo who controlled that particular area happened to notice Yakov laboring over the car. He came up to Yakov, demanding to know what he was doing.

"The Supervisor," Yakov answered immediately. "He told me to make him this bird. He wanted it as an ornament for the hood of his car."

The Gestapo man shook his head slowly, his expression grim. Yakov became anxious; realizing his situation could quickly turn fatal.

"You've taken metal from us and ruined it. Do you know what that is? It's theft and sabotage."

Immediately upon being termed a saboteur, Yakov realized the danger of his situation and became desperate. "I couldn't help it," he pleaded. "He told me to make it for him. I had to follow his orders."

"No," came the dangerously calm reply. "You should never do that."

Yakov was arrested, handcuffed, chained, and put in jail. He was terrified. To be put in jail was the same as a death sentence. He was a young man—21, maybe 22. He remained in the jail for a couple of days, awaiting his execution. As a convicted saboteur, he knew his death would be a public event, used as an illustrative deterrent for the rest of us. He was no longer afraid. Fear comes from uncertainty, the unknown. His future was already determined, set in place. He was miserable, though.

A bone, or piece of wood, wedged between his jaws held his mouth open, somewhat like a horse's bit. A chain attached to either side of the bone and going around the back of his neck held it securely in place. It effectively prevented him from speaking or eating. His hands and feet bound, he moved with difficulty.

His cell provided him no comfort. The ceiling was low enough to prevent him from standing upright, the walls close enough to prevent him from lying down and stretching out. Other people, maybe hundreds of them, chained up awaiting their own deaths, shared the jail with him. Even if his mouth had not been wedged open, making speech impossible, no communication was allowed.

The passage of time lost all meaning for him. He didn't know what time it was or even what day. He only knew that his execution grew steadily nearer. Between beatings he received and the relentless pressure of the chain around his neck pulling tight the bone in his mouth, his entire face began to swell. Puffy, bruised flesh obscured his eyes. He had trouble seeing. He began to look forward to death.

Sometimes, no matter how angry you are with God or how much you try to deny His very existence, an incident will occur that makes you believe in God all over again.

As the time left to him became only hours, a guard came running from the tunnel. He went immediately to the Gestapo officer in charge of the jail.

"The Jew electrician. Is he still alive?"

"Yes. He's scheduled to be executed in three hours."

"Don't kill him. The electricity went out in the tunnel. No one can find the problem. There are hundreds of people in there and they can't do anything without electricity. You have to send him out right away."

They immediately untied him. A guard escorted Yakov out of the prison. They took the bone from his mouth, but the damage was done. They gave him an entire loaf of bread. Unfortunately, he couldn't eat it; his mouth too sore and raw.

I saw him as he tried to make his way into the tunnel. I couldn't see his eyes, the swollen black and blue flesh in the way. Staggering, he tried to walk into the tunnel, pushing the cart with tools in front of him. He kept hitting the walls. He could barely see. I'm surprised he walked on his own. The guards didn't help him, but didn't get in his way either.

Later that night in the barracks, he told me what happened, what the jail was like, how he was treated. I would never have known otherwise. Forkosh tried to help him. There was very little he could do. I could tell it frustrated him to be so helpless when not so long before, when he was in Prague, he could do so much.

The Nazis never admitted that they might actually need Yakov and his skill. After all, he was just a Jew. Even so, they treated him differently after that. They never again laid a hand on him.

Not long after that, the work detail Forkosh and I had been assigned to, digging the ditch for the pipe, neared completion. We dug the ground near a small lake. Each day we worked ten or twelve hours. In that time, a certain amount of work had to be completed. When I finished my own work, I noticed Forkosh laboring nearby me. No matter how much he tried, he fell farther and farther behind. It was obvious he would never finish the day's work assignment in time. The penalty he faced for his inability to finish his job was, at best, a severe beating. Knowing he might not survive such a punishment, I decided to help him.

We worked together quite a bit; my quota completed that much before his. He said very little to me during that time, conserving his strength for the task at hand. He conveyed his gratitude by his expression, the smile he gave me. For me, that was enough. It felt good to be able to help him after all he had done for me. While we knew the SS watched us continuously, it never occurred to either of us that getting the required work done in the allotted time might cause a problem.

Near the end of the day, an SS guard, two dogs trotting obediently at his side, approached us. He had been observing our progress from far away, using his binoculars.

"You there," the guard called, indicating Forkosh. Forkosh and I stopped our work, standing somewhat at attention, waiting for any further instructions from him. The guard stopped in front of Forkosh. The dogs remained still at the guard's side, alert to the slightest movement around them.

"Yes, sir?" Forkosh asked. Neither of us had any idea why the SS guard had singled him out.

"Why aren't you doing your own work? Why does that boy have to do it for you?"

Forkosh didn't respond, afraid that anything he said might turn out to be the wrong thing. I stepped forward, trying to appear and feel confident. It had been my idea to help. I was certain I could easily explain that we only tried to complete the work that had been assigned. Certainly that would be all right.

"Sir," I started, speaking to him in German. He turned his attention to me. "As you can see, I've finished all of my work. I just wanted to help him finish his."

"No," came the automatic reply. The tone of his voice left no room for contradiction or appeal. "He has to do it by himself."

I wanted to protest, to try to explain that Forkosh couldn't possibly do the amount of work expected of him. Before I realized what happened, the two dogs ran at Forkosh. Instead of recalling the dogs, the officer urged them on. He had actually set the animals on Forkosh as punishment.

As the dogs tore at his limbs and bit into his flesh, Forkosh tried to run away. He cried out for help, yelled at the dogs. Nothing mattered. The dogs never slackened in their murderous attack. They ripped hunks of flesh from his body, leaving the pieces on the ground behind them as they continued to rend more from him. Forkosh made it to the nearby lake. He still had no respite. The dogs followed him, continuing their assault in the water.

The dogs soon trotted out of the lake, the fur on their jaws and faces matted with blood, the water unable to wash it all away. Forkosh never rose. He may have drowned in that lake. My guess is that the dogs killed him, literally ripping him apart, long before that could happen. In that way, I lost my good friend Forkosh.

That night, I said nothing. As much as Forkosh's death affected me, I had no tears left to give to anyone, even Forkosh. All I had was my silence. Over the next few days, I said very little. Instead, I carefully watched those around me. I knew I had to survive, to somehow, someday, tell what happened. With the help and knowledge I received from Forkosh, I felt that survival was possible.

Many others felt differently. Many people simply could not handle what was happening. These people felt it was better to end their own lives quickly, rather than wait for a slow, inevitable death at the hands of the Nazis. Usually, the people had been doctors, lawyers, engineers—people of stature, importance, and power— prior to their internment. They threw themselves against the electrified wires. If that didn't kill them, the guards in the towers shot them. Either way, they got their quick, easy death.

Once we finished our work on the ditch, we immediately began work on building roads. It was hard, backbreaking labor. In comparison, ditch digging didn't seem as bad as it had at the time. Part of my survival technique was to focus exclusively on the task at hand, to assure myself that whatever I was doing was as bad as it could be, the next morning would be better. It was difficult to not be discouraged by the fact that the next morning was often worse.

Building the roads was a perfect example. We built the road on a bed of stones. Our first project was to lay the stone bed. We carried the stones, four or five at a time to the end of the road, put them in place, and went back for another load. Carried by hand, with no wheelbarrow or other assistance, four or five was the most any of us could carry at a time.

At first, the stone bed was only a short length; the trip wasn't too arduous. It didn't take long, though, for the length of the road to increase. Soon, we found ourselves carrying stones a mile or so to the end of the road. Then, we walked back and began the trip again. Many of the stones had sharp, jagged edges, easily tearing clothing, damaging shoes. Abrasions and cuts on hands, arms, legs, and feet became common.

By that time, we had laid a small track upon which we had a little cart that we loaded with rocks. We pushed the cart to the end of the track and tipped it over to unload the rocks. Even then, our already damaged, mangled shoes provided us with essentially no protection.

Our only respite during the day came not from any compassion on the part of the Nazis, but because of concentrated attacks by Allied bombers. As I've mentioned before, Dora was the site of munitions manufacturing. Many years after the war, I read in a newspaper that the V-1 and V-2 missiles launched against England from France had been made in Dora. At the time, I had no idea exactly what was being done deep in the mountain. The Germans didn't make a practice of informing the prisoners of such things.

The Allies, though, seemed to know. They clearly intended to destroy the site. The Allied planes came in waves, each of the main countries of the war—America, Britain, Russia—separately sending in squadrons. They flew in low, the better to aim and deliver their bombs on target, I suppose. They flew in low enough that I could see the emblems and flags of the pilots' country on the plane. British followed Russians after a respite of a day, who followed Americans after half a day or so, who followed British what seemed like only hours. Aside from the flags on the planes, we became accustomed to seeing each country's planes coming in from a separate direction.

As the planes approached, the guards shouted orders to us: "Drop!" "Now!" "Down!"

Without further thought, we laid down on the ground where we had stood. We lay down on the dirt, on rocks, on stones. No attempt was ever made to seek shelter. We stayed in the open, unprotected, vulnerable. At those times, I experienced a bizarre feeling of calm. I saw and heard bombs exploding nearby, but it seemed to have no meaning or significance for me. I felt glad to have the rest from work. A bomb might hit its target, destroying something of value to the Nazis. I didn't care enough, nor have energy enough, to shrug my shoulders with indifference.

The Nazis didn't hide or seek shelter during these aerial attacks. They fought back as best as they could, firing at the incoming planes with anti-aircraft weapons. Most of the time, the Nazi fire was ineffective. It certainly did nothing to deter the Allies. Once in a while, though, a plane was brought down.

The Allied bombing runs and Nazi counter-measures quickly became a routine part of our day. While waiting, stretched out on the ground during an attack, I often watched the people around me. Many of them seemed, like me, to be almost bored by the daily repetition. Some people, though, terrified, curled themselves up as much as possible, attempting to make themselves into smaller targets. A rare few actually looked forward to the bombings. They saw it as simply another opportunity to achieve a quick, easy death.

More often than watching the people around me, I lay on my back, entertaining myself by looking up into the sky and watching the Allied planes. I counted how many came from each country, how many all together. Sometimes, I tried to keep count of how many bombs each plane dropped. I found that, at best, I could only estimate those numbers. It gave me something to do. Even as planes came in so low that I could see the faces of the pilots, I didn't have the strength to be scared or worried.

One Russian plane came in low enough for me to see that the pilot was a woman. Unfortunately, her plane was one of those hit by the Nazis. She parachuted out of the destroyed plane. Some of the Nazis ran to intercept her when she landed, not too far from us. They didn't even bother taking her in as a prisoner. They shot her right away.

None of the Allied bombings had any effect on the manufacturing going on in the mountain. They continued making bombs and missiles as though nothing was happening outside. Sometimes, one of the gates leading to the tunnel entrance to the mountain would be destroyed. Sometimes, the railroad tracks leading inside would be hit. It didn't matter. Any of a number of other gates could be used in the interim. With plenty of labor available at a moment's notice, the tracks or gate would be repaired in a few hours. The Nazis needed the repairs done fast. It was our job to do them fast, no question and no complaint.

In case there was the slightest possibility that we might actually achieve some level of comfort, the weather conspired with the Nazis to prevent it. Our thin prisoner clothing was simply not enough protection against the chill and cold. The merest breeze speared through the cloth, leaching the energy and warmth from our bodies. Luckily for me, I found a trick to help me keep at least a little bit warmer.

A moment of good fortune is the only way I can describe finding a discarded cement bag. My few months as an apprentice tailor came in handy as I fashioned a warm undershirt for myself. I cut out holes for my arms and made a neckline low enough to be unnoticeable beneath my prison shirt. As I cut into the bag, I remembered the sight of Yakov: being led from jail, his face black and blue, his eyes swollen shut. By cutting the bag, I knew I was guilty of the same crime: destroying German property. I tried to ignore the thoughts by focusing on the job of quickly and efficiently making a garment from a cement bag.

The moment I put it on, closing my shirt over it, I knew it was worth the risk. It was still cold. The wind still blew through the cloth. Yet, I was definitely warmer. Like everything else, warmth had become a relative thing. In this case, the comparison was to the biting cold without the cement bag.

I knew taking the bag with me into the barracks would be dangerous, if not fatal. It could be easily stolen. Worse, for an extra slice of bread, someone might feel it worth it to tell the Nazis. Despite the inherent risk in any course of action, I decided the safest thing I could do would be to hide it. I kept it under a rock. In the morning, I'd retrieve it, wear it all day and replace it at night. Little by little, the bag tore, became worn out. Soon, I couldn't repair it anymore. It was no longer usable. I never found another, but was deeply thankful for the time I did have it.

Working on the road, I knew I somehow had to keep my strength up. One way to do that was to get extra food. The slice of bread or occasional potato I received from the Italians, when I visited their barracks, was not enough. In order to get at least a little more on a regular basis, I volunteered to bring the food from the main kitchen to the barracks, just as I had done at Auschwitz.

I got up before anyone else, very early in the morning. I went to the kitchen where they gave me soup for the rest of the men in my barracks. I then took the soup to them. For this service, I was given an extra bowl of the soup for myself. I quickly discovered that if I looked around the kitchen carefully, I could find scraps of food being thrown away. I often found potato peels, which I hungrily added to the thin soup. Once, I even found a discarded potato, small even by the standards of the camp, but to me a rare prize.

During the time I struggled to keep warm, I also struggled to keep working. Walking on the sharp stones took its toll, damaging my shoes. Soon, the shoes had rips and unrepairable holes. With little or no protection from shoes, my feet bore the brunt of walking miles a day on jagged stones. On a daily basis, I got cuts and abrasions.

"Sick days" and "time off" were alien concepts in the camp. I had no time to rest, to allow the cuts to heal before receiving new ones. In a short time, one foot became infected. The weight of the rocks I carried bearing down and the stones stabbing up made each step tortuous. Instinctively, I favored the infected foot. Limping, though, created an imbalance that made it increasingly difficult to haul rocks for such long distances each day.

Day by day, the pain grew as the infection progressed unabated. The foot inexorably increased in size, each day swollen more than the day before. Many mornings when I got up, the pain was so severe I wished I had died in my sleep. Even so, I forced myself up and suffered through another day. I had to keep trying because I never gave up the hope that maybe, maybe tomorrow, something will happen.

One morning when I got up, I could not even pull on my pants. My foot had swollen to the point that it no longer fit through the pants leg. I already knew well that no excuse for not doing my work would be tolerated or accepted. In order to simply get dressed, I opened a seam on the pants leg. As the size of my foot increased, so did the amount of pain whenever I put weight on it.

I did my best to ignore it and do what I had to do. I really had no choice. For the most part, I was able to limp through the day. The pain, as bad as it was, became a constant and I became used to it. Only when I stepped on a sharp rock or stumbled slightly, creating more pressure on my foot, did the suddenly sharp increase in pain bother me.

At that time, we had finished our work on the road. No time was wasted in beginning a new project. This was building a barn on top of the mountain to raise rabbits. They decided to raise the rabbits for their fur. Eventually, they had created a small industry in rabbit fur coats and stoles. Tanners worked the skins. Tailors then used them to make the garments. I don't know what they did with the rabbit meat or the fancy fur garments. Maybe some of the SS officers gave the custom-made coats to wives or girlfriends, helping to raise their own status.

For two weeks, I helped haul bricks up the mountain to build the rabbit barn. We carried five or six bricks at a time, left them on the mountain at the building site, walked back down and picked up another load. It was repetitious, monotonous, and exhausting. I didn't go at night to visit the Italians anymore. I was simply too tired and my foot hurt too much. I hoped that by staying off it as much as I could, it might heal.

That hope never turned into reality while I continued hauling bricks. Each morning felt worse than the morning before. Finally, one morning when I tried to stand, I almost passed out from the pain blazing up my leg.

For those two weeks, I managed to do whatever work was required of me despite the pain. I had even begun to believe the pain might eventually diminish and go away. Each day, I convinced myself the next day would be better. It was difficult to imagine it being much worse. That morning, I realized how wrong I was.

It felt as though a dog had taken my foot in its jaws, its incisors impaling my flesh. I was certain it was how Forkosh must have felt when the dogs ripped him apart. My attempts to put my full weight on the foot sent waves of pain searing through it and up my leg. Each step I took, that put weight on the foot, increased the level of pain. I stopped trying to convince myself it could not be worse. Each step confirmed the fact that it could.

I managed to bring the soup in for the other men. I was thankful that morning, not for the little bit of extra food, but for the opportunity to sit down while I ate. I found the relief short-lived. As soon as I got up to join everyone else for the day's work, the pain returned, more intensely. The imagined dog, biting my foot, dug its teeth in, twisting and turning its head to get a better, firmer grip. I wondered if it was possible to die from such pain. At that point, I came close to hoping it was.

I limped out of the barracks with the rest of the men, favoring my infected foot as much as possible. No one tried to help me or said anything to me. I didn't take their lack of action as rebuff or rejection. Some had injuries equal to or greater than my own. A few remained among the living only by the most precarious thread. In any case, there was nothing that anyone could say or do. None of us had the power to change or improve the situation.

The day's work began as every other day had begun for the past two weeks. I gathered up my load of bricks to carry up the mountain and started walking. I moved slowly, each step causing another stab of pain in my foot. I was afraid that by moving so slowly, I would not be able to finish my work. If that happened, I knew I might easily end up with the same fate as Forkosh.

To keep from thinking about that, I concentrated on simply placing one foot at a time, balancing the bricks on my shoulders, and focusing on the top of the mountain where the barn was being built. When I finally made it to the top of the mountain, I felt as though I had achieved one of the greatest accomplishments of my life. Going back down for the next load of bricks was far less difficult. I began to imagine that I just might possibly be able to do my work for the day. Thinking as far ahead as the next day was pointless.

My speed (or more accurately, my lack of speed) earned me no reprimands or reprisals either on my way up or on my way down the mountain. I grew confident enough to put that concern out of my mind as I collected the bricks for my next trip. As I balanced the bricks on my shoulders, I had no choice but to place my full weight evenly on both feet. An acute bolt of pain, originating in my foot, spread throughout my entire body.

Only a few minutes before, I had allowed myself the luxury of thinking ahead to the end of the day. From that moment on, anything of importance in my world compressed to one, basic thought: Take a step. Concentrating my complete attention on that single objective, no longer thinking ahead even to the step beyond this one, I began the walk up the mountain.

Each step was a concerted, focused effort. I thought of nothing else. That would have required too much energy. I was vaguely aware that my pace, slow to begin with, was slowing even more noticeably. I didn't dwell on that, or what might occur if I happened to slow to some arbitrarily unacceptable point. There was only one thing that had any meaning in my life, one goal. No matter what pace I was proceeding at, I was accomplishing my goal.

Gradually, I began to lose my sense of time and place. My world compressed even further. Pain, at each step, reminded me that my foot touched the ground. It was almost a surprise when the amount of pain and area the pain affected changed. I was halfway up the mountain when I had fallen, the bricks I carried crashing on top of me. Instinctively, I put up my hands to protect my face from the falling bricks. That act drained me of what little energy I had.

I remained on the road, unable to move. I wanted to get up, continue my job. It simply was not possible. No muscle responded. I looked up into the sky. No planes flew overhead, no sounds of engines and explosions from deployed bombs drowning the shouted orders from the Nazis. The Allies had evidently decided to take the morning off. The pain from my foot continued unabated. Just the pressure of having it rest against the road was enough to irritate it.

I have no idea how long I remained like that. It felt like hours. It felt like moments. Still no planes, but the face of an SS guard looked down at me. Thinking back on it, I can only imagine that it wasn't very long before the SS came to find out why I had stopped working.

"Why aren't you getting up?" The SS man's tone demanded an immediate answer.

I tried to sit up and show him my right foot. I could barely move my leg. The effort sapped what little strength I had. I collapsed back against the road. "I can't do it. I'm in terrible pain." Explanation or excuse, it didn't matter. It was deemed unacceptable. The SS deigned to keep me alive for one reason and that was to work. I wasn't working.

"Get up, you filthy pig!" the SS man yelled at me. He hit me with the butt of his rifle. At the first blow, I wasn't even aware that he had hit me. It was just a temporarily more prominent pain in my side. "Get back to work, you lazy Jew!" he continued yelling at me while hitting me with the rifle, using the terms "pig" and "Jew" interchangeably. I didn't try to protect myself. It wasn't worth the effort. For a brief moment, I experienced the terrible fear that he might kill me. For a brief moment, I experienced the freedom of release that came with the thought that he might kill me. After that, I tried only to ignore the rifle coming into contact with my body.

He paused, resting for only a moment before continuing. I no longer had anything to lose. I looked up at him, not in defiance but in honesty. "I'm not going to get up. It's not possible. I can't carry anymore."

The statement angered him. He lifted the rifle, ready to hit me again. "You can do one thing for me," I continued. He paused, probably surprised that I had the audacity not only to continue speaking to him, but also to ask him for something. "You can shoot me. Kill me now."

He changed his hold on the rifle from using it as a club to using it as a rifle. He aimed it at me. I was certain he planned to grant me my request. Rather than tensing, every muscle in my body relaxed in grateful anticipation of the relief from torment. To my surprise, he lowered it, studying me.

He continued staring at me. I had no idea what he might say or do. The uncertainty disturbed me. I don't know why, but I was more frightened of him, at that moment, than when he was yelling and hitting me.

Finally, he relaxed a bit, the rifle loose in his hands. "I'm not going to shoot you," he told me. "You're going to die anyway. I don't want to waste the bullet."

"Okay," I told him. "Do whatever you want. I can't move anymore." My foot, black and blue and swollen to at least twice its normal size, lent credibility to my statement.

We reached an impasse. I couldn't move and he had decided not to kill me. I knew that he could easily change his mind at any moment, deciding a single bullet was not such a tremendous waste, after all. If such a thought ever occurred to him, he evidently dismissed it.

I couldn't be left lying in the middle of the road. Something had to be done with me. It did not take him very long to reach a decision regarding what to do.

He called two men away from hauling bricks up the mountain. He gave them the job of taking me down to the hospital. Where they took me might more accurately be described as a field hospital, though it really wasn't much of a hospital at all. It consisted of a large tent, covering some tables. To this day, I don't know why he didn't kill me. I'm sure it was not for any humanitarian reason. Maybe he felt compelled to go out of his way not to comply with the request of a Jew, even if that meant keeping him alive.

The men placed me on one of the tables. Following directions from the doctor in charge, they tied my hands and feet to the table. They stuffed paper into my mouth. It had nothing to do with any thought of comfort for me. Even as they took the time to operate on my foot, my well-being was not a major consideration for them. They just probably didn't want to hear my screams as they worked on my foot. The doctor cut into the flesh on the top of my foot, probably to allow the accumulated pus to drain out, without bothering to waste time giving me any anaesthetic or painkillers. I passed out at that point. I don't remember anything else about being in that tent.

The next thing I remember is waking up in a room that was part of the regular hospital. Actually, the term "hospital" is misleading. The beds consisted of wooden bunks, only slightly more comfortable than the barracks because not as many people crowded onto them. Also, instead of the two or three tiers common in the barracks, only one level existed in the hospital, making the doctors' access easier. Several other beds in the room made the space appear even smaller than it already was. No extra space was wasted on those who could not work and earn their stay. I opened my eyes and immediately closed them. The glare of bright sunlight coming through the window was painful.

Slowly, as I regained full consciousness, I opened my eyes again. Each of the other beds in the small ward held a man who was either too ill or too physically incapacitated to work. Vaguely, I knew it was dangerous not to work, but I was too weak to form a coherent thought about it.

The man in the bed next to mine stared at me, almost hostile. "Why aren't you eating your food?" he demanded. Hungry himself, he felt it was sinful for me to waste food.

"What kind of food?" I asked. I really had no idea what he referred to.

"That food," he pointed out to me. "It's been sitting here for five days."

In that way, I learned I had been unconscious for five days. Hungry as he was, he had not taken the food. He had been warned against stealing the food placed there for me. The warning was not some altruistic effort on the part of the Nazis to make certain I had food to eat. It was a method the hospital personnel used to find out how long it took for me to regain consciousness. Looking at the food, it was obvious it had remained next to me for the full five days.

In the best of circumstances, the food given to us was not particularly appetizing. I ate it as a necessary alternative to starvation. Hungry as I was after five days of not eating, the food waiting for me did nothing to entice me. I let it remain on the table next to my bed.

The ward was one of several in the hospital. The hospital itself was a pretty nice size—not huge, of course, like some modern hospitals, but not small either. That first day, after I woke up, I began talking with some of the other men in the room. They told me this was an experimental hospital. It didn't quite make sense to me. At first, I thought it meant they tried new things to find better cures for people. That notion quickly passed. As far as I could tell, no one received treatment for any injuries or illness.

One of the other men finally explained it all to me. The experiment, at least one of them, was to find out how long a man could survive with a particular injury that wasn't treated. Of the selected men who did receive some treatment, it was simply to test the efficacy of different medications. We provided the Nazis with perfect test subjects. They hoped to find answers to such questions by observing us and our reactions and rates of physical deterioration. When a particular patient no longer proved to be of any value, he was executed. Sometimes, the man was simply poisoned. Usually, though, hanging was the method of execution.

The window of the room overlooked a courtyard. Three gallows stood in the yard. At least once a day, prisoners marched to the gallows, the guards holding machine guns, directing their movements. Knowing how they often attempted to hide ongoing executions, it seemed unusual to me that they would allow the hangings to take place in full view of any patient who happened to look out the window. It was at odds with what I knew of the German sense of efficiency.

It didn't take long for me to realize the reason for the apparent lack of discretion. Like those who worked the crematoria at Auschwitz, they had no intention of allowing any patient in the hospital to leave alive. They had no concerns about what we might witness because our inevitable death insured our silence. The other men in the ward knew this as well as I did. Many of them had already resigned themselves to the idea of ending up in the courtyard, the weight of their bodies pulling the rope taut. Conversations among the doctors that I overheard confirmed this. Again, they took few precautions in being careful what they said near us since they had no reason to believe any of us would survive to repeat it to anyone.

At least once a day, the doctors, mostly German, came into our room in two's or three's. They administered drugs or took tissue samples. We never learned the purpose behind the drugs we received or the skin taken from our bodies. The tests, though, seemed very important to the doctors. They watched us closely, making careful notes on their charts. They wrote a lot, documenting everything they observed. There was a certain reassurance for me in watching the doctors as they made their meticulous notes. At least, it was consistent with what I knew of the German mindset.

Despite all of the tests, notes, and samples, as far as I know, nothing was ever done for my foot. It's just common sense to realize that an open wound needs to be closed in order to heal properly. That didn't happen. The open wound on my foot remained that way. I don't remember any balm or medication of any kind. Only a paper-like bandage or wrapping was used to cover it. At the time, I prayed it would heal on its own. In retrospect, I'm astounded that it actually began to heal, instead of developing gangrene, or worse.

I feel incredibly fortunate that, little by little, my foot began to get better. It was certainly due in large part to my not having to walk or march for miles and miles every day. Instead, I remained in bed, not putting any weight on it at all. Over the next few days, I rested and started eating again.

One night, two of the SS doctors came in, doing their rounds. One of them was Hungarian. I recognized him from other visits he'd made to the ward. Perhaps they thought we were all asleep. More likely, they simply did not care if we overheard anything since they didn't expect any of us to leave the hospital alive. Their discussion revolved around how many patients they planned to execute the next day. Hearing that conversation confirmed everything I had been told and had observed on my own in the hospital. I knew my only hope for survival was to be released. I decided that somehow I would arrange that.

My foot had improved to the point where I could put a little of my weight on it. I practiced walking, a little bit at a time. As soon as the pain started again, I went back to my bed to rest. I felt that the little bit of exercise might help me regain some of my strength. If I was to leave, I knew I had to be able to immediately go back to work.

One morning, the Hungarian doctor came to the ward to check on some of his patients. I can't explain why, but I felt this man was more of a doctor than an SS officer. While he wrote himself notes about the man a few beds over from mine, I walked up to him as best I could. I walked with a definite limp, favoring my still painful foot. It didn't matter to me. I was determined to speak with the doctor.

"Excuse me, Doctor," I said in Hungarian, getting his attention. He looked up from his notes, surprised to see me standing in front of him. Almost everything about me right then appeared unexpected. He didn't imagine I was walking at all and he certainly had not expected to hear me talking to him in Hungarian.

"Your foot is better?" he asked me. He glanced at my foot, lowering the tip of his pencil toward the floor to draw my attention to it as well. He was skeptical. He certainly knew when something was better and the way my foot looked didn't qualify as healed.

"Good enough," I declared. I knew as well as he did that my foot was far from better. I had to convince him otherwise. I had already decided any chance of survival depended upon my rejoining the general camp population rather than staying in the hospital. I had no illusions that if I stayed, it would only be a matter of time before I received orders to march out to the gallows in the courtyard. "You should release me from here." I was ready to plead, beg if necessary.

He tilted his head slightly, genuinely puzzled by my request. "You sit here all day, relaxing, eating our food. You don't do any work of any kind. It's very comfortable for you. Why would you want to go out there and work when you can rest in here all day?"

I didn't want to tell him I knew what was really going on here. I decided to agree with him to a certain extent. "Yes, you're right. I have been comfortable here. But I'm better now."

"Number . . . " he paused briefly as he checked his notes to make certain he got my number right. "9-8-5-7-6, you should be in bed," he stated, sounding almost like a doctor concerned about a patient.

"I don't need to be in bed," I pressed on. I really believed I could change his mind. "See? I can walk okay now and I want you to release me."

He didn't say anything. For a moment, he seemed to be just a doctor, not a member of the SS. I took that as a good sign and began to hope. He glanced down at my foot. He was much taller than I was, so I had to look up to him; but my eyes never left his face. He looked back at me, meeting my gaze. He shook his head slowly, "No. No, I can't do it. Go back to bed."

His voice was almost sad. As he spoke, though, I was too devastated to notice it right away. Before I had a chance to say anything more, to try convincing him I really was okay, he placed his pencil in his breast pocket and walked out of the ward. He looked straight ahead, no longer acknowledging me in any way.

I went back to my bed, not because he had instructed me to do so, but because I no longer had the strength or desire to do anything else. Sometimes, I liked looking out the window when the courtyard was not being used for executions, just to see the sunlight. Right then, I knew the sun would only show me all the details of the gallows. It was enough to see the image of them in my mind. I didn't need to see the reality.

I closed my eyes, trying to think of some way to get out. Only then, did I recall the doctor's tone of voice. With no other idea how to proceed, I decided to try asking again. At that point, I honestly had nothing to lose.

The next night, he came in again to check us and make notes on our reactions to one or another of the drugs they tested on some of the patients. I approached him again. "Doctor," I said, getting his attention, "I'm feeling much better. I'm strong enough to work. Do me a favor and check me out from here." I continued speaking to him in Hungarian. That got his attention more than anything I actually said. He crossed his arms, holding his notes against his chest as he studied me.

"Number 9-8-5-7-6, are you from Hungary?" he asked me in an almost conversational manner.

"No, sir. I'm from Rumania." I took the chance to tell him my history, how I moved to Budapest, about owning a business there for several years. For some of the story, I spoke German. He listened patiently. We even spoke a little about Budapest. He wasn't from there, but had visited the city often. We talked about some of the sights and places we enjoyed seeing there. I had no idea what he was thinking. Watching his expression told me nothing. "Please, Doctor," I begged as our conversation continued, "I don't need to be in a hospital anymore. Please release me."

For the first time, his expression changed. He smiled at me, checked his notes, and then nodded, "Let me see what I can do." He made some more notes, checked another patient, then left.

I went back to my bed and lay down. My heart pounded, excited by the hope of release. Moonlight, soft and diffuse, came through the window. I didn't even bother trying to sleep. I knew I wouldn't be able to.

Early the next morning as sunlight replaced moonlight through the window, I woke from a light sleep to the noise of two of the doctors entering the room. The Hungarian wasn't there. The doctors checked their notes and had one of the patients stand. They examined him, made more notations, and then had him follow them out of the room. No one said a word. We all knew where he was going. My heart began to beat faster, no longer from excitement, but from a growing fear.

We received no more visits that morning. A little before noon, I went to the window. Each of the gallows had a prisoner hanging in it. The far one held the body of the man marched out of the ward earlier in the morning. I went back to my bed and stared up at the ceiling.

One of the other patients had been watching me. "What did you expect?" he asked.

"I had hoped. . ." My voice trailed off. I had really hoped not to see him hanging in the courtyard because if he was released and allowed to live, then maybe I would be, too.

The other man shook his head. "There is no hope, boy." He lay down on his bed and turned on his side, his face away from me. I couldn't allow myself to believe him. My survival depended upon my believing that it *was* possible for me to survive.

Late in the afternoon, the Hungarian doctor came into the ward with an SS doctor whom I had not seen before. They looked at several patients before stopping at my bed. "Number 9-8-5-7-6," the Hungarian read off in German. I sat up, but neither of the doctors paid any attention to me. They spoke together, quietly. I tried to hear what they said, but they talked in voices too low for me to hear. The SS doctor did most of the talking, the Hungarian nodding in agreement. Finally, the Hungarian spoke. The SS doctor did nothing for a moment, then shrugged in response. He walked out of the ward. The Hungarian remained at my bedside.

"9-8-5-7-6, look at me." The order came in German. To this day, I cannot tell you my number in any other language unless I think of it in German first and then translate it. I sat up, facing him. It never occurred to me not to do as he said. "You are not yet well enough to return to the work you did." I tried not to hold my breath, waiting for him to finish. "But you have been here too long, doing nothing to earn your food."

I finally took a deep breath, swallowing. I glanced toward the window. He seemed not to notice. Though he continued speaking to me in German, his voice was softer. "Come with me."

Dora Departure

I walked beside the Hungarian doctor, trying not to limp, afraid to say anything. Almost as soon as we left the ward, he spoke to me in Hungarian, his voice kind, almost gentle. "I've arranged a new job for you. You are to sort clothes from the prisoners. Standing all day may not be easy for you, but at least you won't have to walk all day." I didn't know whether to smile or cry, my heart beating too hard to do either. My worst fears turned out to be groundless.

I have no idea how he managed to get me that job. I had already learned that some things are never questioned, just accepted. The job itself was simple enough. People, hundreds of them, came to Dora from all over Europe. Many thought, at first, it was the promised protective camp where they expected to wait out the war. That notion always disappeared within the first few minutes. Some people had clothes other than the ones they wore. Most people, transferred from other camps, had only their prisoner clothes.

All of the clothing, mostly civilian, had to be sorted according to quality. Bad clothing, torn or damaged beyond repair, was discarded. Clothing in good shape was packed and kept separate. I don't know what was done with those clothes. Clothing that was damaged, but repairable, was taken to the tailor shop maintained at Dora. There, tailors made whatever repairs the clothes needed. Then it was all packed. Again, I never really knew what happened with all of that clothing.

I stood on one side of a long table with several other prisoners. Other prisoners brought us piles of clothing and dropped them on the table in front of us. Standing all day long, in one place, with no breaks wasn't always comfortable; but it allowed me enough of a rest to give my foot a chance to heal. Compared to the kind of labor I had been doing, the work as a clothes sorter was easy. If not for the time I spent there, not having to march and walk miles and miles a day, I'm certain I wouldn't have made it.

Sorting clothes may sound easy; and to be honest, in many ways, it was. But like any other task assigned by the SS, it required focus and concentration. Guards, as well as SS officers, watched us as we worked. Everything had to be done in a specific manner, quickly and efficiently. We commonly found valuables as well as personal, sentimental items hidden within folds of cloth. Religious items—such as tallit, teffilin, and kipot—were also items that we found on a regular basis. We separated all such items from the normal clothes. I'm certain the SS officers kept most, if not all, the valuables and destroyed the rest.

Standing for twelve or fourteen hours a day was difficult in itself. By the end of the day, my foot would hurt and I would limp back to the barracks. I never complained, of course. I knew I had few alternatives, none of them pleasant. Going back to the hospital was simply not an option. I could return to the hard labor; but as badly as my foot hurt after a day of standing in one place, I knew at least it was being given the chance to slowly heal. If I went back to the hard labor, my foot would worsen in a short time, sending me back to the hospital if they decided I was still worth that much bother. I decided the best thing I could do would be to remain silent.

On my first day, I had only been working a few hours when I heard someone call my name, not my number. I ignored the call, focusing my attention on the task in front of me. Besides, I was no longer accustomed to answering to my name. On the other hand, I'd respond immediately anytime I heard my number, always in German, almost always yelled.

I heard my name again, the voice speaking in Yiddish. "Benjamin, Benjamin Samuelson, is that really you?"

I finally looked up from the clothes in front of me to the speaker on the other side of the table. At first, I couldn't believe who I saw standing in front of me. My Uncle Mordechai, my mother's brother, had been in Dora for a few months. At that time, he was in his late 40s but appeared much older. I remembered him as a tall, robust, hearty man. He must have been close to 6'2". The man standing in front of me seemed much smaller, thin from lack of food, his shoulders hunched over. His job was to bring the piles of clothing to the table for sorting and then remove the sorted piles. We hugged each other across the table. We talked as fast as we could, each asking about family members, neither having time to answer. A voice yelled out a number in German. My uncle stood up straight as we both came to attention and immediately became quiet.

"Yes, sir," my uncle automatically replied when the German guard called his number. As the guard approached, we both stood still, my uncle stiffly at attention, his expression fearful.

The guard told my uncle to stop wasting time and get back to work. Uncle Mordechai quickly followed the guard's instructions as the guard himself walked away. My uncle winked at me as he continued with his work. From then on throughout the day, each time he came by, he asked about someone. I had enough time to answer before he had to move on. Sometimes, I would ask him about someone. There was one person I knew he wanted to ask about, but seemed afraid to. It was late in the day before he brought himself to ask about his sister, my mother. I told him I hadn't seen her since our separation upon arriving at Auschwitz. I didn't have to tell him what I thought happened to her. He thought the same thing. Neither of us asked any more questions that day.

That night before I went to sleep, I remembered all the nights when I felt the only reason I had to survive until the next day was the hope that it might somehow be better. I had to admit that, given the conditions in the camps, my individual situation had indeed improved. I could occasionally sit down to work, so my foot had at least some chance to heal. I worked indoors, so I didn't have to contend with the extremes of weather. My uncle told me that two of his sons, Joseph and Hertz, were also in the camp. I now had family nearby me, so I no longer felt completely alone. I derived a feeling of comfort in having my uncle and cousins nearby.

Uncle Mordechai was a very religious man. He managed, along with some of the other deeply religious men in the camp, to maintain his ritual connection to God. The men got together when they could and held their own private services. They kept track of the days, so they knew when it was Shabbat as well as the different festivals and holy days. Like many of the men in that group, my uncle knew large portions of the Torah by heart. They didn't need the parchment in front of them to recite passages and prayers.

On more than one occasion, my uncle asked me to join them. Because of my fear of being discovered and summarily punished, I nearly always turned him down. On the other hand, I never tried to talk my uncle out of meeting with the other men. He found some comfort in it, and any comfort in any form was rare and precious. I was happy for him that, even in the conditions of the camp, he felt he could still praise God and feel at peace with Him. I would never try to take that away from him.

In some ways, perhaps, I envied him that he could find even that small sense of peace. It seemed to me that every day brought something that reminded me that "better" was still to be forced to live at a subhuman level. As I mentioned before, when I lived on our farm, we treated our animals with more care than the SS gave us.

My "better" conditions applied only to the kind of work I did. As far as food went, I received no more than I ever had at the camp. In a way, I got a little less because, during the time my foot was healing, I could no longer bring the soup in the morning. Not only did I not get the extra portion for doing that job, I no longer had the chance to pick up scraps from the kitchen.

Starvation was something we dealt with on a daily basis. Sometimes, people did things out of desperation that they would never have considered otherwise. I'll never forget what happened one time when the bread truck came in. The Germans brought in truckloads of baked bread. It was never enough to feed all of the prisoners. The bread came in small loaves. Each loaf was expected to feed three or four prisoners for the day. How we divided it up was of no concern to the Germans. It was more common than not for a person to wind up with no bread at all for the day. Again, this state of affairs was of no concern to the Nazis.

The truck, filled with bread, came into the camp and stopped near the kitchen. As usual, two SS guards armed with machine guns stood next to the truck. That truck contained a commodity more valuable than gold or gems. Every prisoner wanted, desperately, what was inside. The guards knew that. Once in a while, hunger will impel a man to risk his life for a bite of bread. The guards knew that, too.

I'll never forget that morning when the truck arrived. It came in, as usual, to the eager anticipation of the prisoners. The back of the truck was opened to unload the bread. One prisoner, hungry to the point where he no longer was capable of rational thought, ran at the truck. He seemed to come out of nowhere. I saw him only as he was near the truck. So unexpected was his action, even the guards didn't react right away. The prisoner grabbed a loaf of bread and bit into it, too hungry to wait. The brief pause gave the SS guards enough time to respond. One of the guards shot him before he took a second bite. Even if he had run away immediately, he would never have made it. At least this way, he died with food in his mouth.

Uncle Mordechai told me of something my cousins did in order to help not think about their hunger. Joseph and Hertz worked in the tunnel. On their way out, they would pick up a small piece of coal and put it in their mouths. By sucking on the coal, it was sometimes possible to trick your body into thinking you actually had something substantial and nutritious in your mouth. It didn't stop weight loss or physical weakness or possible death from starvation, but it was enough to help ease the hunger pangs.

Every morning and evening, all of the prisoners went to the apel plotz. Here, as in the other camps, it was a large, open area where the SS guards counted us to determine how many had died during the night, or to make certain that no one had escaped during the day. This was such an ingrained part of our day that on any morning they changed the routine and got us out early, we knew something was going on.

That particular morning was one in which we had to get out early. Apprehensive to begin with, we gathered outside, standing in even rows, facing about 25 gallows, already prepared for a mass hanging. Gestapo men surrounded the yard and camp. We had become used to the sight of the SS; but any time the black-suited Gestapo showed up, especially in such numbers, we knew something very serious was happening. At such times, the fear naturally existed that it had been decided to simply eliminate the entire camp population. If they intended to carry that out, it would certainly take some time; but it could certainly be done. Seeing the gallows set up in front of us did little to alleviate that fear.

Of the approximately 10,000 prisoners gathered that morning, forced to watch the executions, I happened to be among those prisoners in the first row nearest the gallows, not more than a few feet away. We all stood in the yard, quiet and still. If you moved, the Gestapo shot you. No one moved. It must have been close to nine o'clock in the morning when they started bringing prisoners out from the jail. They reminded me of how Yakov looked when he was released, but worse. Yakov had been in the jail only for a short time. The men being led to the gallows—all Russian prisoners of war—had been in the jail for days, maybe weeks. None of them could speak because of the wooden bit chained into place in their mouths, causing their faces to swell, sometimes to the point where it was no longer possible to see their mouths.

The weather was very cold that morning, but the Russians wore only their pants. It seemed to take a long time for all of the Russians to be marched into place. There was at least 200 of them, each one handcuffed, each with a rope already around his neck.

The Gestapo had the first 25 Russians to be hanged move into place. Before the actual hanging, one of the Gestapo men stood in front of us all and read a paper, explaining what crime the Russians had committed. Their crime was sabotage, and execution was the punishment. I immediately thought back to Yakov and his crime of "sabotage," but it turned out the Russians really had committed such an act.

As I mentioned before, they had the Jews dig trenches for a pipe that was to bring gas to the interior of the mountain where it would be used for the manufacturing done there. The Russians laid the pipe into the trenches. The pipeline had been completed about two weeks. The Germans turned on the gas, and nothing made it into the mountain. They immediately investigated the problem. It took them awhile to find the cause of the blockage. They found that many of the pipes had been stuffed with dirt, making the flow of gas impossible. Since they knew exactly who worked on which length of pipe, they knew that the Russians had purposely stuffed the pipes, then buried them. Naturally, such an act could not be discovered until the entire job was completed. By their act of sabotage, the Russians effectively negated months of work.

When the Gestapo man finished reading the charges, he stepped away, giving a signal for the first group to be executed. We had to stand, facing the Russians in silence. The Gestapo wanted to teach us a lesson by forcing us to watch the hangings. They viewed public execution as an effective deterrent to crime. If any of us committed an act of sabotage, of any kind, we would be executed. We already knew that, of course, but we still had to bear witness.

When someone is hanged, he does not simply drop straight down, the weight of his body breaking his neck, killing him. Being in the front row, forced to watch the hangings taking place, at most a few feet away, I learned that death is rarely immediate or even quick. A man struggles. Sometimes, his own struggle kills him. Sometimes, he chokes himself to death. In almost every case, he will writhe, kick out, fighting to the last possible moment to stay alive, even if that life is harsh, brutal, and painful.

The first Russian in front of me did exactly that; fighting desperately to hold onto the merest thread of life. I was so close to him that I was kicked in the chest by his final movements. I could do nothing about it. None of us were allowed to move. I couldn't protect myself in any way. The very real threat of being shot if I moved kept me standing still, looking directly ahead. Finally, the last Russian of the first group died.

Some appointed prisoners cut down the bodies, piling them to the side of the yard as the second group moved into place. The Gestapo man repeated to us the crime they committed and the punishment for it. Again, I was kicked by the Russian in front of me as he struggled to hold onto life as long as he possibly could, his muscle spasms diminishing, and then eventually stopping. My chest began to ache from being hit by the swinging feet of the Russians in front of me as they died, but I simply remained silent. Many of us thought we, too, might be killed as part of the punishment.

After the second group lost their struggle for life, a third group was moved into place. The entire process lasted several hours before all the Russian prisoners had paid for their crime with their lives.

One of the Russians in the last group moved his mouth as the rope around his neck was tied into place. The bit in his mouth moved, the chain holding it in place having worked loose at some point. He wasn't directly in front of me, but just to one side. After a moment, I realized he was not simply moving his mouth, but was actually speaking, repeating the same phrase over and over again. Not knowing the Russian language, I had no idea what he was saying, why it was so important for him to say it again and again. Through his repetition, I remembered the phrase. Decades later, I asked someone who spoke Russian what it meant. He looked surprised and a little embarrassed when he told me it meant crudely: "Screw you, Nazis."

When the last Russian was cut down from the gallows, the Gestapo man warned us again about the fate of any prisoner caught committing an act of sabotage. To our relief, he then released us to return to our normal routine for the day.

I had been sorting clothes for only a couple of days when I found the teffilin, the leather straps which the very religious Jews use as an integral part of their prayers, carefully wrapped in a prayer shawl, hidden within the sleeve of a shirt. During the weeks I sorted clothes, I would eventually find many such items, but that was the first. Someone had taken great care in trying to hide his personal, religious objects.

I took the prayer shawl out of the shirt and unwrapped the teffilin. They were obviously old and well used, but also very carefully taken care of. I could easily imagine a devout, old man who had been using this same prayer shawl and set of teffilin for perhaps decades. As Uncle Mordechai passed by me, I showed it to him. His face lit up with an inner joy and excitement I don't remember ever seeing before. Certainly, I don't recall ever seeing him as happy. He touched the items, very gently, as if afraid they might disappear. He seemed to forget that I was even there. Only because I was so close to him was I able to hear what he said as he murmured quietly in Yiddish, "It's been so long."

Afraid of attracting the attention of a guard by staying in one place too long, my uncle gathered up the piles I had made and moved on. I gave the incident no more thought, as I began to find other things that people felt had value, sometimes of value only to the individuals who hid them. I realized my family and I had done the same thing, by making buttons out of gold. I knew our clothing, too, was in a pile somewhere, the buttons and buckles I had worked hard to craft long gone.

On my way back to the barracks that night, I happened to see my uncle. He was standing behind a building, trying to make himself as inconspicuous as possible. I saw immediately what he was doing. Somehow, he had managed to smuggle both the teffilin and the prayer shawl out of the sorting room. I have no idea how he accomplished this, with guards watching us so closely, but he had succeeded. It was something very important to him.

He had his arm wrapped in the thin leather strip of the teffilin as prescribed by thousands of years of ritual and tradition. His head bent slightly in prayer, he did not notice me or anyone else around him. He had chosen a place as out of the way as he could. In that, too, he had succeeded. Few people passed by, those that did ignoring him. Unfortunately, one of the few people to notice him was one of the guards. The guard saw my uncle before I even noticed the guard. It was only when he called out, demanding my uncle account for himself, that I saw him approach. He raised his rifle like a club, yelling "thief!" as he ran at my uncle.

My uncle looked up in time to try to ward off the first blow. After that, he simply curled up as tightly as he could, trying to make as small a target as possible, trying to protect his head as the guard rained down blow upon blow.

I knew that the safest thing for me to do would be to run as far away as I could and to do it as fast as I could. Even knowing what might be best for me, I couldn't leave my uncle there, being beaten to death, the guard showing no signs of easing his assault. As far as I knew, he and my cousins might well be the only family I had left. Not only that, watching the guard beat him, I thought of what must have happened to my father, and how no one was able to help him.

With no further thought, I ran toward them, crying out, begging the guard to stop. "He's my father," I said in German. "Please, please, don't kill him." I came as close as I dared.

The guard stopped, looked at me, his anger spent. Momentarily, I feared he might continue the beating on me, but I was lucky that time. He looked back at my uncle, his rifle lowered next to his side, my uncle's blood still moist on the stock. The guard looked back at me, an expression of genuine surprise on his face. "He's my father," I repeated in German. I knew a pleading quality remained in my voice. I didn't care. I meant it. Only then, did I learn what had caught the guard by surprise.

"You speak German well. When did you learn to speak it, boy?" the guard asked me.

"When I was ten," I told him truthfully. "To be really educated, you have to learn German." I automatically repeated my father's words to me. He had deeply believed that, as had I when I was ten and learning the language, reading everything I could find written by Germans or in German.

The guard nodded slowly, impressed by my education, and the fact that I acknowledged the necessity of knowing German to be truly educated. "You're a nice boy," the guard told me. He looked at my uncle with an expression of disgust I can envision to this day.

"How come such a good boy like you has such a thief for a father? Why would he do something like that?" He had not stopped staring at my uncle, his grip on the rifle tightening.

"Sir, please," I continued to beg, "he made a mistake. That's all. Please save his life." I saw my uncle move slightly, though he continued bleeding. Knowing he was still alive gave me greater courage. "I promise it will never happen again."

"If it does, I won't be so lenient next time," the guard said as he cradled the rifle under his arm and walked away.

As soon as he was gone, I knelt beside my uncle, trying to see how badly he was injured. Bruised and bleeding, at least his breathing was strong and even. It could have been much worse. I held him in my arms as he began to relax.

"Don't ever do that again," I said softly in Yiddish, more plea than warning. "Promise me, please. If you ever see anything like that again, leave it alone. You see what happens."

He nodded his agreement, not yet able to speak. He still wore the teffilin on his arm. He put his other hand on the leather strap, now stained with his blood. Only then, did he begin to cry.

Uncle Mordechai kept his promise to me. For the rest of the time we worked together, he never again tried anything like that. Soon after that, he was transferred to another camp. One day, I came to work and he simply was not there. Such transfers happened all the time. At that point, I lost track of him and my cousins for almost a year. I felt very much alone, not knowing if I had any family left.

This abrupt displacement occurred with such regularity that many people refused to make more contact with someone than was absolutely necessary. To become friends with someone meant there was one more person whose loss became personally meaningful. This happened even with superficial acquaintances. The boxer from the next barracks was like that.

The barracks next to mine housed mostly Hungarian Jews. Because I spoke the language, I got to know some of them. One of the men was very well built and appeared much healthier than the rest of the men, even when he took on the emaciated appearance that was normal, given the starvation rations in the camp. I never spoke with him. But from some of the other men in that barracks, I learned the man was a professional boxer, an unusual profession for a Jew. And he was good at it.

One day, when I didn't see him at the apel plotz, I asked about him. I was told he had been killed the night before. The murder of a Jew was so commonplace as to no longer be remarkable. Even so, I was curious and asked what happened.

Somehow, the Nazis discovered that the man was a boxer and they wanted to set up a match between him and one of the SS officers. The Nazis appreciated diversions of many types and in this one, they could prove the superiority of the Aryan race when the officer beat the Hungarian boxer. Of course, they had to make certain that the officer would win. Even in his starvation weakened state, the boxer was a professional athlete and might, through technique and training, beat the Nazi, something which simply could not be allowed to occur in front of the audience of SS officers and camp officials.

To ensure that would not happen, he was told to lose the fight. In return, he would be rewarded with an entire loaf of bread and the opportunity to fight again the next night, once again losing the match for a loaf of bread.

The fight was held outside the camp's gate. Evidently things did not go exactly as the Nazis planned. The boxer, actually given permission to strike a man who had the authority to kill him for no greater crime than being in the way, did as well as his training permitted. Grimly enthusiastic, he hit the SS officer and ultimately won the match.

His execution was based on a couple of things. First of all, he embarrassed the SS by showing that a lowly, hungry Jew could beat a Nazi in a fair fight. Secondly, he did not follow orders and lose the bout as instructed. I often wish I had been able to see the fight, watching as a Jew hit a Nazi with impunity. In any case, he ended as thousands before him, gone in a moment on the whim of the Nazis.

My sense of isolation and being alone deepened shortly after losing track of my uncle when an announcement came during the morning count at the apel plotz. It was a common practice to move prisoners from one camp to another. This happened when one camp became too crowded, or another camp needed additional slaves to complete a particular project. An officer, usually an SS officer, pointed to a person or a group, said, "Go!" And you went. No further accommodation was ever made. In that way, losing track of friends and family happened on a regular basis. That's what happened with my father, Uncle Mordechai, and my cousins.

This particular morning, another camp needed workers. They got us out early and told us to get undressed. No one ever thought to disobey such an order, because we all knew the price we would pay for such an act. We each got undressed, leaving our clothes in a small pile on the ground next to us. We stood in lines, naked, waiting for whatever came next.

An SS doctor came to inspect us. He walked along the rows, looking at each person, checking to see each one's strength and health. I imagine he was trying to decide how much labor each person was capable of, before dying from exhaustion. That more than anything would determine if it was worth the effort to transport someone from one camp to another.

I thought of all these things as I watched him move from one prisoner to another, checking muscles and so on. I tried to second-guess him, think what he might be looking for and why. It wasn't possible. It might be anything. Slowly, prisoner by prisoner, he approached me. I stopped thinking, stopped trying to guess what might be. He came to my row, continuing his inspection of each prisoner in turn.

When he came near me, still a prisoner or two away, I pulled in my belly as hard as I could. Already emaciated from months of near-starvation, the bones from my chest stuck out, the skin pulled taut, prominently displaying each rib. He came by me, glanced at me quickly and gave me a direct order.

"Get out," he demanded. "You're half-dead already."

He didn't have to tell me twice. I grabbed my clothes and ran from the line. I joined a couple of other men who looked near to death. I put my clothes back on as we watched the process continue.

Thinking about it now, I can't explain why I did that or exactly what I was thinking about at the time. The action may very well have been instinctive in some way. I can only describe the results.

After the doctor finished his inspection, only five of us from the population of several thousand prisoners gathered that morning had been sent out. One of the five in our new little group was a rabbi from a town not far from my hometown. I could easily see why he had been excluded from the work force. At some time, not long before, he had been attacked by the dogs. His arms were badly mangled, the flesh bitten and ripped. He obviously had some infection since they didn't seem to be healing. Instead, pus oozed from open wounds, causing his arms to appear sore and raw. I was surprised he was able to do any work at all. It certainly must have been painful for him to hold or lift anything. I have no idea how he managed to carry anything with his arms so mutilated.

The Rabbi had quite a few friends in camp, not only many of the congregants from his synagogue imprisoned in Dora with him, but others as well who came to admire him for his wisdom and compassion. He continued to act as the leader of those people, listening to them, giving advice, providing a spiritual connection to a life which daily became more difficult to think of as real. He made a point of speaking briefly in farewell to each man he knew. He couldn't allow what was likely to be a permanent separation to take place without a word or two of emotional and spiritual support.

So focused was he on saying goodbye to his friends that he did not hear the order to move out. The look of surprise on his face was almost comical when everyone began moving. Still waving one last time to his friends, he tried to get out of the way, to join me and the other men who had been culled from the herd of laborers. One of the guards saw him walking away from the large group and towards us. The Rabbi had made it close enough to us for us to hear the exchange with the guard.

"Where are you going, old man?" the guard demanded of him.

"They told me to get out," the Rabbi replied simply. He honestly did not imagine any problem.

The guard did not believe him. No matter what the Rabbi said, the guard demanded he join the group leaving the camp. The Rabbi held up his arms, trying to show why he couldn't possibly be of any use as a laborer. He began to beg, plead, all to no avail.

The guard made him go along with the rest of the people. Neither the Rabbi nor any one of the 5,000 or 6,000 men sent out of Dora that day ever came back. I never knew the name of the camp they went to, only that it was a hard labor camp.

A few days after the transfer of prisoners, the officer in charge made a general announcement over the loudspeaker. During the previous days, more prisoners had come into the camp, replacing those who had left. Usually, such announcements never boded well, but this was different. They asked if anyone was a tailor. Sometimes, when a specific job needed to be filled, they simply asked if anyone knew how to do that job. That's how Yakov became an electrician, working in the tunnel.

A tailor, I imagined, would be an easier job than even sorting clothes. I thought to myself, "Too bad I'm not a tailor." The next moment, I realized that I could tell them that I *was* a tailor. My short apprenticeship in Budapest which, at the time, I thought so terrible now gave me the right to raise my hand in response. For the first time since telling Mr. Katz that I quit, I thanked him, grateful for my time with him. Because of him, I could honestly say I was a tailor and since neither I nor anyone else there had any papers or documentation of any type to either prove or disprove our claims, there was no reason to admit it was only for a few months.

I stepped out of line to join the other men who answered the call. We stood together, a large group, all of us hoping for the same thing, that a job as a tailor would be easy compared to any other job we'd been doing. I looked at the other men, all old-timers, men who had probably made their livings as tailors for decades. I wouldn't be surprised if many of them came from families also in the tailor business. There I stood, a little kid in comparison to them. I was determined to continue. I certainly could not go back at that point.

The SS officer in charge of finding a tailor briefly questioned each man about his experience. I listened to what he asked the other men. He conducted it very much like a normal job interview, with a group of applicants eager to fill the position he offered.

I grew more and more confident, certain I could answer any question he posed to me.

His approach to the job interview changed when he came to me. He stared at me a moment, saying nothing. He glanced quickly at the other men before returning his gaze to me. I stood up straight, trying to show some of the confidence I felt a short time earlier. I hoped to appear a little taller, maybe a little older. He did not appear impressed by either attempt.

"Are you really a tailor, boy?" he questioned, his tone accusing me of lying before I had the chance to reply.

"Yes, sir," I answered with as much assurance as I could.

"How long have you been a tailor?" He obviously did not believe me and seemed to be looking for something to prove me wrong.

"For three-and-a-half years," I quickly told him, trying to sound as if it was the simple truth, the only answer I could possibly give. He was still unimpressed. Afraid he might send me out of the group, or worse, I pressed on without waiting for him to say anything more. "I was apprenticed very young." I thought, "That much, at least, is the truth." Had the situation with Mr. Katz been different, I might very well have become a tailor, and been one for the past several years. I wanted the job very badly. My foot was still healing and I knew, as a tailor, I would be sitting down all day. I felt that the opportunity to sit, rather than stand all day, inside a nice warm building would help me a lot.

"Make certain you are a tailor, or you know what will happen," the SS officer stated. He didn't have to say anything more. His threat was blatant, not implied. I was determined to prove myself as capable as any of the other men there. As they led us away, I reviewed in my mind everything I had learned at the tailor shop. I ignored my treatment by Mr. Katz, focusing instead on what he and the other tailors at his shop had the chance to teach me.

They took us to a large warehouse, which had been transformed into a factory for tailors. Row upon row of brand new sewing machines greeted us when we entered the room. The beautiful machines, just in from Italy made me think again of Mr. Katz and how much he would have loved to have had only one of the machines.

The machines didn't impress me as much as the building itself—large, warm, and dry. Any prisoner would do anything to work there. Being a tailor would be the perfect job for me, giving my foot time to heal. I saw being forced to sit for hours on end as a privilege. It all seemed too good to be true. Then came the test.

I was concerned that we might be expected to sew new clothes. No matter how much I tried to remember from my early days in Budapest, I knew I would never be able to do something like that. I glanced at the other men. Many of them tried to give an appearance of confidence, some seemed beyond caring while a few appeared as worried as I felt. I wondered if they might have lied about having experience as a tailor. If that was the case, they really did have something to be concerned about.

Each of us was assigned to a machine and told to prepare it for work. At least, having worked a little bit in Mr. Katz's shop, I was able to thread and use the sewing machine. If not for that, I would have failed the test before I had a chance to start. We each sat down at our given machine, silent, as the test was explained. Each of us would be given a bundle of clothes. At a signal, we were to open the bundle and sew the clothing. They would time us to see how long we took to do the project. To have a fair assessment of who was capable of the job and who was not, they gave each of us the same number of garments. The bundle you got held ten pants or ten shirts—all prisoner clothes. The job of the tailor was to repair the prisoners' clothing. They realized how prized this job was and knew the people would easily lie about their abilities in order to get away from the hard labor of the regular camp.

The guard handed me my bundle without a word and walked to the next man, handed him a bundle, and so on until each hopeful tailor had clothing to work on. I closed my eyes, for a moment, before opening my bundle. All I could do was hope the clothing was not in very bad shape. As with everything the SS had us do, speed and efficiency were high priorities. I feared that it might take me too long to fix the clothes.

When instructed, I opened my bundle. I'll never forget what I saw: pants, just ten pairs of pants that actually seemed in pretty good shape. I was extremely lucky in that the only thing wrong with most of the pants was a ripped seam. All I had to do was sew straight lines to repair the seams. Everything around me disappeared as I concentrated on the machine and the seam I repaired. I wasted no time in checking my work, knowing it had to be right that first time or it wouldn't matter anyway, but immediately went on to the next pair of pants. I continued like that, never looking up, not even taking time to sit up and stretch, until I finished sewing the last seam on the last of the ten pairs of pants.

As soon as I finished, I went to the SS officer in charge. He happened to be the same man who was skeptical of me earlier. As I walked up to him, I passed a lot of the other men, still working at their machines. Only then, did I begin to have some idea of how quickly I had completed my bundle. I told the officer that I was done. He checked the time. For a moment, he didn't seem to believe that I had, in fact, finished. He walked over to my machine and quickly checked each pair of pants.

He nodded in approval. "Yes," he said, trying not to sound impressed. "It seems that you are a good tailor."

I didn't realize I had been holding my breath until I sighed in relief. "Thank God for that," I murmured softly to myself.

I was chosen as one of the men to work as a tailor. Being able to sit in that nice, warm building was the best thing that could have happened to me then. Gradually, my foot continued to heal. It no longer hurt to walk. I was there for quite some time, though I don't recall exactly how many months.

Within a short time of my working as a tailor, I got a promotion. The factory had at least 75 tailors working, probably more. I was made head of the warehouse. My job was to accept the finished product from the tailors in the factory and make certain the work was done correctly. With that many tailors working, different shifts, work continuing close to 24 hours a day, I could never have done such a job by myself. I had a big staff of people working for me. Within that small domain, I had become a relatively important person. I never lorded it over the men working for me. Every person's situation was precarious, mine no less than theirs.

It embarrassed me to be responsible for checking the work of these men. Many of them had been making their livings as tailors for longer than I had been alive. They brought their work to me to give it a final okay. Sometimes, I could see their legs shaking, fearful that I might not approve of their work. They often looked down, staring at the floor as if looking me in the eye might threaten me. They went out of their way not to do anything that might result in my rejecting a new seam in a pair of pants.

Once in a while, a jacket might not have been repaired quite right or a pair of pants hemmed crudely. I'd simply replace the garment with a good one, but make certain to tell the tailor to be more careful in the future. My life, as well as his, depended upon it.

The tailors did much more than simply repair seams on the prisoners' clothing. Sometimes, they created new clothing and often altered many of the garments that came into the camp. Some of the tailors became quite good at making fur coats.

They got the fur from the rabbits being bred in the barn on the mountain. Just as an announcement was made looking for tailors, tanners and leather workers came forward to work the rabbit hides. They became a part of the clothing factory.

One of the men who came forward as a tanner was Itzak, a friend of mine from my hometown. As with most people I had known in Rozavlea, we lost track of each other during the deportation. I didn't even know he was in Dora until I saw him among the tanners. I ran to him, calling his name. We hugged each other, relieved and happy to see a familiar, friendly face in the crowd of strangers. Of all the people I could possibly have seen, Itzak's presence surprised me the most. He was of average height, but very strong. He also had a short leg, giving him a permanent limp. It was also difficult, if not impossible, for him to bend that one knee. He put paper or cloth or anything he had into his shoe to try to make his legs more even and his limp as unnoticeable as possible. I have no idea how he managed to survive the selections that the Nazis used to weed out those with any deformity or physical abnormality. Somehow, he made it, hiding his bad leg any way he could.

Itzak had as much right to call himself a tanner as I did in calling myself a tailor. Back home in Rozavlea, he was a butcher. He knew how to skin animals quickly and efficiently, two qualifications of importance to the Nazis; but beyond that, he knew little. At first, he concentrated on the part of the job he knew best: skinning animals. Within a couple of days, he lost count of the number of rabbits he skinned. While he did his job, he watched everything the old-time tanners did and learned quickly, soon becoming one of the better tanners in his group.

In the course of my job, I went to the tanners to see their work. I was responsible for making certain the tailors received the best skins. Itzak and I had the chance to see each other and talk during each of my visits. He took pride in the work they did and showed me the entire operation, explaining each procedure. I learned how quickly a rabbit could be skinned. Despite all Itzak had learned, it was still what he did best.

"Where does the meat go?" I asked.

He shrugged in response. "It's separated and packed," he explained. "After that. . ." His voice trailed off, accompanied by another little shrug. "All I know," he continued, "is that I don't get to eat any of it." He tilted his head slightly in the direction of one of the ever-present guards. He didn't have to say anything. We both knew what the penalty would be for stealing the meat.

He showed me the process for drying the hides. First, a board is laid flat and covered with salt. Then, a hide is stretched taut and pinned to the board over the salt. The salt draws all of the moisture out of the hide, curing the leather. Once that process was done, the hide was dry, but stiff and unmanageable. It was then worked to make it soft and pliable, something the tailors could work with. That was the point at which I collected the pelts and took them with me to the tailors in the factory.

The tailors made custom garments for other people as well. Near the top of the mountain, across the valley from the rabbit farm, was a special barracks where the SS kept some young women to use for sex when they felt like it. It might offend the Nazis sense of esthetics to force these women to wear drab, threadbare prisoner clothes. They had to wear new, elegant clothing.

I went to the women's barracks with one or two of the other tailors. There, we measured the women, brought partially completed garments for them to try on, pinned gowns and dresses for custom fits. Nice, good-looking Jewish women, most of them felt embarrassed and ashamed by what they did. Few looked directly at us while we did our jobs. In addition to the tattoo of the regular prisoner number, they carried another small tattoo, located under their upper arm, given only to the women used for sex. Like branded cattle, they would forever carry on their bodies a mark announcing how they managed to survive.

Once in a while, the tailors made a gown or other garment for the women from scratch. Usually, though, they simply altered one of the thousands of dresses that came into the camp. Beautiful, elegant, expensive dresses wound up being worn by women who could never have afforded them prior to the war and who did not want to wear them now. Despite good food, better living conditions, and no manual labor, I did not meet a single woman who was happy in that barracks on the mountain. Doctors routinely checked the women, making certain they remained healthy. Some pretended that they enjoyed the easy life and fine food, especially when the guards or SS stood nearby, watching as the tailors worked; but they could never look us in the eyes when they said it.

I also noticed that when the guards stayed farther away, leaving only the tailors and myself close to them, the women tried to keep the extra tattoo from showing. As far as I know, after the liberation, the women had the tattoo removed. A lot had it done in Sweden, but other European countries did it for the women as well. The resulting scar had no stigma attached to it, thus making it preferable to the tattoo.

Within a short time of my promotion, I began taking a proprietary pride in the quality of work put out by the tailors in the factory. I easily understood how Itzak felt pride in the quality of the furs and pelts that he and the other tanners prepared. It pained me to see a beautiful dress or gown, so carefully made by one or more of the tailors, cut and altered to conform to the Nazi's mandates.

One of the jobs of the tailors was to make any garment immediately recognizable as belonging to a prisoner. For a period of several months, the prisoner clothes were in short supply. Since we had an abundance of civilian clothing, prisoners received those to wear. Before the prisoners got the clothes, though, we had them at the tailor factory. There, the tailors tore a strip out of the side of the leg and put in a corresponding strip of cloth which had previously been used to create an entire set of prisoner clothes. They also cut a large, square patch of cloth from the back of the shirt or jacket, again replacing it with the thin striped prisoner cloth. That way, a guard could immediately see who was a prisoner and who was not.

It hurt me most, professionally, when the same thing was done to one of the dresses for the women in the mountain barracks. A large section from the back of the dress was automatically replaced with the ugly, thin cloth. Those dresses we got from the sorting room were well made, had probably been expensive when originally purchased. It didn't matter. Ripped, torn, cut, and resewn—the dresses proclaimed the status of the wearer, even if she covered all of her tattoos.

I can clearly remember the nightly count at the apel plotz, glancing up at the mountain to the women's barracks. The women did not have to join the rest of us at that time. Instead, they had to walk slowly back and forth in front of their barracks, allowing the SS and guards to view what was available to them for the night's activities.

Any time you have a large group of people together and some desired item is scarce, someone, someway, somehow will find a way to provide that item . . . for a price. The scarcer the item or more difficult it is to obtain, the higher the price. It's the classic economic principle of "supply and demand." A black market will evolve in which items are traded and sold.

One such item was the cigarette. Many people smoked in those days. No one knew how much harm cigarettes did, like they know today. There was no stigma against smoking, people starting at very young ages. I had been smoking ever since I was fifteen and living in Budapest. My father was a very heavy smoker. He used to love the cigarettes I would bring home with me from Budapest. From a big city like that, the cigarettes were much less expensive and of a much higher quality than he was able to get in Rozavlea.

Nobody ever thought of smoking as a bad habit that had to be broken. It was simply something to do that we enjoyed. Only in the camps did I see how strong a habit like that could be, how difficult to stop, how much a man will trade in order to obtain a single cigarette.

I remember one of the first times I saw a prisoner with a cigarette. I was astonished that he had managed to get such an item. He stood a little apart from the others, leaning against the wall of one of the barracks, deeply inhaling the smoke, holding his breath for a moment to feel it in his lungs, and then slowly exhaling. He had his eyes closed, blissfully unaware of anything around him, his expression calm, almost peaceful.

It was dinnertime, when we had our soup and a piece of bread, if we had been lucky enough to get one. Another prisoner came up to the smoker, holding out his plate of food. He tapped the smoker on the shoulder to get his attention. The smoker opened his eyes, at first surprised, then apprehensive at seeing someone. He held the prized cigarette behind his back, trying to hide and protect it. They spoke briefly, the man with the plate holding up his food for inspection. The smoker hesitated, but I saw that his eyes never left the food. In a very short time, the smoker brought the cigarette from behind his back and handed it to the other man in exchange for the plate of food.

Each man seemed satisfied with his end of the bargain. The new smoker immediately took a deep drag on the cigarette, holding his breath for as long as he could to calm the longing of his lungs. The ex-smoker walked away a short distance and sat next to the barracks, leaning against the wall for support. He hunched over the plate of food and ate it quickly, afraid someone might take it anyway from him.

For myself, even though I smoked heavily before arriving at the camp, I reasoned that food was far more important than a cigarette if I expected to survive. I would be lying if I said I never wanted a cigarette or didn't envy those who drew the calming smoke into their lungs. My intention, though, was to survive and anything that might impede that was something I could do without. Seeing that a man will trade his food for the chance to smoke a single cigarette stayed with me. I thought that if I could get a cigarette, I could then trade it for food. For a long time, I could do nothing about that thought, but it was always in the back of my mind. As the prisoner in charge of the clothing warehouse, I was in a position to finally take advantage of the thought.

One of my responsibilities was to deliver the finished products. Sometimes, that meant going up to the women's barracks on the mountain to bring them the dresses we had made. Sometimes, it meant going to the SS officers or guards to deliver clothing they had ordered, like the fur coats. Sometimes, it meant bringing a jacket or pair of pants to another barracks.

The Nazis routinely searched each prisoner every time he left the tailor factory. They knew we might be tempted to steal an extra shirt or pair of pants for either our own added warmth or for trade, and the easiest way to do that would be to wear an extra layer of clothing. Upon leaving, each man was required to open his shirt to prove another shirt was not there. The same thing applied to the pants. I never once tried to do that. I knew I would be caught immediately and already knew what the consequences of such an action would be. Instead, I stole extra clothing in a different way.

Ever since I was a little boy, I had heard that the best place to hide something was in plain sight. I can tell you for a fact that it's true. Each time I left the factory, the guard searched me for extra clothing. Over my arm, I always carried some clothes for delivery somewhere. Every other day or so, even if I was going to the women's barracks and had dresses that I carried, I also had an additional shirt or two, or jacket, or pair of pants. I opened my shirt and pants, proving to the guard that I wasn't trying to sneak out of the factory with extra clothes. I then picked up my pile of clothing that I had to deliver and was sent on my way. They automatically assumed that in taking the pile of clothing, I was doing my job, taking the clothes to deliver to whomever they were intended for. They never questioned whom each shirt was going to, whom each jacket was meant for. I never had to account for all the extra clothing I stole in that way.

Once I made my actual deliveries, I had to dispose of the extra clothes. Sometimes, I gave a jacket or shirt to someone who didn't have it. For something like that, I never asked for anything in return. Most of the time, I used the clothing to trade for food. As the winter of 1944 took hold, a new jacket could bring me an entire portion of bread or serving of soup with a potato peel in it.

Sometimes, I found the men who somehow managed to obtain items like cigarettes. Like any business transaction, we negotiated price; so many cigarettes for a shirt, so many for a jacket. The price was never the same, either due to the amount and quality of the clothing, or the abundance or scarcity of the cigarettes. We worked together quickly, neither of us wanting to take or increase our chances of being caught. With the cigarettes in my hand, I felt safer and more confident. It was far easier to hide a few cigarettes than to try to hide some shirts or extra pairs of pants. At those times, I looked forward to dinner.

It didn't take long before it became known among the hardcore smokers that I might have a cigarette or two to trade. I never had to worry about not making a trade. There was always at least one person willing to give me his own meager portion of food for one of my cigarettes. It was a trade that satisfied us both. It never ceased to amaze me how one man could be so hungry he would willingly risk his life for a mouthful of bread, and another man who is just as hungry will give away all the bread he has for one cigarette. The thin soup and small chunk of bread were never filling by itself; but with twice as much, it was actually possible not to feel my stomach cramp with hunger when I went to sleep at night.

By February of 1945, life had taken on a common, if not necessarily pleasant, routine. Every morning, no matter how cold, in rain or snow, we gathered at the apel plotz to be counted. We stood as still as possible during the daily ordeal in our thin clothing, even our jackets doing little to help keep us warm, not even daring to stamp our feet in an attempt to generate warmth. Once the SS completed the count, we immediately went to our assigned work area. As the winter grew colder with snow covering the ground, I looked forward to going to the tailor factory, where we did our jobs in the dry warmth of the huge building.

It had been a while since we had been called out earlier than usual to the apel plotz. That morning early in 1945 is one that I remember well because it was so unusual.

The morning began with an eerie familiarity. By the time we gathered at the apel plotz, the area was surrounded with SS guards. The ominous sight of a corresponding number of Gestapo imbued in us a sense of dread. As was normal in situations like this, we had no idea what was going on, what was going to happen. None of the SS or Gestapo spoke to us. None of us dared to speak to or question them. We lined up, quickly and efficiently, and then waited. It began to lightly rain.

As we moved into place, I noticed that the Gestapo men began to arrive. More than seeing the others, this concerned me.

Whenever this many SS showed up in the shadow of the Gestapo, we knew whatever was going to happen next would not be good. The last time the Gestapo showed up in such numbers was for the mass executions of the Russian prisoners of war. I wondered if someone or some group had committed another act of sabotage. Spending most of my waking hours running the clothing warehouse, I no longer saw as much of the regular camp activity as I had when I first arrived.

We filled the apel plotz. No room had been reserved for mass hangings, no gallows set up. My next thought began to frighten me. Each man who guarded us carried a machine gun. For the first time, I imagined them opening fire and killing us all where we stood. Thinking quickly, I reasoned they could easily eliminate all of us, given a little time. Disposing of the bodies might be inconvenient, but they would find a way.

The rain continued, not hard, but enough to begin soaking though our clothes as we waited. So many things began racing through my mind, that when they started having us reform into lines of five, I felt relieved. They obviously intended to take us somewhere. Naturally, none of us had any idea where it might be. The thought briefly came to my mind that it might be even easier to kill us in lines of fives, outside the camp, than gathered in one large group at the apel plotz. Disposing of the bodies might certainly pose less of a problem.

I did not have time to think too much about it, nor would I have been able to do anything at that point except follow their orders. For whatever reason, the Nazis had decided to transfer the entire population of Dora. Thinking about it now, I suspect that with the war nearing its end and little hope of emerging victorious, they decided to abandon the munitions factory deep within the mountain. I tried not to think about things I had no power to control or change. Formed into our lines of five, we marched out of Dora under the watchful eyes and ready machine guns of the Gestapo and SS guards.

Bergen-Belsen

We marched, not knowing where we might end up, trying not to think beyond the next step, never having the option of even looking back. Our clothes began to weigh us down because even thin cloth grows heavy as it absorbs water. The rain, still light but steady, eliminated what little snow might have remained on the ground. I walked in my line, head down, shoulders hunched forward, arms folded tightly against my body, trying without much success to remain dry and warm. I noticed grass, lots of grass on the sides of the road. The grass at my feet was crumpled and broken as I and every other prisoner marched the fresh shoots into the mud.

In a short time, we came to a halt at a makeshift railroad station. The only thing there was the train, an enormous behemoth made up of hundreds of cars, mostly enclosed boxcars but some open cars as well.

Seeing the train, I knew that, at least for a while, we had no fear of being killed. They intended to transport us, most likely to some new camp. I felt relieved, knowing that as long as we were needed, even as slaves, we had at least a chance of staying alive.

They began to load us into the cars, sharp shouts and curses in German punctuated by prods from rifles and machine guns, occasionally accented by the sound of a gun being fired. The Gestapo and SS yelled orders to the guards who violently passed them along to us. No mention was ever made as to our destination. None of us expected it. I wonder if the guards themselves knew what the destination of the train was.

Food was distributed to the prisoners as they entered the cars. A loaf of bread was to be shared between five or six people. The same group was also given a can of what was called pork beef, maybe a pound or a little bit more to be shared equally. The only instruction anyone was given was to hurry into place. At no time, did I hear anyone being told how long the journey was likely to be. As soon as a car was full, its doors closed and sealed, the next car immediately began loading. The process repeated without variation with each successive car.

The rain had not stopped during the entire time we spent loading into the boxcars. Since I was near the end of the lines, I kept hoping I might be lucky enough to be in one of the enclosed boxcars, dry and warm, out of the incessant rain. I tried to keep a count in my head as to how many prisoners went in a car, how many enclosed cars remained, what my chances might be to get into one. Seeing how many boxcars remained, my chances did not look good, but I tried to remain optimistic. As the rain began coming down harder, I gave up any attempt to remain dry. My clothing was soaked, hanging heavily on me. I simply looked forward at the lines ahead of me, hoping I might be one of the fortunate ones. I viewed the boxcar as safety from the weather.

My heart sank when, only two or three rows in front of me, the last boxcar filled to capacity, its doors drawn shut and sealed. Only the open cars remained. I thought to myself, "This is bad."

Without a pause, they began loading us into the open cars. Each group of five or six people was handed the small loaf of bread and can of meat. It was of no concern to the guards that our bread soon became soggy and inedible in the rain. They knew we would eat it anyway. We did.

By morning, the rain had stopped. At the front and back of the car was a little bench where the SS guards sat, two per bench, already there as we entered, watching us in silence. Even though they wore heavy coats to keep warm, they appeared no happier about being in the open cars that we felt. We sat on the floor of the car, four rows across, facing one way, each man sitting in the lap of the man behind him. In that way, the maximum number of prisoners could be fit into a single car.

I happened to be in the last row, the legs of one of the SS guards touching my back. I tried to sit straight, not to press against his legs, not to make him any more uncomfortable than he might already be. None of them spoke to us. We waited as the door to our car was shut and the procedure continued with the next car. The prisoners spoke in whispered tones with each other, speculating as to where we might be going. The SS men told us nothing.

Finally, the last prisoner was loaded into the last car, its door shut. Shouted orders reverberated along the length of the train. With a soft jolt as the engine started, we began our journey away from Dora.

We tried to make the food last as long as possible, since no one knew how long our trip was going to take. Even though we tried, one can of meat and a loaf of soggy bread, divided five ways, does not last long. We finished the food within a few hours. Even if we had wanted to and tried to ration, it would not have been possible to divide so little food among so many people. We had not been given any water, and the salt used to preserve the meat contributed to making our thirst almost unbearable.

Sitting in the open car turned out to be a blessing. We mitigated our thirst that first night by licking the walls of the car which had been made slick with water from the rain, any moisture being a precious commodity. Even with that minute amount of water helping alleviate the worst of our thirst, it was far from quenched, our mouths and throats still dry and parched. And then God came with a nice, fat rain. I knew that I was one of the lucky ones to be in that open car.

At first, our thirst was so bad we simply tilted our heads back, opened our mouths and let the rain fall in. After a few minutes of allowing our mouths and throats to become moist, we found a better way to drink. Some of the men had blankets with them. We opened the blankets, capturing the rain as it fell. We then took the metal plates which had been given to us for our food and poured the water onto the plates. The best wine in the world could never come close to the exquisite taste of that fresh rain water. In all the years since then, I have never enjoyed or appreciated a drink more than I did that day.

Later that day, the train stopped. We easily saw why. Allied bombers, a few coming in low enough for us to see which country's flag was painted on it, targeted the railroad tracks. They came, wave after wave. I was accustomed to the sight from Dora; but maybe because we now sat out in the open, there seemed to be more than I ever remembered. The bombers seemed to take care to avoid hitting the train, while taking equal care to decimate the tracks.

We had to remain in the cars with no food to eat and only what rain we might capture to drink, while the tracks were repaired. As usual, available labor was never an issue in any construction or repair project. It was a relief when, the tracks repaired, the train started again.

The last car of the train contained the food and water stored for the SS guards and Gestapo. Whenever the train stopped, our guards had a break and food. The prisoners, naturally, received nothing.

The Allies continued their bombing of the tracks, forcing the train to stop several more times. The second time it stopped early in the morning when the dew still lay heavy on the thick grass at the sides of the railroad tracks. I felt the legs of the SS man behind me press lightly into my back. I immediately sat up as straight as

I could, trying to move a little bit forward, fearful I had annoyed him. I found it impossible to give the SS man any more room than he already had, the man in front of me locked into place by the density of men in front of him. I felt the nudge again as the SS man tried with no success at all to stretch his legs. I heard a slight sigh of resignation behind me and then a low voice speaking in German.

"Where do you come from?" the SS guard asked.

At first, I wasn't certain he was talking to me, so I remained silent. He sighed again, a hint of boredom potentially seeding irritation. He nudged my back again, a little harder to make sure to get my attention.

"What country are you from?" he asked again.

I had no reason not to respond, and every motivation to try to keep him from becoming angry. "I'm from a small town in Rumania," I told him, speaking in German. Truthfully, I was also bored, sitting in that car. Engaging in conversation, even if it was with the man holding a machine gun over my head and willing to kill me without a moment's extra thought, was a welcomed diversion.

"Really?" he asked, sounding genuinely interested. Then, to my surprise, he began speaking in Rumanian. "What's the name of your town? Where is it?"

I finally understood why every time I spoke German, it took the individual I spoke to off guard. It was unexpected, as much as I never imagined this SS man to speak fluent Rumanian. We began talking a little bit, switching easily between German and Rumanian. I found out that he was also from Rumania, though his family still considered themselves German. After a while, we spoke only Rumanian as if somehow agreeing, without words, to leave that aspect of Germany behind us and speak the language of our home and childhood.

I could not help looking out the side of the car through the wooden slats to the open field which the railroad ran through. If I stretched my neck, I was able to see even more of the passing landscape. Thick, high grass moved with a slow, gentle wave in the slight morning breeze. The dew reflected the early sunlight, enticing, mocking, proclaiming water a few feet away and impossibly distant.

"I have an idea," I finally said to him. "It may be a while before the tracks are repaired. Why don't you let me go down and pick up some of that grass?"

He laughed a little bit. "You have to be kidding," he said, amused by the thought. "Can you imagine it? They'll see you from another car, standing out in the middle of the field. They'll shoot you right away. You probably wouldn't even get far enough to stand in the grass."

I listened to him, regretfully having to agree. I wouldn't get a foot away from the train before being shot and killed, no questions asked, no answers even wanted. Still laughing, he leaned over to the SS man sitting on the bench next to him and, speaking softly in German, relayed my insane request. The other SS man laughed. I knew their laughter came at my expense, but I didn't care.

Even as the two SS men chuckled softly to themselves, I knew I had to find a way to get out of the train. The water from the rain was gone, even the sides of the car no longer moist. I didn't even have enough saliva to wet my lips. The more I looked at the dew on the grass, so heavy as to form drops of water, the faster my mind worked, trying to think of a way to get there.

The SS man behind me moved his legs again, attempting to find a comfortable position after sitting for hours on end. That provided me with the motivation I needed.

"I have an idea," I told the SS man in Rumanian. He began laughing softly, already enjoying whatever new words of amusement I might have.

"Well," he prompted, "what is it?"

"Why don't you come down with me? You can stretch your legs a little bit. You hold the gun on me, guarding me. Nobody will bother us. They're not going to shoot *you*." I spoke rapidly, afraid that he might cut me off, unwilling to listen to my entire proposition. When I finished, he said nothing, made no sound, not even that of derisive laughter. I had no idea whether or not that might be a good sign. I could only hope it was. Nervous, I tried to swallow, but didn't have enough moisture in my mouth to do that.

After an uncomfortable few moments of silence, he said, very thoughtful, "Do you know something? That's a good idea."

Under his guard, we got out of the car and walked the few feet to the grass. I could see he was almost as relieved as I was. He stretched, shaking his legs to loosen the cramped muscles and increase the circulation. He kept his finger on the trigger of his machine gun, ready at his side should I make the slightest move aside from what we had agreed.

For myself, as soon as we reached the grass, I paid no further attention to him, the train or anything else in the world except the tall, wet grass all around me. The first thing I did was to grab a handful of the fresh, sweet grass, rip it from the ground and stuff it into my mouth. At that moment, no meal in the world could remotely compare to the pleasure I got from eating that grass. The water, still on the blades, soothed my dry, parched mouth. The grass itself filled my stomach, making me feel satisfied for the first time in almost as long as I could remember since my deportation.

Before I finished swallowing the first handful, I tore another handful from the ground delighting in the feel of the dew moistening my hands. I stuffed that second handful into my mouth, this time chewing a little more slowly, enjoying every bite. After a few handfuls, I couldn't eat anymore; but I still pulled up clumps of the grass and licked the water from the stems, throwing it aside when I had licked it dry.

I finally glanced up to see the SS man several feet away, watching me, his machine gun lowered at his side, ready for use at the least provocation. Every so often, he bent his knees slightly, giving him the appearance of bouncing. It seemed funny to me, but I dared not laugh. I imagine watching me eat grass with more enthusiasm than a fine gourmet meal provided him with some amusement. He made no move to hurry me or pressure me to leave. Finally, he said, "Are you ready?"

"Yes," I replied automatically, "I'm done."

"Okay," he said, "let's go." I thought he sounded a bit disappointed. I guess the prospect of returning to sit in that cramped car was little more enjoyable for him than for me.

On my way back to the train, I grabbed at handfuls of grass and stuffed them in the pockets of my shirt, into my shirt, anywhere I had extra room. Clump after clump, I ripped from the ground as I walked by, until I had no more room in my clothing for storage, but was forced to carry a large armful into the train's car.

Suddenly, I was the wealthiest man in the world. In a carload of starving people with nothing to eat, I was bringing something edible. I passed the grass in my arms to the men around me and then emptied my shirt and pockets, trying to get the grass to as many of the men in the car as possible. I saw my own reactions played back over and over again, men hungrily eating the grass without thinking, then gradually chewing more slowly to taste the fresh water and make the treat last as long as possible.

Over the course of the next several days, we repeated the trip down from the car to the grass every time the train stopped, which happened almost daily. We developed a routine, a system. The same SS man came down with me, guarding me as he stretched out his legs, luxuriating in his own freedom from the cramped sitting position on the bench behind me.

Every time, I ate as much as I could, drinking the water left on the grass before it dried in the day's sunshine. I'd then grab as much as I could hold and carry back into the car and give it to the other men there. I was the only one who ever went down from the car. I took great care in never making the slightest move to jeopardize my life or the privilege I was given in leaving the car. I have no doubt in my mind that even a fellow Rumanian would not hesitate to kill me instantly if I overstepped my bounds.

Because of the constant bombing of the railroad tracks, forcing us to wait for hours, sometimes up to a day while repairs were made, a trip which should have taken only a few hours stretched into five or six days. Finally, the train stopped, not due to Allied bombs but because we had reached the end of our journey. They never told us the name of our destination, where we went or why. As appeared to be common for the SS, the train did not end its journey at an established station. It seemed to stop in the middle of nowhere, no town or even buildings in sight.

Waiting for the train was a large contingent of SS, accompanied by Gestapo. As always, the appearance of so many Gestapo created a sense of foreboding among us. We never trusted them, mostly because they never gave us any reason we could trust them. Large numbers of Gestapo had come to mean a large number of prisoner deaths. It was impossible not to equate one with the other.

The car doors slid open. For the first time since leaving Dora, everyone was ordered to stand and get out. Many of the men in the car had trouble standing and walking after sitting, almost immobile for so long. They received shouted curses and blows for not moving quickly enough. I was fortunate in that I had made several trips out of the car and so my muscles responded with much greater efficiency to my needs.

Only as the SS slid open the doors of the enclosed boxcars did I realize how lucky I was to have been placed in an open car. Like us, those put into the closed cars received no food or water. Unlike us, they received no benefit from the rain, which at least allowed us the chance to have something to drink. While we had the benefit of traveling in the open, fresh air, they suffered in the suffocating enclosure.

We stood near the train, waiting as each boxcar was opened. More often than not, the men crowded inside could not come out of the car by themselves. In most cases, the SS had to pull corpses out of the tightly packed car to allow any living prisoner out. The men died from dehydration, starvation, and suffocation. What I originally looked at as protection from the elements turned out to be a portable coffin.

I watched as body after body was pulled from the boxcars, thousands of them. At first, I didn't hear the man who called out my name. Finally, fairly close to me, he called loudly, "Benjamin!" I turned, surprised to hear the voice of my father's cousin Abraham, whom I had not seen since before leaving Rozavlea. He was a horse trader from a nearby town. I remember when I was a child visiting his family, especially my cousins Peri and Miriam, who were close to my age so we often played together. Looking at him then, I could see only the merest shadow of how I remembered his appearance, when I was a child, represented in the emaciated man standing in front of me.

During my entire stay in Dora, I had no idea he was also there. By some miracle, he had managed to survive the trip from Dora in one of the enclosed boxcars. Most of the men crammed into the boxcar with him had perished. He wouldn't have survived another day in there.

We embraced, crying without shedding tears; for neither of us had enough moisture in our bodies to create them. Thin and frail myself, I was still shocked at the sight of Abraham's appearance. His bones showed clearly against skin stretched taut over them. The skin itself was thin, looking like it might tear at the slightest pressure. Bruises and cuts, which might be new or weeks old, appeared unable to heal. His clothes hung on him like nothing inside was there to fill them out. I don't even know how he managed to find the strength to call my name and walk over to me. He looked very much like one of the bodies pulled from the boxcar, only he stood in front of me.

He held me at arm's length, studying me as I had him. "You were always thin, Benjamin," he said to me. "But never like this." We both laughed, for some reason thinking it very funny.

The grass I had eaten during the trip was not ultimately filling or substantive; but when the only other option is starvation, grass is a welcomed alternative. In my cousin Abraham, I saw what

I might easily have become had I gotten my wish to be in the closed car. He had trouble walking, so we held each other for support as we moved into line, responding to the orders shouted by the SS over loudspeakers.

We stayed next to each as we formed into the obligatory lines of five, leaning against each other for support, both physical and emotional. We never asked each other about family members. I knew he was alive. He knew I had survived. Probing any further would drain what little energy and physical reserves we had.

We formed into the lines as commanded, the corpses still being dragged out of the boxcars, piling up haphazardly next to us as we stood waiting for further orders. The instructions to us continued through the public address system that the SS had set up.

"The walk to the next camp is not far," came the reassurance from the SS man making the announcements. "However, if you are tired or feel that you cannot continue, simply step out of the line and wait by the side of the road."

I shook my head, having heard this speech before. Uncle Abraham looked at me, puzzled. I put my arm around his back. He was much taller than me and put his arm around my shoulder. "Just stay with me."

He squeezed my shoulder a little. "Of course, I will, Benjamin."

The announcement continued, repeating over and over, in case we missed any part of it: "Just walk to the side of the road. Don't be afraid. Nothing will happen if you can't walk the entire way. A truck will come by to pick you up."

It was almost the same story I heard upon being deported from Rozavlea. I had long since stopped trusting anything the SS told us and felt stupid for having ever believed anything they had said. I made up my mind that, no matter what, I would not step out of line. I had no idea where or what our destination was, but I was determined to walk the entire way.

Finally, all the survivors formed the lines of five and, under the watchful eyes of the SS and Gestapo, began walking away from the train. Thousands had died on the train, but thousands more of us remained. I can't say exactly how long we walked, perhaps seven hours, perhaps more.

I saw friends of mine from the camp, thin as Abraham and myself, no longer able to place one foot in front of the other. For some, stepping out of the line and walking to the side of the road were almost more than they could manage. They must have known as well as I did that no truck would carry them to wherever we were headed. It was of no consequence. They had no energy left to go on.

Abraham and I held on to each other, between the two of us able to walk, however slowly, where one might have fallen. Each man I saw by the side of the road filled me with greater determination to move forward under my own power. A few hours into the march, I felt Abraham beginning to slow down, each step taking more from him than he had to give.

"Benjamin," he whispered to me, "I'm so tired." I saw him looking toward the side of the road with longing. The look of his frightened me. If I had enough strength, I would have carried him to keep him beside me as we marched.

"Don't," I begged him. "Don't wait for the truck."

"Why?" I couldn't believe he even asked the question. I can only imagine that it was only the thought that the Nazis might have, for the first time since the deportation, told us the truth. It was enough for him to hold on to. It was a fantasy, made real by his growing inability to continue. With no option left, he had no choice but to believe.

We walked a little while more, but I could feel him gradually dragging more and more until he could no longer provide the mutual support we had counted on. I held him, helping him walk with each step. My own strength was dissipating, slowing my own steps.

"Benjamin," he began, his voice weak, apologetic.

"Please, don't," I cut him off. "They're going to kill you."

"I'm sorry," he said. "I can't make it anymore." He embraced me briefly, tightly, then walked away from me, slowly, barely able to move on his own, out of the line, and sat at the side of the road.

I continued walking, looking back over my shoulder at my cousin, sitting at the side of the road, his head lowered. Not until he was out of sight did I look forward again. Behind us, we heard the sounds of machine guns. Wasting a bullet no longer concerned the Nazis. The truth was that the trucks did come by, SS on top wielding machine guns, killing each and every man who had stepped out of the line.

The march ended at Bergen-Belsen, where we were met with a lot of SS and Gestapo, already there, waiting for us. There was nothing unusual about our not being told anything. They assigned us to a barracks, so many for each one. We had no other provisions, no food, no water. Nor was there any work. Unlike Dora, where we worked to essentially build a small city, at Bergen-Belsen, the only thing expected of us was to die.

Within a day, prisoners began fulfilling that expectation. Bergen-Belsen was a death camp, no matter what sense that phrase was used in. Nothing seemed to be alive there. Grass tried unsuccessfully to grow. Birds found little reason to fly overhead and less reason to sing. Only two things of any note happened in that camp: People slept and people died.

The Nazis did not bother taking any extraordinary measures to kill us, as they had at Auschwitz and, I imagine, at any of the other death camps. We did the job for them, dying by the hundreds. The living, dying, and dead coexisted so closely, the line differentiating one state from the other blurred, becoming almost impossible to define.

Our daily routine began by dragging the bodies out of the barracks of those who had died during the night. Each morning dozens and dozens of bodies had to be taken outside. Whether from hunger or from any of a wide variety of diseases or from some combination of reasons, person after person crossed that fine line, demarcating life from death.

From my first day in Auschwitz, I had seen death so often, in so many forms, that it had become commonplace. In Bergen-Belsen, the sheer number of commonplace experiences became numbing. After about a week there, I saw something that even in those circumstances seemed unusual, but over the course of the next month or so became, itself, common.

The line between life and death had become so fine as to be crossed within the time it took to go from one breath to the next. I was standing near one of the barracks, conserving what little energy I had when one of the other prisoners walked by. He was older than me and much thinner, though I hadn't thought that possible. He walked slowly, with nowhere to go and little strength to get there. His pace gradually slowed until he stopped walking completely. He collapsed, falling to the ground right where he stood. He was dead probably before he reached the ground. He may have died while he was walking and it simply took his body a few extra moments to realize the fact.

Over the course of the next month or so, this same thing occurred often enough that it also became a part of the day's routine. In the weeks just after my arrival, I would take my belt, wrap it around the legs of one of the bodies that had fallen in place and just pull it out of the way. After a while, that act required more strength than I had.

I sometimes found myself staring at the body in front of me, trying to decide if I had the energy to pull it out of my way or to walk around it. Sometimes, just standing in one place and trying to come to that kind of decision required so much from me that I simply sat down to rest.

Most of the men in the camp were fairly young. A few were middle-aged. You never really saw old men. They died long before reaching Bergen-Belsen. If I saw someone who might have been as old as fifty, it was extremely unusual. I had turned nineteen only a couple of months earlier.

Another part of the day's routine involved trying to find something to eat. Those efforts proved to be uniformly unsuccessful.

More often than not, the meager amount of food we could find never was worth the effort expended in finding it.

Each day, we heard the war growing louder, growing closer. At first, I wasn't certain what the distant noises were. Certainly, I was familiar with the sounds of planes and bombs, but those were only two of a wide variety of sounds that helped define war. As the sounds grew steadily in volume and decreased in distance, the SS guarding us, officers and enlisted men alike, became increasingly tense, more agitated.

At night, the sounds continued, unabated. One thing I learned is that war is very loud, even when it is far away. I found that I was able to sleep, even with the noise of the approaching war. I simply didn't have enough strength left to stay awake. Once in a while, I wondered if that was what it was like for those who fell down, dead, while walking. Perhaps it was easier for them to just fall asleep, or die, instead of trying to keep walking.

By the beginning of April 1945, I no longer could pick up my feet when I walked. I have no idea how much I might have weighed then. I might have weighed eighty pounds, maybe a little less. I only know that when I walked, picking up my feet required far too much effort. I got around by pushing one foot forward, then dragging the other foot up and pushing it out in front of me. It took a while to get around from one place to another, but I had no time constraint to be concerned with.

By this time, there was little or no separation of the prisoners. At one time, Russian prisoners of war stayed in a different barracks from the Jews who stayed in a different barracks from the political prisoners and so on. By the first weeks of April, such distinctions no longer existed. Everyone stayed together while we watched each other die.

One morning, early in April, I saw one of the Russian prisoners pass me, carrying a beet. I was so astounded to see an entire beet, let alone possessed by one man, that I forgot to conserve what energy I had. I called to him as he passed by me. He stopped for a moment, covering the beet protectively in his hands, looking at me with suspicion.

I pointed at the beet he carried. He glared at me, unmoving. I wished I spoke Russian. I tried German, hoping he had picked up enough of that language to understand me. I pointed again at the beet.

"That beet you have. . ." I began to say. I didn't have a chance to finish my thought before he moved it up against his body, away from me.

"Mine," he said peremptorily, in heavily accented German, leaving no room for discussion or negotiation.

"I know that," I assured him. "I just want to know where you got it."

He simply continued staring at me. I tried again, using fewer words, and adding gestures to my comments. He finally relaxed, convinced I was not interested in taking his prize from him. He pointed toward the far end of the camp. "Over there," he said. "Lots of them in a huge hole in the ground."

He left as he took another small bite out of the beet, determined to make it last as long as he could. What he said made sense to me. Back home, we would dig a large hole and use it for storing fruits and vegetables during the winter. Dug out deeply enough, the earth itself acted to preserve the food while insulating it so that it would not freeze.

I looked in the direction he indicated. I was so far away, I saw nothing; but I started walking. Soon, I noticed other people, energized by the promise of food, moving in the same direction. By the time I reached the area, I was only a part of a growing crowd. I could barely see the hole, so many people pushed at its edges, oblivious to those around them except as irritants, preventing them from obtaining whatever food they could.

I had always been a little small for my age and at that time, I was also painfully thin. With only a little effort, I managed to push myself in among the throng until I was able to reach down into the hole.

It wasn't easy to reach anything. I pulled myself forward, leaning in as far as possible without falling in. The weight of those behind me provided an anchor, allowing me to reach farther down than I normally would have been able to. My fingers brushed against a beet. I stopped, knowing what I felt, unable to actually believe it was real. I almost slipped as the positions of those behind continued changing. I grasped at whatever was beneath my hand and pulled it up to me.

I crawled back from the edge of the hole, not yet even certain what prize I had. Pushing my way out from the crowd was more difficult than pushing my way in. Finally, I saw what I held in hand. From the storage area dug deep into the earth, I had managed to retrieve a single large beet.

My joy was cut short by the sound of machine-gun fire. The sight of the crowd of people drew the attention of the guard, stationed in the watchtowers. The only attempt made to restore some semblance of order was to kill anyone making a disturbance. People fell around me, this time from the bullets hitting them.

I automatically fell to the ground, the beet underneath me; for I was just as protective of my prize as the Russian had been. I lay still, seeing the people on the ground near me staring, lifeless, where they had fallen.

Screaming, cries of pain, shouts of anguish—all gradually decreased in amount and volume as the dead covered more and more of the ground near the hole. I dared not move, certain any attention I drew to myself would elicit the response of a bullet. I waited, motionless, for several hours, my precious beet pressing painfully, reassuringly, against my chest.

When the day waned, nightfall giving me the courage to open my eyes and end my pretense of death, I knew I had to leave. I feared that they might come from the towers and make certain that no one lived by shooting, at close range, the bodies on the ground. I saw no movement around me. Slowly, gradually, I rolled to my side, picked up my beet and held it to me. It didn't take very long for my vision to become accustomed to the night. Nothing and no one around me moved. I knew if I was to leave, I would find no better time to do so. Grasping the beet tightly in my hand, I got up and made my way as quickly as I could back to the barracks.

All the way to the barracks, I imagined how wonderful the taste of the beet was going to be. I knew I would be like the Russian prisoner, taking small bites, slowly chewing each one, making it last as long as I possibly could. I planned on sitting in the barracks, getting myself as comfortable as possible and beginning my feast in peace.

I walked into the barracks and almost dropped my beet in shock. Sitting on the floor, his back against the wall for support, was Uncle Mordechai. In his arms, he held my cousin Joseph. His other son Hertz sat next to them, his head down, too exhausted to cry. I had no idea they were at Bergen-Belsen. They may have arrived that day or been transferred from another barracks. To me, it didn't matter. I had family with me again.

I ran to them, showing them the prized beet. Seeing the condition Joseph was in, I wanted to hand the beet to him. Uncle Mordechai slowly shook his head. "Too late," was the only thing he said. Joseph, a handsome man, like a movie star, stood over six feet tall. A man of that size requires more food simply to stay alive than a small man like me. I could survive, however tenuously, at perhaps eighty pounds. Joseph couldn't. He had died in Uncle Mordechai's arms not long before I arrived.

Even if I had arrived earlier, one beet would not have been enough to save my cousin. I offered the beet first to Uncle Mordechai, then to Hertz. Each took a single, small bite and chewed slowly, not so much to want to make it last, but simply out of instinct. Uncle Mordechai never let go of Joseph or took his eyes from his son. Hertz sat next to his father, not saying anything.

I sat down near them and bit into my beet. I don't remember finishing it or what it tasted like.

The next morning, I helped them drag Joseph's body out of the barracks. By then, none of us would have been able to do it alone. Thin and emaciated as he was when he died, it was still too much to ask of people as weakened by starvation as we had been. For the next couple of days, I stayed near Hertz and Uncle Mordechai, thinking they might well be the only family I had left in Europe.

During that time, the activity level of the SS and guards in the camp increased, though none of it seemed directed toward us. They appeared agitated, on edge. No one got much sleep anymore, the sounds of the war now so close and so loud as to make sleep, even from sheer exhaustion, nearly impossible.

On the morning of April 15, 1945, the world changed again. We left the barracks to find that most, if not all, of the Nazis had departed during the night. The sounds of the war were no longer heard in the distance, but right outside the camp. The unmistakable sound of an approaching tank grew louder. It did not stop at the gate, but came barreling through.

I did not witness the tank's entrance, but I saw it as it clamored to a halt. We held back, initially fearful that the Nazis had returned to finish a job our continued existence meant was undone. It took several moments for us to realize the tank was not a German, but a British one, the Union Jack emblazoned on the side. No one dared imagine that the Nazis might have captured a British tank.

We gathered around the tank, curious, not certain what to expect. The hatch opened and a man wearing the distinct uniform of a British officer climbed up, surveying his surroundings as we studied him.

The British had arrived at Bergen-Belsen.

PART THREE

Life After Death

Liberation

The British officer continued watching us, while we watched him, no one saying anything. Many decades later, I found out that the name of that first British officer to enter Bergen-Belsen was Robert Daniel. He seemed slightly confused, certainly surprised to see so many of us.

"What kind of people are here?" he finally asked.

Many of us spoke several languages each, but few of us spoke English. One of the men, who did speak English and understood the officer, tentatively came forward. "We are Jews," the man answered, slightly bewildered at finding himself speaking on our behalf.

Daniel looked around him, not even trying to hide his surprise. "So many Jews are still alive?" he asked, incredulous. I was surprised that so many of us managed to survive. I can only imagine what he must have seen, arriving at camp after camp, to also find it surprising.

A second tank arrived, easing to a stop near Daniel's tank. A British army chaplain, a rabbi, got out and spoke with Daniel.

I couldn't help staring at the British rabbi, so unlike any rabbi I had ever seen. Slender, standing tall and straight in his British army uniform, he was clean-shaven with close-cut hair. The Rabbi looked at us, tears in his eyes. For a moment, he didn't speak, either unable to find the right words or unable to articulate anything to us right away. Finally, he took a deep breath and addressed us in Yiddish. It sounded strange to me, hearing Yiddish tempered with the British accent. We automatically stepped in closer to the Rabbi, none of us wanting to miss anything he might say. He probably never had so eager and attentive a congregation.

"Don't worry," he began, reassuring us. "You're going to be free. Within a day or two, the rest of our army will be here."

His Yiddish was excellent, his words clear and distinct. Even with that, my mind could not quite comprehend what he was saying. The concept of freedom, something I had hoped for from the moment I stepped out of the train in Auschwitz, had also taken on the aspect of fantasy. Now, the Rabbi was telling us our hopes and fantasies would become reality. I was not even certain for a while what that meant, to be free. Free to do what? Free to go where? As far as I knew, my entire immediate family was gone. I had no desire to return to my home in Rumania, effectively leaving me with nowhere to go. I had nothing and no one. Even those fleeting thoughts required more energy than I had to give. I stood still, listening to the Rabbi as he continued speaking.

"We just liberated another camp near here," he explained to us. "It's a women's camp. I'm certain that many of your sisters, wives, and mothers are there. Hold on for a day or two, any way you can."

None of us knew another camp was close by. Many of the men visibly brightened at the hope of seeing loved ones again. The Rabbi continued speaking for a little while longer, his words encouraging us, attempting to comfort us in any way that he could. At that moment, simply hearing a voice speaking to us with decency and compassion was enough.

Just prior to the arrival of the British army, many of the SS and guards disappeared, deserting their posts, afraid of being held accountable for their actions by the advancing Allied troops. Some left the camp to take their chances in the woods or maybe in the hope of finding a local villager to take them in. Some thought to masquerade as prisoners, hoping to avoid punishment that way. They dressed themselves in prisoner clothes, presenting themselves to the British as victims, not victimizers.

The sight of the costumed Nazis was almost comical in comparison to the rest of us. Not one of the pretenders got away like that. They filled out their clothes, strong, healthy men, maybe even carrying a little extra weight. The contrast between a prisoner who was so thin lacking the strength to lift his feet to walk and an SS officer who might have last eaten a few hours earlier was too great not to be immediately apparent.

The Russian prisoners took it upon themselves to mete out justice, killing the Nazis who tried to hide. Sometimes, they took the time to report the Nazis to the British, but usually did not want to wait for them to slowly work their way through the British legal system.

The Rabbi kept his word to us. Within two days, the British army took over the running of Bergen-Belsen. The first thing they tried to do was give us those things we needed most. They brought in food, water, established medical care, and cleaned the camp as much as possible. At times, though, the most compassionate of acts can have unfortunate results.

When one encounters thousands of starving people, the humane response is to provide food, immediately and in large quantities. The British reacted in exactly that way. They gave each of us a whole can, maybe a pound, of pork beef, as well as plenty of bread and a lot of water. That one serving for me was more food than I had eaten, in total, since my arrival at Bergen-Belsen. I responded to the gift of largesse differently than most of the other starving men did.

Staring in disbelief at the can, I remembered my mother's voice so clearly as to easily imagine her standing next to me. "Be careful, Benjamin. Eating too much on an empty stomach can make you sick."

Hungry as I was, recalling my mother's admonishment, I somehow, intuitively, understood what she meant, feeling that so much food, especially the rich, salty canned meat, would be difficult for my emaciated body to handle. I ate some of the bread, slowly, along with the water. It didn't take much for me to feel full. I sighed, happy and content not to feel my stomach cramped with hunger.

Many of the other men had reached the point of hunger where thought and reason no longer come into play. They ate everything the British gave them, ready to eat anything more as soon as it was made available. The British, taking pity on us, gave anyone as much food as he wanted. Unfortunately, what one wants and what one's body can process are very often two different things. The men ate everything they could, making up for months of eating nothing.

Unaccustomed to food of any sort, their bodies shut down in protest at the sudden internal assault. They died quickly, by the hundreds, killed by food where hunger had left them alive. Once again, walking through Bergen-Belsen, bodies lay everywhere, forcing you to pull them out of the way or walk around them, whichever was more convenient at that moment. The British, shocked and appalled at what they felt they had done, immediately cut back our food allotment, giving out extra only in a few, special cases. By then, they operated a kitchen at the camp, making it easier for them to control how much food they gave us.

A few days later, we learned that an entire trainload of bread was sitting not far from Bergen-Belsen, left at the last moment by the departing Nazis. The Nazis had planned on bringing the bread in for us, finally feeding us before the imminent arrival of the British. The British evidently trusted the Nazis even less than we did, if that was possible. They tested the bread before giving any to us by feeding it to some dogs that remained around the camp. The dogs died quickly, the bread poisoned.

The Nazis had hoped that, hungry as we were, we would eat enough of the bread to die quickly, leaving no living witnesses for the British to find. By arriving a day, maybe even hours earlier than the Nazis had anticipated, the British forced the cancellation of our mass extermination.

Something had to be done with all of the bodies, both the ones dead from before the British Army's arrival and those who died after the liberation. The British soldiers dug mass graves for the bodies. To help keep my mind active and alert, I tried to count how many bodies went into the grave. I reached 30,000 before the British had completely finished their task. Some, like my cousin Joseph, had remained unburied since before the liberation. Many, though, died afterward, from disease too far along for the British to cure, from starvation, from too much food. So many of us lived so close to that line separating us from death that anything, even things meant to help us, easily pushed us over.

The British kept their word to us in another way. Within a few days of their arrival, they reunited the women and men. I honestly feel that did more to encourage us to hang on to life than anything else they could have done. For many of the men, finding wives or sisters was far more important than even the food we received.

I remember one day when I was standing in line to get food from the kitchen. Several women also stood in line. One woman, maybe in her late forties or early fifties, stood a few people behind me. I can only guess at her age since the conditions in the women's camp, being no better than ours, left most of the women, like most of the men, appearing much older than their actual age.

A young British officer walked along the line, making certain we kept order, not pushing each other, and so on. No one commented, having already become accustomed to the British routine. He talked briefly to some of the people, offering compassion and sympathy. Some of the people found it a little irritating; they wanted food, not pity. Most, like myself, wanted kindness as much as bread and responded to his words. To our surprise, he spoke Yiddish and spoke it very well.

As he walked along the line, I couldn't help noticing that as he passed near me, his expression seemed almost confused. He walked by, no longer speaking, looking at each person carefully, and paying special attention to the middle-aged woman behind me. Finally, he stopped in front of her.

"What's you name?" he asked gently in Yiddish, the concern in his voice evident. The woman barely looked at him. Before she had a chance to speak, he went on. "Is your name 'Miriam Cohen?'"

She looked at the young man, her eyes widening in shocked recognition as tears clouded her eyes. She put her hand to her mouth, closed her eyes and collapsed, the officer catching her before she reached the ground. He called out loudly in English. One of the men near me spoke English and told me the young man was calling for help from the other officers for an ambulance.

An ambulance arrived quickly, the young man having held the woman tenderly until it did. He explained quickly to the medics what happened and left in the ambulance with the woman. The man near me told me what had happened. The woman was the young officer's mother. The young man had left home when he was a boy to live with relatives in England. He had lost touch with his mother at the beginning of the war and had assumed she was dead. Seeing her had been as much a shock for him as for her; but while he was strong and healthy, meeting her son, after all she had been through, had been more than the woman could handle. I'm certain he made sure she was well taken care of. Sometimes, things are simply meant to be. There's no other way to explain the chances of that woman's son being one of her liberators.

Another promise that the British kept was to take care of the sick. They set up a hospital, one that actually cared for and tried to help the people who went there. They found the job overwhelming with so many people sick and dying, but continued the task in any case, their humanity preventing them from turning away someone who needed help.

Since, at the time of our liberation, the war was still going on, the British soldiers left after a short time to continue their fight. In their place, they left Yugoslavian soldiers to guard us. Some of the Yugoslavians had themselves been prisoners of war, trained to handle weapons, many still in uniform. I can imagine a few reasons why they felt it necessary to keep us, guarded, in the camp.

One reason, I'm certain, is that as many of us became healthier and stronger, the fear existed that we might try to exact our own revenge on any Nazi or even German citizen we might find. Conversely, they feared that Nazis and SS officers who had escaped might not think twice about the opportunity to kill another Jew. There was a certain amount of truth in both of those reasons.

Along with the Yugoslavian guards, many British stayed in the camp as well. Most of those who remained were doctors and nurses working at the hospital and the people who made certain we received three meals a day.

I was lucky in that I was fairly healthy, just emaciated from lack of food. Little by little, as we became accustomed to eating more and better food, our health improved, my own included. It didn't take long before some of us became disillusioned with the food the British served us. They had learned their lesson and our food, while filling and healthy, was extremely bland. For the first few weeks, having enough to eat, no matter what it was or what it tasted like, was enough to satisfy me. Once my stomach was full and I was secure in the knowledge that more food was available, taste gradually became important once again.

Some of the other men and myself formed what we called a "hunting party." I had found an entrance to the sewer system. Some of the other men explored it with me. We had no idea where it might lead us, but we had nothing to do and lots of time to do it. The strong, pungent odor was definitely unsavory, but not enough to keep us from trying. To our relief, we found the system opened outside the camp, providing us with a convenient, if not particularly savory entrance and exit to the camp. The best benefit was that we completely bypassed the Yugoslav guards. Ironically, none of us took the chance to escape the camp. Few of us had anywhere to go. In a strange way, the camp had become our home.

We went through the nearby woods to local villages. From the farmers and local villagers, we stole chickens, sometimes even killing a cow and taking it back with us. We always went in the middle of the night, finding that the best time for foraging in someone else's barnyard and the time least likely to be caught doing it. It was also the best time to find and kill the cows. The local farmers, leaving them in pastures, made them easy targets for us.

I remember one time when we killed one of the local cows. Naturally, we had to cut it up because there was no way we could drag an entire cow with us, let alone maneuver it though the sewer system back into camp. When we returned to camp, the first person to greet us was Itzak, the butcher-turned-tanner who found himself acting again as butcher, taking care of the animals we brought back with us. He never joined us on any of these expeditions because of his pronounced limp when he walked. We had to move and move quickly in unfamiliar or unknown areas. At least, he no longer felt the pressure to hide how he walked. More relaxed, he was once again the friend I knew at home.

Itzak saw how we had butchered the cow, our basic ineptitude as butchers hurting his professional pride. All we cared about was killing it and cutting it up quickly into manageable pieces we could take back with us. He spent close to half an hour, lecturing us about all the things we had done wrong and giving a quick lesson in how to properly butcher a cow. None of us minded since I noticed, and I'm certain the others did as well, that Itzak smiled the entire time.

We then set the meat out over an open fire, providing ourselves with a makeshift, very tasty barbecue. We always shared with anyone who wanted some. No matter how much we brought back, we never had enough to give everyone all the food they wanted.

It just gave us another reason to go out again in a day or two and bring back more.

Thinking back on those hunting parties, we acted very foolishly. We could have easily been killed by one of the Nazis hiding in the woods, providing one less Jew to bear witness. After several weeks, we felt confident in our ability to elude potential dangers and risks. Our naivete became apparent one night after yet another successful raid. On this particular hunting expedition, we came close to getting killed, but not at the hands of the Nazis.

Our hunting party was on its way back to Bergen-Belsen, bringing several chickens, eggs, as well as fruits and vegetables along with us. We walked along the side of the road, the woods beside us. As usual, it was the middle of the night. We felt pleased with ourselves, confident and happy with the amount of food we carried. Some of the men even began referring to it as "going shopping." In some ways it was similar. We began to pick and choose what we felt was the best food to return to the camp with.

As we walked back to the outside sewer entrance, we heard the approach of a truck, its bright lights destroying our night vision, momentarily blinding us. Our first, natural reaction was to run; but before we even had the chance to drop what we carried, we heard loud, sharp orders in English.

"Halt! Don't move!" We knew the meaning by the tone without having to understand the specific words.

While none us spoke enough English to understand the command, the order stopped us in our tracks. The tone was unmistakable, identical to every order we had heard shouted at us for as long as we remained in the Nazi camps. After so long of responding immediately to such orders, a few weeks of freedom could not alter our reactions.

A British patrol had found us. They wasted little time in questions, which none of us could answer anyway in English and none of the patrol could pose in any language we knew. They arrested us, putting us in handcuffs, and piling us into the back of the truck. They then took us to a small building not far away which they had set up as a kind of headquarters for the various British patrols combing the local area in an effort to create and maintain order.

They put us in a small room with no chairs to sit on. We loudly protested such treatment, proclaiming them no better than the Nazis. In a short time, we had chairs to sit on, like human beings. Some of the men in our group, tired of being victims, went to the other extreme, ready to fight, literally and figuratively, against any imposition of authority. With the language barrier exacerbating the tension, it was not long before we came uncomfortably close to fighting with our British liberators.

Finally, one of the officers found his captain, the man with the highest position at the headquarters. It was our good fortune that the Captain was Jewish and happened to speak Yiddish very well. He came into the room, not so much to formally question us as to try to find out what was happening.

"Who are you and where are you from?" he wanted to know, asking us in Yiddish.

Several of us began talking at once. No one was able to make himself clear or understood since we each spoke different languages.

"Wait, wait," the Captain interrupted, getting our attention and our silence. "One person talk or one at a time. Do any of you speak English?"

We deferred to one of the men in our group who happened to speak a little English, making him the best spokesman for us in dealing with the British Captain. He explained we came from Bergen-Belsen, had been prisoners there. Before he had a chance to explain exactly why we had left the camp, the Captain interrupted him.

To our surprise and relief, he didn't automatically accuse and threaten. Instead, he seemed genuinely concerned for our welfare. "You should stay inside the camp," he told us. "It's not safe for you to leave like that. Our patrols are finding a lot of escaped Nazis, so if they see you walking around, they have no way of knowing who you are. And usually they don't have time or want to bother asking questions. You're lucky they didn't shoot you on the spot."

We remained quiet for a moment, not certain what to say. The Captain made it easy for us by asking, "What were you doing outside of the camp, anyway?"

"We were looking for food," answered our spokesman.

The Captain looked at us, his turn to be surprised by us. "Isn't there enough to eat there?" he asked, looking like he was ready to take to task whatever officer failed in his responsibility to provide us with sufficient food.

"Yes, there's enough to eat," our spokesman admitted. "We just don't like the food you're giving us."

This time when the Captain looked at us, he laughed, reducing much of the tension in the room. "All right," he said. "I'll see what I can do about the food. You, though, have to promise not to leave the camp."

We, a little grudgingly, accepted the compromise. In all honesty, we had grown to enjoy our trips out of the camp. For myself, it was much easier to think of myself as actually being free when I had a choice of where to go and when to leave. Even though the camp was more of a home than anything else I had, being forced to remain there still made it a prison, despite the change in jailers.

Sweden

For the first time since I was a boy listening to my sister Chana read to me about establishing a Jewish State in Palestine, I began to seriously consider the possibility of living in the Holy Land. It was as much a dream in Bergen-Belsen as it was in Rozavlea. I had no money for travel, no other means to make the dream a reality. In the back of my mind, I kept alive the hope that, someday, things would be better for me. I already had a sister living there, perhaps the only close relative I had left. In the meantime, I had to decide what options I had available, what I wanted to do, and where I wanted to go. Even if I wanted to, I certainly could not live the rest of my life in Bergen-Belsen.

It didn't take long before my options narrowed and a goal became clear, as the British allowed people to leave the camp. Many people had illnesses and diseases that the doctors and nurses at the camp simply did not have the resources to treat effectively. In addition to complications from starvation, pneumonia and tuber-culosis were common, along with many other things that our conditions made us susceptible to contracting. The Red Cross came to the aid of such people. They arranged for those, who needed more specialized or extensive medical attention than the doctors at the camp could provide, to go to Sweden.

One of the things I have to give the British credit for is that they made a real effort to keep families together. So many people, myself included, had come from large families, only to finally have freedom and find themselves with only one or two relatives left to enjoy it with, if that. If someone was to be sent to Sweden and that person had any immediate family in the camp, the relatives went with them.

I saw that as a way to get out of Bergen-Belsen, but I wasn't sick and I had no immediate family. I knew for a fact that my father and little sister had been killed. I never saw my mother again, but I have no doubt as to her fate. I had no idea if my older sister Frieda managed to survive, but I had no reason not to suspect that her fate was similar to the thousands of others I saw led to the gas chambers.

I wanted to leave the camp, and going to Sweden seemed at least possible with help from the British and Red Cross. I wanted to put as much distance as possible between Germany and myself. The Nazis had taken everything from me and I wanted nothing more to do with anything that might remotely remind me of them or of my time under their control. I felt that anywhere would be better. Already, we heard rumors about how generous and kind the Swedish people treated those of us who came from the camps. They opened their country and their hearts to those who, literally, had nothing left and nothing to give in return but hard work. It was a perfect exchange.

Through sheer luck, I found out that a woman in the hospital had the same last name as I did. My first thought was that, maybe, somehow, Frieda was in the camp. I told myself it was possible she had been in the nearby women's camp. I went to the hospital as soon as I heard, hoping to see her and yet afraid of the disappointment I would certainly feel if it weren't my sister.

I entered the ward, but stopped just inside the door, no longer anxious or confident. One of the nurses saw me. She came up to me, concerned that I might be sick.

"No," I reassured her. "My name is Benjamin Samuelson. I had heard . . . I thought that maybe . . ." My voice trailed off. The nurse had heard the same kind of story from so many different people that I didn't need to finish. She knew what I wanted. Everyone was desperately trying to find any relatives that might still be alive. In that respect, I was no different.

"Right over here," she gently told me, smiling. She had also learned to refrain from building hope and expectation. Many names were common and we certainly did not need further disillusionment.

She led me to a bedside. I looked down, disappointed and happy at the same time. As soon as she looked up at me, I felt a weight on my chest. It was my cousin Peri, the daughter of my father's cousin Abraham. I knew I had to tell her what happened to her father, but I couldn't say the words right then. She turned to the woman in the bed next to her. "Miriam," she said and I immediately recognized her sister. "Look who it is."

They both looked up at me, tears in their eyes. "Benjamin?" Peri finally spoke directly to me. "Is it really you?" The nurse left us alone as I sat next to her on the bed and held her hand.

"Peri," I said to her, "I just found out you were here." Her eyes never left me, even as the tears clouded them and rolled down her face.

"I'm glad you came. I was afraid that Miriam and I had no family left."

"Peri. Miriam." I stopped, unable to mar a reunion with news of death. She grasped my hand tightly.

"Go on, Benjamin," she said, giving me strength. "We want to know. It's better than always wondering."

I told her about meeting her father after the train ride from Dora. I told her about how he stumbled to the side of the road and the sounds of gunshots when I could no longer see him.

"Like all the others," she commented quietly. "All gone. May they rest in peace. And your family?"

"The same," I answered. Neither of us went into more detail than that. After recounting the story of Abraham, none of us cared about the specifics of how each one died. It all ended the same way. Our families were gone. We talked for some time, not wanting to let a relative go away again.

Finally, she spoke to me with sadness in her voice. "They're sending us to Sweden, Benjamin. Miriam and I are going to a hospital there. Now that I know I have family here, I don't want to go."

"Tell them I'm your brother," I instructed her. "We have the same last name. There's no way for them to know otherwise. I can go to Sweden with you."

Her eyes lit up, smiling before her lips moved. "That's a wonderful idea!" Her enthusiasm was contagious. If I hadn't looked forward to going to Sweden before talking to my cousin Peri, I had no choice but to get caught up in her excitement. We began making plans before the nurse had a chance to return.

As soon as the nurse came back, Peri and I began talking at once. The nurse smiled and put up a hand, signaling us to be quiet. She put her hand on Peri's forehead, then took her pulse, glancing from her watch to Peri and myself.

"I can see that meeting...your brother is it?...has been very exciting for you," the nurse said to Peri, before we had a chance to say anything else.

"How did you know?" Peri asked, her eyes wide with the question.

"I've seen it enough," the nurse told us, smiling at me. "Don't stay too much longer," the nurse cautioned me. "She needs her rest. But you can come back tomorrow." The nurse patted Peri's hand tenderly and straightened her blankets.

"Can he come to Sweden with me?" Peri asked.

"I don't see why not." The nurse smiled and left us alone again while she went to check on other patients. Peri and I smiled, too. I talked a little bit to Miriam; but Peri and I, nearer to each other in age, had always been closer when we were children. Miriam, who was the more quiet of the sisters to begin with, was several years younger and had other interests and playmates. For the moment, it seemed, we would be one family.

She squeezed my hand in enthusiasm, every bit as happy as I was. I only stayed a little while longer. Even I could see that Peri was getting tired, despite all of the excitement. As I tried to leave, she begged me to remain. I promised her I would be back. The slight fear in her eyes told me that while she wanted to believe me, she knew that circumstances might prevent anything I intended to do.

As soon as I could the next morning, I returned to the hospital. Seeing Peri's relief and joy at my arrival was as therapeutic for me as for her. As soon as we could, we told the staff that I was her brother and that I wanted to accompany her to Sweden. They registered me right away, happy to facilitate any reunion they could.

She and Miriam were scheduled to leave for Sweden soon, but we did not know exactly when. Each day, I went to the hospital and visited with them, spending as much time there as I could. We all talked for hours, catching up on everything while not mentioning most of the details of our lives over the past year; for it had been exactly one year to the day from my deportation from Rozavlea to my liberation from Bergen-Belsen. We talked a lot about times back home, reminiscing about relatives who passed away long before the war. It all seemed so remote, yet so important to remember that it was only a little over a year for us, since some of the events we discussed. It was important for us to remind ourselves that at one time we had full, rich lives so that we might begin building foundations for the rest of our lives.

No matter what you think or plan, events sometimes have a way of ignoring anything you try to do. One day, while I sat with Peri and Miriam, talking about what we would do in Sweden, one of the British officers in charge of making the arrangements to transport the sick and injured came to speak to me. He was very apologetic as he told me I would not be able to go with the women he knew as my sisters. It had something to do with schedules and wounded, and I don't remember what else. All I heard was that my hope to leave was not going to come true.

"After all this, you'll send us away without our brother?" Peri asked, not wanting to believe it. I held her hand, which she gripped tightly.

"I'm sorry," the officer told us, not looking any of us in the eye. "I really am." He left quickly, wanting to avoid what might potentially become an uncomfortable scene. I can't say that I blame him, but I had hoped for so much more.

Peri seemed even more upset than I was, and certainly more vocal about it. I was still stunned by the news while Peri was ready to protest the decision. Before I could begin to think clearly, I had to calm her down.

Brushing the hair away from her forehead, I told her, in as reassuring a tone as I could, that she shouldn't worry. "I'll find a way," I promised her. "You just get some rest right now. I'll be back tomorrow to see you."

I walked around the camp for the rest of the day, thinking only about what I could do to accompany my cousins to Sweden. I must have walked around the camp several times, my head down, feet kicking the dirt, trying to think of something. No matter how hard I tried, nothing came to mind. I felt helpless, my life choices dictated by people wearing uniforms whom I had no ability to sway. For the moment, it was difficult for me to care much who was wearing what uniform. It all seemed about the same to me.

Once in a while, I have noticed that God makes His presence known, even when you may no longer think of making Him a part of your life. As I continued walking aimlessly around the camp, kicking at the dirt, I noticed something gleam at my feet. I had seen enough gold in my days in Budapest to have a good idea what it might be. I picked up a gold bracelet from the dirt. I brushed it off, shining it as best I could with my shirt. It wasn't very heavy, but nicely crafted, stirring my appreciation for fine work done with pride in its appearance.

Holding the bracelet in my hands, I knew I had found a way to join Peri and Miriam on their journey to Sweden. It was the same reason I had a successful business in Budapest. People always want to own gold, either for its beauty or the way it works to make the wearer appear sophisticated or the fact that it can always be traded for the essentials of survival. There are as many different reasons why, for centuries, people have sought out gold for personal adornment and use as there are people seeking it out.

I put the bracelet safely in my pocket, certain I could find someone willing to trade it for my passage. I spent the rest of the day debating as to who best to approach with the offer. I had a feeling I might only be able to do it once, so I had to make sure I chose the right person. My first thought was to approach the officer who came to tell me I could not go. I quickly dismissed that, since he already had the power to allow me to leave if he was so inclined.

I made a point of observing the different people in the hospital. I wanted to learn who had influence in making decision and in scheduling. My attention kept returning to the nurse.

The next morning, I went again to visit my cousins. Her spirits had not improved since I left the day before. The nurse was checking up on her when I arrived, looking concerned about Peri's condition. Seeing me, they both brightened a little bit: in Peri's case simply because she was happy to see me; the nurse because she hoped I might cheer Peri up.

Without thinking any further, I went up to the nurse and carefully took the bracelet from my pocket. I held it out in my hands for her inspection as I had thousands of times before at my store in Budapest, showing jewelry to its best advantage.

"I found this," I told her before she had a chance to say anything. She looked quickly from my hands holding the golden bracelet to my face. I immediately became afraid that she might do something very noble and British, like suggest trying to find the rightful owner. I didn't give her the chance to think of it. "This is for you," I continued. "A gift from me. I only have one request. All I ask is that you put me together with my sisters when they go to Sweden. I want to go with them."

The nurse slowly took the bracelet from me, holding it up to allow the light to reflect off of it. She put it on her wrist, admiring how it looked on her. Women have a much greater appreciation of jewelry than men do. "I'll see what I can do for you," she told me. I had heard that same thing many times while a prisoner under the Nazis, but I was willing to allow myself to believe she might honestly try.

Once again, the British kept their word. Evidently, the nurse did do everything she could on my behalf. Within four weeks, Peri, Miriam, and Benjamin Samuelson, listed on the British registers of displaced persons as "brother and sisters," began their journey to Sweden, together.

I was happy to be in my cousins' company and thrilled to be leaving Bergen-Belsen and any territory that had been controlled by Germany far behind me. Peri, though still sick, was every bit as happy as I was to be going to a decent hospital in a country far from the memories of the camps. Miriam felt much as I did, wanting to put as much distance as possible between her and the camps. We each thought of Sweden as the start of a new life, born from the depths of experiences we had already stopped discussing, trying our best to forget.

Our transportation was all arranged for us. We traveled for the better part of a day by buses until we reached the port. There, we had passage on a ship. The whole time we talked about what it might be like, what we would do. Peri and I became even closer during that time than we had been as children. She might very well have been my sister as we looked after each other and cared for each other, including each other in our plans to make new lives for ourselves. Every plan, every conversation included Miriam. Any family was far too precious to be put aside.

Our arrival in Sweden turned out to be a little bit different than any of us had anticipated. We knew, basically, what to expect, but the experience is never the same as what you imagine. Whereas the Swedes generously opened their country to hundreds, if not thousands of refugees, they also had practical matters to attend to. Many of us, like Peri and Miriam, came for treatment of illnesses. Some of us might be sick with contagious diseases, like typhoid or TB and not realize it. They had to protect their own citizens. On arriving, the Swedish authorities put us in quarantine for thirty days. Peri and Miriam spent the time in a hospital while I was placed in another facility. I believe that it, too, had once been a hospital. I still remember the name: Lanscrona.

While the quarantine facilities had everything we needed, including well-stocked cafeterias, they separated the men from the women. Lanscrona was one of the men's facilities. I can still remember some of the food served in the cafeteria, like fried liver, did not appeal to me; but they felt we needed the nourishment and virtually forced us to eat it.

At first, I didn't mind the quarantine because I understood why they took such precautions. To be honest, though, being put in a restricted area and watched over again, I began to feel little different than I did in Bergen-Belsen under the British. No matter what the reason or rationale is behind it, confinement is still confinement.

They did go out of their way to treat us well. The thing that stays in my mind most about those first few days in Sweden is how nice and generous the people acted toward us. They provided us with anything we needed, all kinds of clothes, food, toiletries, whatever the situation required. They even gave us some pocket money, so that we might be able to buy anything else we might want or feel we needed.

It was not only the government that had philanthropic policies toward us, but the people themselves. This greatly impressed me during my first few days in quarantine. Lanscrona had a lot of volunteers, regular citizens who gave of their time and energy to help us adjust to our new surroundings. Most of the volunteers were women, many of them quite wealthy, who simply felt they had to do something to help. I remember how some of the women would drive to the camp in large, expensive cars and spend their entire day doing whatever they could. It was not uncommon to see these women crying as they left the camp, either frustrated or ashamed that they couldn't do more. Sometimes, they gave us some money in addition to the clothing and food; but most of us would accept only the essentials.

Many of us deeply appreciated the gestures from these women as they opened their pocketbooks for us, but felt awkward about accepting charity. In my own case, I came from a family and background that emphasized giving to others in need and working for whatever you had. It felt vaguely uncomfortable to me to be the one needing to receive charity. I was used to working for everything I ever had, doing without if I couldn't earn it myself.

The Swedes understood this and made an effort to give us the opportunity to feel productive and useful. They accepted our help as volunteers within the confines of Lanscrona, keeping it clean, making certain it was well maintained. While we didn't have to do anything there if we didn't want to, they insisted on paying us for any work we performed. In that respect, we didn't volunteer in the same way that the women did who came to help. They would probably have been insulted to take money for their time and effort; but being paid, for the work we did, certainly did a great deal to help us feel better about the money they gave us.

In some ways, the thirty-day quarantine was very strict and restrictive. The only personal, outside contact we had was the people who worked at the camp and the volunteers who came each day to help. Soon, though, it was common for some of the Swedish girls to try to make contact with us, throwing love letters tied to rocks over the gate.

One other thing that the Swedes did to help us was to establish and maintain lists naming each survivor in every facility and hospital in Sweden, as well as those throughout Europe, that had refugees staying there. The lists then circulated so that we had another way of, hopefully, finding friends and relatives. From my first day in Lanscrona, those lists never left my thoughts. In every way I can think of, those lists had far greater importance than the new shoes or suits they gave us. Those lists of names embodied every hope and prayer any of us ever made while imprisoned by the Nazis. A name on the list meant that a prayer came true, a loved one or family member survived and, despite what anyone went through, we knew we were no longer alone.

With not much to do while spending my time in quarantine, those lists became extremely important. Everyone, myself included, anxiously awaited the arrival of a new list, bringing with it the hope of reconnecting with a loved one. I always read every name carefully. When I had a chance, I would reread those lists, always in the back of my mind keeping alive the hope that I might see the name of my mother or my sister, neither of whom I either saw die or heard of being killed. As the days passed, the hope grew dimmer, but no matter what I thought the reality to be, I looked anyway.

Naturally, my name was also added to the list from the quarantine camp I was staying in and circulated along with everyone else's. It came as no surprise to me that the reaction of those in our camp to receiving a new or updated list was duplicated in each and every place a list of names appeared. That's how I found out what happened in Stockholm.

A few days, maybe a week, after my arrival, my name, by then on a list, made its way to a hospital in Stockholm. There, people like Peri went for treatment for illness or diseases or to obtain operations that they needed but never had the chance to get while under the Nazi regime. In the Stockholm hospital, was a young woman who had gone there to have an appendectomy. She had just had her operation, perhaps a day before. She read my name on the list circulated at that hospital. She became so excited at seeing the confirmation of my survival that she wanted to immediately run from the hospital and join me. Naturally, the doctors wanted her to remain in bed and rest such an invasive surgery.

"It's my brother!" Frieda cried, explaining to them. "He's made it. He's alive. He's here in Sweden." She wanted to leave the hospital right away and go to Lanscrona to find me. Afraid she might run away to find me, they tied her in bed, assigning a nurse to watch her 24 hours a day. Only the solemn promises from the hospital staff that as soon as she was better, they would in fact reunite us, kept her calm enough to remain where she was. They allowed her to call me, though, that day.

The last thing I expected was to be told that there was a telephone call for me. I had no idea who it might be or what it could mean, but the unexpected novelty caused me to feel anxious. By the time I reached the telephone, I could feel my heart pounding heavily in my chest.

"Hello?" I asked, tentatively, not certain what to expect.

Immediately, I heard crying on the other end. "Benjamin! Benjamin, it's me. It's Frieda." I began crying, too. While I had always hoped to hear her voice again, the reality of the recent past had made the hope seem more fantasy than reality. Hearing my sister's voice, knowing she was alive and in a hospital in Stockholm, was the best news I could ever have been given. I felt happier at that moment than probably at any time since leaving Budapest.

I don't remember who gave me the handkerchief to wipe my eyes but, at some point, I felt the piece of cloth in my hand and was thankful for it. The people near enough to overhear at least my part of the conversation smiled, happy in seeing that another reunion could take place.

Frieda never spoke much about her experiences under the Nazis; but over the years, I pieced together an idea of what happened to her. During the initial selection at Auschwitz, she was assigned to a labor group, transferred almost immediately to another camp. She spent the majority of her time in the labor camp until the end of the war. No one could have any idea that forces outside the reality of the camps continued to operate. Negotiations for the release of women prisoners took on greater urgency as the war drew on. At one point, an exchange of 10,000 trucks for female prisoners was made, the women to be sent to Denmark. At the time that was going on, near the end of the war, the Nazis had marched Frieda and a group of women from her camp into the forest for execution. While the women lined up, ready to be shot, the order came to send the women back to their camp. The deal for the trucks had been finalized. Frieda became one of the women sent to Denmark.

During my last weeks in Lanscrona, Frieda and I kept in contact with frequent telephone calls. We spoke of many things, but had no set plan at that point. Neither of us actually knew what was available to us.

By the time Frieda's health had improved to the point where the doctors felt she could safely leave the hospital, I was released from Lanscrona. Neither of us had anywhere to go; so we went to another facility, much more like a camp, called Krompton. Once again, demonstrating their kindness and compassion, the authorities went out of their way to keep their word to us. They sent Frieda to join me in Krompton, never separating us from that point. What I mean by saying they went out of their way was that, Krompton, too, was a men's facility. The population in Krompton fluctuated between 300-400 men, depending upon how many arrived and how many people left. Frieda became the only woman to live there, sharing a room with me.

Seeing her, living with her again, watching her grow stronger and healthier, was the best thing that could have happened to me at that time. She often mentioned to me that knowing I was alive and with her was better medication than anything she received in the hospital. Naturally, I told her what had happened to our father and I could feel my anger rising. When I told her about our little sister Gitel Marim, I couldn't stop crying. Neither of us harbored any doubt as to what happened to our mother. The first few days, we spent a lot of time holding each other, supporting each other, and making solemn vows to stay together, no matter what else might happen.

Initially, the Swedes in the area did not want us there. The camp had been a Russian POW camp operated by the Germans. Evidently, it had not been unusual for a POW to escape, kidnap one of the local girls, take her into the nearby forest, and rape her. The people who ran the camp spent a lot of time with the locals, explaining who we were and giving assurances that we presented no threat. Gradually, they came to trust us and treat us without fear or anxiety.

During the time in Krompton, they sometimes took volunteers for work in the nearby woods to cut lumber. It was work that they paid us for, so we could begin to earn and save a little money on our own. Sweden has a lot of forests, something I never had given any thought to before my arrival there; and cutting down the trees was useful for the economy. In the morning, anyone who wanted to go was encouraged to do so. We piled into the backs of trucks and drove to whatever part of the forest was scheduled for harvesting. We then spent the day cutting down trees, returning to the camp in the evening. When we got back to the camp, they paid us for the work we did that day. Every time I worked in the forest, I came across old, used mattresses, put there by the Russian POWs. I could understand why the local people might initially fear us.

The Swedish government went out of its way to do whatever it could to make our lives easier. The Swedes sincerely hoped we would stay in the country, making it our new home. They looked forward to having us contribute to, and be a part of, the growing strength and success of the nation as a whole. I know of many people who did exactly that, happy to have a place to call home, where being Jewish didn't mean that others had the right to kill you. They felt safe, protected, and useful; and that was enough.

Another thing that impressed me about the Swedish people was their honesty. Where I grew up, we never had legal papers or written contracts between people. If people conducted business with each other, they discussed what was to be done, shook hands and that made the agreement binding on each party. No one took advantage of anyone else. A man's word was something you could trust and have faith in. Yet, even given my background and upbringing, I was surprised at how the Swedes conducted business.

One of the first things Frieda and I did was to go on a bus tour organized by the government. It was their way of showing us some of the industry and opportunities open to us. The driver of the bus explained the country to us, where things were, what kinds of jobs had openings. We passed a large dairy farm, which drew the attention of both Frieda and myself, bringing back the memories of our home in Rozavlea.

We slowed as we passed a man driving a cart filled with milk cans. We watched as he pulled to the side of the road, delivered full cans of milk and picked up the empty ones. He picked up the empty can that stood waiting for him at the side of the road. Underneath the can was some money. He took the money, then placed a full can in the same spot. I asked what the money was for. Our driver explained that the local people paid, in cash, every day for the milk. They put it under the can to keep it from blowing away in the wind.

Naturally, I wondered if that was really safe. Anyone walking by could easy tilt the can, take the money, and no one would ever be able to find out what happened. Further, it seemed to be a widespread enough practice that everyone knew where the money was. Putting it under the can or under a rock was not an effort to hide it. The guide looked at me a moment, as though he honestly did not understand my concern.

"Why would someone take the money?" he asked. "It's payment for the milk. Everyone knows that." The driver of the milk cart kept the money he collected in a basket on the seat next to him, a rock sitting on top of it. Again, the rock he kept was not intended to conceal it, but simply to keep it from blowing away.

When asked about where we wanted to work, both Frieda and I volunteered to go to work on a dairy farm, a huge ranch that not only had animals, but the equipment needed to do all of the manufacturing of butter, cheese, milk, and so on. Frieda and I felt extremely comfortable in that familiar environment. I worked with the animals, while Frieda did much of the cooking. During the entire time I worked at the dairy farm, I never saw a can that did not have the money underneath it, waiting exactly where it should be, in the amount that should be there.

As much as I liked the country and appreciated the way I was treated, I never intended to stay there. Even though, to this day, I can't say often enough or in enough ways how much the Swedes did for me and how nice and decent they treated me, I never considered the country as a permanent home. To me, it served as an interim, transitional place between being a homeless refugee and establishing a foundation for myself. From the time I was a little boy in Rumania, I wanted to go to Palestine. That dream was a deep part of me. I felt going to Sweden was simply a step toward making my way there.

I can't explain the attraction, the need to go to the Middle East. Partly, I think, because my sister Chana lived there, so it was another connection to my family. Partly, it was due to religious considerations. From my earliest memories, we always would say, *"L'shana haba Yerushalayim."* "Next year in Jerusalem." The automatic litany became fixed in my mind and soul as the place I needed to go as part of my life's journey.

Since I no longer had a home of my own, it made sense for me to want to go to the homeland of the Jewish people. I knew that somehow, I had to find a way to get to Palestine. Many other young people, homeless like me, many left without any other family save the Jewish people as a whole, felt much the same way I did.

I easily found a group of people, most around my age, who began organizing to find a way to enter Palestine. The British, controlling what was called the Palestinian Mandate, restricted legal immigration to about 1500 people per month. They used soldiers on land and warships at sea to try to enforce that quota, doing whatever they felt necessary to prevent illegal immigration. We knew receiving dispensation to enter Palestine legally would be almost impossible to obtain. We prepared ourselves to enter the country by illegal means.

Adequate preparation takes time, planning, and money. We set about making certain that when we actually began our trip, we would successfully complete it. We constituted a large group, perhaps 650 strong. Our first priority was to establish a base for ourselves. Together, we pooled our resources and rented a huge building which, at one time, had been a kind of hospital or convalescent home. Located near the forests not far from where Lanscrona was, it provided us a place in which many of us already knew some of the area.

We had a kitchen, cafeteria, everything we needed. Each of us paid out of the money we made to keep the place running. Many of us managed to earn money by working in local businesses and factories. Along with several others, I got a job in the city working at a brush factory. In the morning, a bus came to pick us up, take us to the factory, then return in the evening to take us home. The money we received went to a general fund to build the financial base we needed to move so many people to Palestine. It took close to eight months before we had the opportunity to board a ship that eventually took us from Sweden to the Middle East.

During that time, I was able to save up a little extra money for myself from the salary I earned at the brush factory. While I continued giving most of the money to our general fund, I kept some of it as spending money for myself.

After a while, I had saved enough to afford a nice Omega watch. I wanted that watch, not only because it was one of exceptional quality, but also because it was one of the first things I was able to purchase for myself, with my own money, since my deportation from Rozavlea. That gave me a sense of independence and confidence in my own abilities that I had not really had since my time in Budapest.

I loved that watch and wore it all the time. The only thing wrong with it was that the band was a little loose, sometimes opening without my wanting it to. Trying to fix it myself, I thought I had the problem solved. I was disheartened one day, to arrive at the brush factory to find that, at some point, my watchband had opened and the watch had fallen from my wrist. I hadn't even noticed it until I tried to check the time. I was disheartened enough that other people noticed. One of the Swedish workers in the factory asked me what happened.

"I don't know, exactly," I told him. "My watch must have fallen off somewhere. I have no idea where it could be."

"Have you gone to the police station?" he asked me. "Maybe someone found it and it's been turned in."

I didn't believe that, if someone had found it lying in the street, they would bother taking it to the police. After all, this wasn't the same as leaving money under a milk can, where everyone knew what the money was for. I couldn't help feeling cynical about the entire idea.

My co-worker merely shrugged. "What have you got to lose?" he said reasonably. "It might be there."

I had to admit that he was right; going to the police station would take only a few minutes of my time. During lunch, I walked to the station, not very far from the brush factory. I felt a little silly, taking up their time to ask about a watch I was certain was not even there, but I asked anyway. To my surprise, the police officer I spoke with simply asked me if, looking at the watch, I could identify it. I assured him that I could.

He left for a few moments, going into another room. When he returned, he was carrying a string that held over a dozen different watches. He laid the string out on his desk, taking care with the watches as he separated them so I could easily see them.

"Are any of these yours?" he asked me.

I saw my watch right away, but it took me a moment to answer, so shocked was I to see it, in perfect condition, sitting on the officer's desk among the other lost watches. My respect and admiration for the ethics and honesty of the Swedes grew even greater.

"Yes, sir," I told him. "That one in the middle is mine."

He pulled the other watches off the string to get to the one I identified, took that one off, then replaced the others. "Here you are," he said as he handed it to me. "You may want to get that band fixed so you don't lose it again."

"Thank you, sir. I will." He never asked me for any further identification. I could have told him any watch there was mine and he would have handed it over to me. I began to understand that he operated with the same basic honesty as did most other Swedes that I had met, then assuming my behavior would be consistent with that. It might not have occurred to him that I would lie about which item belonged to me. I smiled, realizing I had that in common with my hosts. It would not have felt right for me to pick out any watch except my own and I would not have done so.

As I left the police station and walked back to the factory, I felt safe and secure for the first time in a long time. It was a very reassuring feeling, one I was no longer accustomed to.

Despite how comfortable I was in Sweden and how much I admired the Swedish people and appreciated their kindness and generosity, my feelings toward Palestine remained. All I could think about was working toward the day when Frieda and I might be able to go to the Holy Land and, with our sister Chana, reunite what was left of our family. I was not alone in feeling a need to go to a country that I already thought of as a Jewish state, a place where no one could make laws condoning discrimination and violence against us.

After approximately eight months of working together, we arranged, with the guidance and encouragement of Haganah, the Jewish underground, to leave Sweden. Haganah helped make certain that we all made it to the port. Six hundred and fifty of us, mostly women who had been in the Ravensbruck concentration camp, got on buses in the middle of the night, arriving at the ship *Chaim Arlosoroff* well before morning.

To the
Promised Land

Frieda and I said our goodbyes to Peri and Miriam. They had decided not to join us in Palestine, but instead went to America, where they had relatives from their mother's side of the family.

We knew a little about the ship's history, but I was interested in finding out more. Anytime I found anything in a paper or book about the ships used by Haganah to bring refugees into Palestine, I read every word, hoping for a reference to *Chaim Arlosoroff*. Over the years, I pieced together a little bit of the ship's story.

Originally, it was a United States Coast Guard cutter named *Unalga*. I remember reading once, many years later, that President Richard Nixon, well before the beginnings of his political career, went on his honeymoon aboard her in one of the four-passenger cabins of what was at that time a cargo ship. During World War II, *Unalga* was used as a repair ship, maintaining and repairing ships at sea. After the war, *Unalga*, along with many other ships, was deemed obsolete by the U.S. Navy and sold off as scrap to the highest bidder.

In the years directly after the war, Haganah made a point of buying ships to be used specifically for the purpose of running the British sea blockades to get as many people into Palestine as possible. In some way, they could be seen as successful, helping 1,000 reach Palestine in 1945; increasing to over 20,000 in 1946; and close to 40,000 traveling to Palestine in 1947. Unfortunately, many times that amount sought entry and, with the British waiting on the shore, most wound up being arrested. Even in Sweden, we knew our chances seemed slim to actually reach the shore, but we wanted to try anyway. With the help and preparation by Haganah, we felt we had a decent chance. Haganah placed their faith in the ability of *Unalga* to reach the shores at Haifa.

Still structurally and mechanically sound, when the U.S. Navy put it up for sale, *Unalga* became the first ship Haganah purchased. After being refitted by the Maryland Drydock Company, *Unalga* met the class standards of the French classification firm of Bureau Veritas and inspection of Lloyds of London. Bureau Veritas standards couldn't qualify the ship for registry in the United States, but it was enough to register the ship in either Honduras or Panama. Legally registered in Honduras and flying her flag, the ship became *Ulua*, named after a river in Honduras.

A largely volunteer crew, made up in great part of young American Jews who wanted to go to Palestine, sailed the ship to its new owners in Marseille. In addition to the volunteers, only some of whom actually had naval or maritime experience, Haganah wanted its own agents aboard, trusted individuals responsible for ship and conduct. Haganah agents became active officers as well as regular crewmen. Either way, the status of Haganah agents was a close secret. As a passenger, I had suspicions that Haganah agents made the journey with us, but I could never point to a specific man and identify him.

In outfitting the ship, codes specified that only supplies equivalent to a 180-day consumption for a 30-40 man crew could be brought aboard. Everything else, from 2500 life jackets to four carloads of Canadian lumber had to be crated and shipped as cargo.

We specifically paid for gas masks with our hard earned Swedish money. Naturally, we hoped for an uneventful passage, but we had enough sense to prepare for the worst. It's possible those gas masks wound up crated and shipped as cargo, because I never saw them.

Haganah made its own modifications to *Ulua*. The most important was creating a wheelhouse in the lower decks of the ship, tied to the one on the bridge, protected by large steel doors which we could lock tight against any potential invasion. In case the British boarded the ship, something the Haganah thought might be likely, we could transfer steering capability to the lower wheelhouse, effectively maintaining control of the ship. Another modification was the steel poles, like telephone poles, welded to the side of the ship, two on each side, the edges beveled to make them an effective deterrent against any ship which might think to ram us.

One other addition to the ship was not done out of planning against eventual conflict, or out of a desire to make room for more people to make the trip to Palestine. The addition was made entirely to compensate for the tremendous amount of bulk taken off *Ulua*. Equipment needed to repair ships at sea is large and heavy, the ship carrying it made specifically to accommodate it. When Haganah removed it all from *Ulua*, replacing it with the cargo of supplies and hopeful human beings was not enough to make up the difference. Ballast, of a sort, had to be added. Two huge containers, filled only with water to provide weight, served as that ballast. One container fastened to the deck on each side of the ship was rather unsightly, but we soon became accustomed to the ungainly appearance.

In Marseille, *Ulua* underwent a few more modifications, among them turning those truckloads of Canadian lumber into bunks and partitions. Once again her name changed, this time to

Chaim Arlosoroff, in honor of the former political head of the Jewish Agency who had been murdered in 1933 on the beach at Tel Aviv by someone whose identity was never discovered.

It was the modified, newly outfitted *Chaim Arlosoroff* which arrived at the port in the middle of that cold night in Sweden to take a group of refugees, most of us not more then twenty years old, to the Promised Land. One of the older refugees, a man perhaps in his mid-30s, boarded with his daughter who was probably the youngest passenger at about ten years old. That the little girl had survived at all was amazing to me.

We didn't simply go to the port and walk on the ship. We had spent a lot of time and money, making our own preparations. The most important had to do with our stated destination. I have a suspicion that Sweden had an informal understanding with the British that no ship leaving a Swedish port would be bound for Palestine. Needing to work within that restriction, we had to find a way to carry legal papers, visas, and so on, while keeping to our plan to go to Palestine.

We found allies, of a sort, at the Cuban consulate, representing a country which the Swedes had no aversion to our going to. I can only assume that a great deal of the money we worked so hard for found its way to one official or another who worked there. The underground obtained official documents from the Cubans, probably for a price, stating our intended destination as Cuba. Each of us received all the proper, legal papers we needed, giving us the ability to show anyone who needed to know where we planned on going that, by a particular date, we expected to reach the port at Havana.

At the same time, the Cuban ambassador had us sign declarations for their private records which confirmed that we had no intention of going to Cuba. Everyone was happy with the arrangements. We had visas for Cuba, allowing us to leave Sweden with no problems and the Cubans had our promise that we would never be near their country. None of us cared about that. Finally, headed to Palestine, Frieda and I felt our dreams coming true.

In the latter part of 1946, Haganah tried to keep the trip as secret as possible. Arriving at the dock, they loaded us onto the ship, quickly and efficiently. They allowed only those from our group on the ship. A reporter was there, somehow having heard about the ship and, maybe, even some of what we planned to do. He asked questions, giving only vague answers when questioned himself.

We never found out who the reporter was, where he was from, or what paper he represented. He was thrown out, some of the Haganah agents making certain he had no access to the ship. As far as the rest of us went, we cooperated with any instruction they gave us. We knew speed was of the essence and we complied, even though once we got inside the ship, we had to deal with severe overcrowding.

They had taken out all of the equipment which the ship had when it was being used during the war. In place of all that, the Haganah built beds, really not much more than planks where we could sleep. Under any other circumstances, I doubt any of us would have tolerated such conditions, feeling and appearing as it did so close to the confinement in the boxcars we had been lucky enough to survive. No one minded being stuffed into makeshift rooms so tightly, but we had difficulty making use of the beds. We felt this was simply part of the price we had to pay to reach Palestine and the fulfillment of our dreams.

Along with our few belongings, food, cargo, and necessities for the trip, we carried items for trade. The most important item was cigarettes: small, light, and negotiable anywhere in the world. I wasn't certain where Haganah expected to use the cigarettes, since I imagined we would travel directly to Palestine; but they knew better what to prepare for than I did.

Our first stop was a port on the northern coast of France. We brought on extra stores of fuel and water, preparing for another stop later in our trip where more people planned to join us. In the middle of the night, another ship—a heavy cargo ship—pulled up near us, effectively blocking our way.

I happened to be standing near one of the crewmen who I had suspicions might be a Haganah agent. He looked out at the ship and said in a low voice, "We're in trouble." I was disheartened to hear that from him. I said nothing to him, silently hoping he would be proven wrong. For a while, it seemed our journey would end before it really began. What happened at that point, I can't tell you exactly. I have a suspicion that Haganah paid someone off, using our money to ensure passage through the universal exchange of bribery.

In the middle of the night, my hopes coming true, we cut the ropes and sailed out from the port, heading to international water. I looked for the ship that had blocked our way only a short time before. I couldn't find it anywhere.

After that, the trip progressed smoothly and uneventfully, until we reached Gibraltar, the entrance to the Mediterranean. There, we encountered a storm which became increasingly violent. It was not very long before we found ourselves in the grip of a what I can only describe as a hurricane. Waves, dwarfing the ship, crashed down on us. The ship, ex-U.S. Navy though it was, simply was too small to effectively contend with the brutal forces of nature unleashed against it.

It felt as though the ship rode straight up on some of the larger waves, only to come straight back down. It finally got to the point where even the Haganah agents on board felt the need for secrecy had come to an end. They radioed an SOS, the need for assistance outweighing all other concerns. Unless we could survive, none of us would enter Palestine.

From our ship, we could look out at the storm and see, sitting not far away, five British destroyers, battling the storm like us—but in ships much more suited to survival under those conditions. All of us sailed in international waters. Normally, when a ship sends out an SOS in international waters, any other ship, from any other country, which is in a position to assist, is expected to do so. In our case, we watched the British ships as they remained close enough to see despite the storm, without having to use binoculars, but making no move to respond to our distress calls.

I'm certain they must have hoped we would sink in the storm, solving their problem for them before it ever really became an issue. Their lack of action made it clear to us that we had a new enemy, wearing a British uniform and speaking English.

The storm couldn't have lasted more than a couple of days, but seemed far longer, rarely letting up in intensity during that entire time. Most of the people on board the ship became ill from the exaggerated movements of the ship and sea. Even most of the crew—seasoned, professional sailors—became incapacitated in one way or another. For some reason, I remained healthy, though I have no idea why I wasn't affected like so many others.

Along with the sailors who remained unaffected, I helped in any way I could. For the most part, that meant looking after some of those who had become very ill. With the help of some of the other crewmen, we tied the epileptic and the very sick ones into their beds, so they wouldn't risk falling to the floor as the ship was buffeted by the unrelenting storm.

We feared that, unable to eat or drink anything, people might easily become dehydrated. To combat this, we fixed some tea, which I brought to each person I could, opening their lips a little bit for them and dripping some of the tea into their mouths. I felt it was important to make certain they had something wet in their mouths and, hopefully, the tea in their stomachs might help calm or end the vomiting. For the duration of the storm, it was the rare individual who was able to keep down even the few sips of tea that I managed to give them.

To make movement on the ship possible, the sailors strung up ropes across the decks. They then tied ropes around me, attaching them to the ropes on the decks. Even if I slipped or fell, I always felt the security of the rope around my waist.

At one point, I saw the little girl on the deck. I don't know how she got there. I think she may have been trying to find her father. Water came flowing across the deck, its momentum and force washing away anything not tied down. I ran to the girl, grabbing her as more waves came crashing along the deck. I could see her crying; but I couldn't hear her, though I held her against my chest as I made my way below deck with her. Not until I placed her on the dry floor did I finally hear her sobs.

At the height of the storm, one of the containers of sea water came loose from the forces of nature railing against the *Chaim Arlosoroff* and fell overboard, lost in the depths of the Mediterranean Sea. I saw almost immediately how important those containers had been to us. Weighed down by the one remaining container, the ship began to list to that side. The waves and wind conspired to push us farther into the sea. With the weight on deck no longer evenly distributed, the ship had more and more trouble coming up out of the waves which tried to beat it down.

I have to give the sailors on board credit for their skill and professionalism. Several of them, working together as quickly as they could in a race against the storm, cut the lines holding the remaining tank in place on deck. It fell over the side, any sound of its entry into the sea swallowed up by the sounds of the storm. Almost immediately, the ship came up on the next wave, riding higher than it had for a while.

Without the weight of the tanks, the ship took more of a beating, yet at the same time, seemed less likely to go under and stay there. Had the sailors been unable to remove that second tank, I have no doubt the ship would have sunk.

When the storm passed, we could still see the British destroyers, waiting for us. In spite of our repeated distress signals, we never received a reply from any of those ships. All I could think of was: once again, when we needed help the most, others found it easier to ignore our pleas. My gratitude toward the British for the liberation of Bergen-Belsen began to wear very thin.

The destroyers never came close to us. As long as we remained in international waters, there was little they could do. They followed our progress at a discreet distance, preparing for the time when we no longer had that slim veneer of protection.

Soon after the storm was over, we stopped the ship, taking care to remain in international waters, close to Northern Africa. All kinds of small boats came from a variety of different African countries. Loaded with fruits like oranges and grapes as well as many other things to eat, they came prepared to trade. The crew got the cigarettes out of the cargo hold—our highly valued, tradable commodity which appeared to be better than any currency. A package or two bought us an entire bushel of fruit.

I had no idea how scarce cigarettes were in this part of the world, but I saw what some of the people coming to trade were willing to do to get them. Having them was better than gold. Some of the men of the little boats began fighting among themselves, each wanting to be the one to make it to our ship to have the opportunity to receive a package of cigarettes for a little extra fruit. After several hours of brisk trading, we had all the fresh food we could eat.

We paused in Taranto, Italy, only long enough to load another 700 people into the ship, these refugees brought by Haganah, somehow, using overland routes to arrive at the port. How Haganah managed to move, protect, and feed that many people is still somewhat of a mystery to me. *Chaim Arlosoroff* became even more crowded with the addition of the refugees from Italy. Again, no one complained.

While we remained in the safety of international waters, we did not see any more British destroyers, though I knew they had to be nearby. As we neared Palestinian waters, a British plane flew by, low overheard. The crew instructed us to go below, informing us the British used the plane to take pictures of us for identification. Not wanting ourselves to be identified, we readily complied with the orders. Less than an hour later, all of us below deck and out of sight, we heard the plane flying by again. It was then that the destroyers made their appearance, seeming to come out of nowhere.

We had a plan as to what to do when we reached the shore. We headed for the beach at Haifa, where the people from that city would meet us. Our plan was to beach the ship, jump off, and mix ourselves up with the people from the city. Short of arresting and processing every person, a task we hoped would prove too daunting, there would be no way to tell which of us came from the city and which came from the ship. The British had their own plans about how to deal with us.

It wasn't very long before the waiting game at sea came to an end. We left the safety of international waters behind us and entered the waters of the Palestinian Mandate, controlled by the British, who took the job of preventing illegal immigration very seriously.

Off Bat Galim, one of the two destroyers escorting us came alongside and ordered us to stop. We ignored the message, just as they had ignored our calls for help during the hurricane. Many of us had come back out on deck, wanting to catch a glimpse of Palestine as soon as possible. At about that time, a British plane came in toward the ship low enough that many of us instinctively dropped to the deck. It reminded me of Dora, where the Allied planes came in low enough for me to see the faces of the pilots.

Our response was not only to ignore the warning, but to do whatever was necessary in order to reach Haifa. *Chaim Arlosoroff* went to full speed, making a run for the beach.

The last thing the British wanted was for us to reach the shore. One of the destroyers came at us, ramming our ship from behind, where the threat of the poles was nonexistent. We slowed out of necessity, the British taking advantage of the situation by sending a boarding party onto our ship.

We had come too far to give up our dream without a fight. I don't think they expected us to fight them, perhaps imagining us to have nothing to fight with. While it was true that we had no traditional weapons, we instead struck out with anything that came to hand. We assaulted the invading British sailors as they came on board with anything we could find, mostly bottles and tin cans. So many of us, hurling so many objects, overwhelmed the British troops. Some of them got injured, hit by one of our projectiles more by chance than design.

We hardly had time to celebrate before they tried a new tactic. Determined to keep us out of Palestine, they next shot gas bombs at us, hoping the tear gas would force us into compliance. While we cried in pain, rubbing our eyes to no avail, they sent a second boarding party to back up the first one.

Without the gas masks we had paid for, we found ourselves at a further disadvantage. For many of us, it meant only that we had to fight harder.

This time, they tried to wrest control of the ship from us by taking over the steering. What they didn't know was that we controlled the ship from the modified steering below decks, protected by the steel doors installed by Haganah. Frustrated by what they saw as only a temporary failure, they tried to break into our actual wheelhouse, all to no avail.

Instead of yielding, we became more resolute, again fighting back in any way we could. Not expecting so much resistance, especially after using tear gas against us, they found themselves overwhelmed. We actually managed to force them to abandon our ship—most going back to the destroyer, some just jumping into the water.

Deciding it was time to use any means necessary to stop us, they opened fire on us with machine guns, wounding some and killing a few. We went below, safe from the bullets, once we left the deck. The men steering the ship kept to the plan we had formed before leaving Sweden. We finally ran *Chaim Arlosoroff* onto the beach at Haifa, exactly as we wanted to.

Somehow, the British seemed to have found out what, in terms of the arrangements with the people from Haifa, we had planned to do. Without our knowing what happened, they had instituted martial law, preventing anyone from the city of Haifa from leaving their homes. Maybe it was something they began implementing after our departure from Sweden as a matter of course, but it always seemed to me to be suspicious that it just so happened on that particular day that only British soldiers stood on the beach.

None of us knew, at the time, that the residents of Haifa could not make it to the beach. With nowhere else to go, our ship stuck on the sand, just as we wanted, we jumped down from the ship into the surf and ran to the beach. It was disheartening—after all the work, planning, sacrifice, and fighting—to literally walk into the hands of the British. We fought a little bit. But not being any match for soldiers with machine guns, they had little trouble arresting all of us and loading us onto their ships. If anyone escaped that day, I would be very surprised.

They had to do something with us, take us somewhere. The last thing they wanted was to imprison us in Palestine, while taking us to England was never even an option. Along with the Palestinian Mandate, the British also controlled other interests in the area of the Mediterranean. One of those areas under British control at the time was Cyprus. There, they had two detention camps, Caraolos and Xyletymbou. The trip, for some reason, took almost a full day. Maybe they wanted to make sure the prison was ready for us, close to 1500 people to be processed and interned.

Arriving at Cyprus, they took our names, assigned us to barracks, a routine with which we all had become familiar. Separated into one of the two camps, assigned to barracks, barbed wire penning us in like animals, the perimeter patrolled by machine-gun carrying soldiers in uniform—we once again became prisoners. Admittedly, life in the camp on Cyprus was very different from life in any of the camps under the Nazis, but prison is prison. We adapted as best we could.

We called the two camps the Winter Camp and the Summer Camp. The Summer Camp, utilizing tents for barracks, was the larger of the two by quite a lot. The Winter Camp had actual, permanent barracks. Frieda and I wound up in the Winter Camp, called Camp 66 by the British. Normally, women and men stayed in separate barracks, but Frieda stayed with me. We worked it out so that she had her own, little room in the men's barracks where I stayed. We had come too far to allow anyone to separate us again.

None of us gave up the dream of eventually going to Palestine. Toward that end, we made specific efforts to prepare ourselves for when we finally left Cyprus.

The camp I was assigned to with Frieda was one of the more modern ones, complete with nice, clean, roomy barracks. I think this particular part of the camp may have been a British army base during the war. In any case, I felt it was important to do whatever I could to prepare myself. In that, I had a lot of help. Haganah agents, both those captured at Haifa along with the rest of us and those who managed to relay information to those agents to and from the camp, made an effort to train any of us who wanted to learn some of the arts of warfare.

I was among a large group of young men and some women who enthusiastically took advantage of the training. Our experience fighting on the ship demonstrated to us how important it was to learn to fight and defend ourselves. Tin cans and bottles might work for a very brief time; but skill and confidence in using weapons would, in the long run, serve us far better.

Naturally, we didn't announce to the British exactly when and where we had our training. Some things still had to remain secret, at least as much as possible. The Haganah agents came to Cyprus, ostensibly to help us contend with day-to-day life in prison. They helped make sure we had adequate food, clothing, and medical supplies. They brought packages and letters from relatives and loved ones. The "cover" of helping us, used by the Haganah agents, became an essential connection to the outside world for many people. Those of us seriously training with them, though, would never have been prepared for combat without their guidance.

While we naturally could not have any real weapons, we used whatever we could, usually sticks, to substitute for the rifles we someday would have. As much as possible, we trained as regular soldiers, knowing one day, we would use what we learned.

I wanted to be as prepared as possible. I trained under the Haganah with a lot of other young people. We all wanted the same thing: A home in our own country. We knew that to fulfill that desire, it meant ultimately fighting the British and later on, the Arabs who wanted us in Palestine even less than the British did.

Even a stick, knowing what it represented for some future time, can be a powerful weapon. As we trained, becoming more proficient, we also felt more confident and self-assured. Little by little, we felt in control of our lives, even behind the barbed wire fences, and less like victims.

Maybe we needed that time on Cyprus to help change our attitudes. I know that after a while, we no longer behaved like prisoners. If we wanted or needed something, we asked for it. Short of leaving the camp, we received what we requested.

Even leaving the camp, to a certain extent, was permitted. My camp was directly across the road from the much larger Summer Camp. A dirt road separated the wire fence of the Winter Camp from the wire fence of the Summer Camp. Under the watchful eyes of British guards, people felt relatively free to go from one camp to the other. In that way, many young people met future wives or husbands, leading to a lot of marriages.

That ease of association led not only to marriages, but also to a lot of babies being born. It became a regular activity for us to request a baby cradle. We got the cradles when we asked for them, though the commander of the camp began to wonder out loud if we had created a baby factory in the middle of the prison camp. Perhaps, in a way, we had. Children represented to us a continuation of life and hope for the future.

At first, they put up roadblocks twice a day to stop traffic so that we could move easily from camp to camp. At best, this was a major inconvenience because, aside from interrupting the flow of traffic on what was one of the main roads, they had to place extra guards on duty to make certain we did not escape. To make matters worse, some of the men had become so fed up with being a prisoner, they began abusing the guards.

Most of the time, it was verbal abuse—cursing at the guards, taunting them, calling them names. Once in a while, it became more than that. In the Summer Camp, they sometimes had herring to eat. On more than one occasion, I watched as someone took a herring and slapped the face of one the British guards with it. To their credit, the guards never fired their weapons at us, though I'm certain they wanted to on more than one occasion.

To take care of several problems at once, they built a bridge between the two camps, enclosed by barbed wire, so that we could go easily from one camp to another without disrupting the traffic on the road or needing the extra guards to prevent our escape. It also prevented us from abusing the guards that remained.

Some people had even set up shops of one sort or another, so going from camp to camp might entail anything from visiting a friend to going shopping. Thousands of imprisoned people made the entire area seem like a small town.

Training did not take up all of my time. My lifelong interest in business became stimulated by possibilities I saw at the camps. We received packages and money from friends and relatives via the Red Cross and other international agencies. Frieda and I connected with our sister Chana in Palestine, who sent us letters and sometimes a little bit of money. A barter system, of sorts, began to take shape. The only two skills I had, as a tailor and jewelry maker, didn't seem to have a place in the micro-economy of the prison camps. I noticed that people loved to have fresh fruits and vegetables, so I began to think about what I might be able to do to fill that need.

One day, I went to the commander of our camp and asked him if I could have permission to travel to Nicozia, the capital of Cyprus to do some shopping. It took a little explaining, but we finally came to an agreement. Once or twice a week, I was given a license to leave the camp, in the company of one of the guards, to go to the city. There, I made deals with some of the local merchants. I bought truckloads of their fresh food, mostly fruits, for cheap prices. It worked out well for both of us. They got rid of excess food that would probably just spoil, and I got lots of fresh fruit at very reasonable prices. My guard and I came back to the camp, the truck loaded. From there, I sold my fruits and vegetables, making a little bit of money for myself.

The same guard didn't go with me every time; but after a while, I got to know most of the guards who accompanied me on each trip. They had the chance to get to know me as well. They could see that I was an honest man, who was going to Nicozia for exactly what I said I was going there for. It didn't take long before my guard, whichever one it happened to be, became bored by having to stand around while I conducted my business.

I soon came to agreements with each of them. Generally, when we got into town, I gave him a little bit of money, so he could get something to eat or drink. He dropped me off at the market so I could carry out my negotiations with the farmers. Then, for the rest of the day, he spent his time at the bar or maybe even sightseeing. When I was done several hours later, he would come back and pick me up. They knew they could trust me to return when I said I would. Again, it worked out best for everyone. I was given permission to leave the camp, pretty much whenever I wanted to. The person guarding me that day got to go into the city, like having an extra day off.

I also got special permits which allowed the Greek shop owners to bring their trucks into the camp, following the guard's jeep. That way, I only had to unload the fruit once. With a couple of thousand people in Camp 66 alone, it never took me long to sell out my stock. I didn't have the chance to unload the truck. I simply opened the back and sold whatever I had directly off the truck. It soon became a regular routine for me to go shopping in Nicozia a couple of times a week.

We never became complacent or lost our desire to enter Palestine. The British released some people to fill the quotas allowed into Palestine; but the quotas filled quickly, leaving most of us behind. We continued training and Haganah picked specific individuals who they helped to escape. They had very clear ideas about the kind of people they wanted, what age and so on. Haganah needed the help of the people left in the camp to make good the escapes of those individuals they chose, and we willingly aided them in any way we could.

I don't know what they did at the other camp; but at our camp, we found that the most effective method was to dig a small tunnel under the wires enclosing the camp. We dug it out far enough so that someone leaving through the tunnel emerged near the beach, making it easy for them to be picked up by boat, mostly Greek or Turkish fishermen who had been paid by Haganah to transport people from Cyprus to Palestine. Haganah had the arrangements all worked out with the fishermen, who arrived in the middle of the night and received a set amount for each person they brought to Palestine.

Small, long, close to the surface, easily accessible, and easily hidden—the tunnel was an important part of the underground movement within the camp to help prisoners reach Palestine. Unfortunately, the very things which made the tunnel work well also wound up working against it.

The British knew escapes happened, more often than they admitted. As we grew bolder, their efforts to keep us from effecting escape increased, more guards patrolling the perimeter with greater frequency. One of the ways they felt they could deter us was to use a small, open tank as a part of the patrol around the outside of the camp. We simply used it as a measure of exactly when to leave. We knew, once the little tank passed by, we had a window of safety in which to use the tunnel to the beach.

One night, our plans, as well as those of the British, failed. They had tried, without success, to discover the way we managed to leave the camp. The little tank, on patrol, came nearer to the fence than it normally did. By accident, literally, they found our tunnel.

We had never built it strong with a lot of internal support. After all, it was being used furtively, the people needing it only to move through as quickly as possible. It certainly was not built to support anything of any great weight on it. Even a little tank was too much. As it rolled over the top of the tunnel, the weight of the tank collapsed the roof. The tank fell to the ground below and became buried in the sand. Luckily, no one was in the tunnel and as far as I know, no one in the tank was injured.

Though not pleased about having their tank beneath the level of the beach, they managed to accomplish what they set out to do. They found out how we had been getting people out and prevented us from continuing the practice.

Some of the people had radios, which we often listened to in the evenings. On the night of November 29, 1947, we all sat in silent anticipation, as did Jews throughout the world, waiting to hear the vote taking place in the United Nations General Assembly. It was the culmination of 2,000 years of Jewish prayers and dreams, as one nation after another voted for Israeli Statehood.

Listening intently, we enthusiastically cheered with each report of a nation voting for Statehood, knowing we took one step closer to having our own land, a place where we could feel at home at last. With each nation voting no, a silence fell as the dream we shared retreated farther from our sight.

Finally, the vote completed, the camp seemed to echo and reverberate with our cries of happiness and joy. The United Nations General Assembly voted to create a new nation . . . the modern State of Israel.

Within another few months, Frieda and I received word we could leave as part of April's quota of Jews, given permission to enter Palestine. Despite the U.N. vote granting Israeli Statehood, Great Britain still controlled the Palestinian Mandate, continuing to allow only a meager allotment of legal immigrants.

Frieda and I did everything we could to remain together. Part of being included in the quota hinged on our ages, which we lied about in order to receive the dispensation. Because of that, I have two official ages I can quote for myself. I had been a prisoner of the British for close to a year-and-a-half by the time Frieda and I boarded the ship for Palestine. Without a second thought, I left my grocery business in Camp 66 on Cyprus.

On the way to the port at Haifa, all I could think of was the fact that, after all I had planned and hoped for, all I had been through, I was finally entering Palestine to be with my family and my people.

Israel: Fight for Independence

Haganah agents serving as soldiers, waited at the port for our group to arrive. They would take Frieda, myself, and the other people arriving in Palestine with us to Tel Aviv. The road between the two cities passed through a lot of territory controlled by the Arabs, who did whatever they could to prevent any more Jews from reaching Tel Aviv. The soldiers took no chances, using a bullet-proof, armored truck for the journey.

We rode in the back with some of the soldiers, weapons of all description in the truck with us. The weapons came from all over the world, anything the Haganah could borrow or purchase. They even had some weapons given by Jews and Gentiles, throughout the world, sympathetic to the struggle. I sat next to a heavy burlap bag, oddly shaped by whatever was inside. I asked one of the soldiers who rode with us what it was.

"Potatoes," he answered, though by the way he smiled, I expected to see anything in there except potatoes. I reached for the bag to see for myself. He made no move to stop me. Instead, he nodded to me, encouraging me to see what was there.

The bag contained hand grenades, one more way to protect ourselves on the dangerous road from Haifa to Tel Aviv. That particular trip turned out to be uneventful, the need for opening the "bag of potatoes" never arising.

Upon arriving in Tel Aviv, Frieda and I went to see our sister Chana, who by then was married and had two little girls. The time we spent there was wonderful and sad as we explained what happened to other members of our family. Frieda stayed with Chana; and after a short time, I went to a secret camp run by Haganah as a training facility for combat soldiers. For the next two weeks, I received a more practical education in combat and firearms, building on the training I had at Camp 66. I learned to handle and use real weapons with live ammunition.

The most frustrating aspect of that entire period, in relation to the training, was the diversity of our weapons. As I mentioned, Haganah got weapons, of all description, from any source they could. The result was we had a lot of guns, a lot of ammunition—though the ammunition was not necessarily compatible with the guns. One of our tasks was to take a box full of bullets and sort them out according to caliber so that we could then put them with the appropriate rifle. We had lots of boxes, all from different countries, containing bullets of all different sizes. Sometimes, precious rifles had to be left behind for lack of bullets to fit them. We became quite good at being able to tell quickly what bullet went with which rifle.

My first rifle was from Canada, probably from World War I. It wasn't the best weapon in the world, but I was thrilled to have it. My biggest problem was finding the ammunition that I needed to be able to use it as a weapon. I remember, even after I was assigned to a unit, sorting through boxes in the middle of the night, trying to find enough ammunition for that old Canadian rifle to make it useful the next day in combat.

Our clothing was as varied as our weaponry. I remember that my jacket was from Belgium, my pants from the United States, my shoes from France, and so on. I can't remember if I even had two articles of clothing from the same country—probably not, since it would have been unusual enough to have been memorable.

Even the hat I wore was not a regular military hat. It was a little hat, providing just enough protection to keep from getting sunburned. It was one of the many things given to the army. On the inside, sewn to the brim, was a message in Yiddish. In translation, it said, "A gift from a hat maker in America."

One thing I do remember was the day not long after my arrival when we fulfilled the promise made the past November by the United Nations. We officially proclaimed Israeli independence, returning to a Jewish homeland we had been forced to abandon two millennia earlier. I was in a camp near Tel Aviv with my unit, listening intently with the other soldiers who had dedicated themselves to protecting our new home.

Years of struggle and hardship seemed, for a brief moment, of no lasting consequence, only the necessary precursor to having the right to say: "This is my home, my land." I later heard from my sisters, who lived in Tel Aviv at the time, that the celebrations and parties stretched into several days, as I'm certain they did in most major cities. Neither I, nor any other soldier in the new Israeli Army, the Haganah, had the good fortune to celebrate for more than that evening as we sat around a radio, hearing our dreams come true.

Our joy at the event was short-lived as we immediately became the target of massive attacks by the Arabs, who seemed to want nothing more than to pick up where the Nazis had left off, wanting to eradicate every living Jew from the area. Thus began our war for independence. Their dedication to the cause of destroying us seemed as great as our dedication to remain, grow, and prosper.

On May 14, 1948, the British Mandate ended with the declaration of the State of Israel.

One of the most exciting events in the early days of the new Israeli Army was when we received our first regular shipment of modern rifles. They came from Czechoslovakia, complete with ammunition for those specific rifles. It felt strange, at first, not to have to search for a bullet so I could use my weapon. For the first time, I felt a part of a national army. The ancient Canadian rifle simply couldn't measure up.

I almost threw that Canadian rifle away but then, thought better of it. After all, one shipment of arms couldn't possibly protect an entire new nation. I returned it to the warehouse, so someone else might use it while waiting for another shipment of rifles. As for my new rifle, I couldn't have had a more wanted companion during our march from Tel Aviv as we made an effort to protect the cities which had just come under Israeli jurisdiction, securing one area, one city at a time. Whenever I slept, I not only kept my new rifle nearby, I often had it in the bed with me.

That rifle (a rather nondescript product from some factory in Czechoslovakia whose owners had probably, for the right price, sold the same model to the Arabs as to us) represented the culmination of a dream for me. I was no longer in Palestine, but in the country of Israel, a soldier in her army, helping protect her territory and people from incursion. In the history of the Jewish people, we have prayed for such a thing for 2,000 years and I was a part of the fulfillment of those prayers of countless, unknown Jews throughout the centuries. Not since the times of King Solomon had an Israeli soldier, standing on Israeli soil, carried arms in defense of his own country. That rifle was a direct, tangible connection to the past as well as the best way to secure our future as a united, sovereign people.

We knew, from the moment the British left, that we had to fight for every meter of territory which the United Nations partitioned to be the modern State of Israel. The British seemed glad to be rid of their responsibility in controlling the Palestinian Mandate. While they did nothing to harm our chances at survival against the Arabs, they did nothing to assist us either. They pulled out, taking their arms, munitions, personnel, and any other support they might have given. They abandoned us to the fate which might await a small, largely untrained population under constant assault from all sides by millions of hostile neighbors.

Our fledgling army had rifles, like my new one, along with ammunition for them, plenty of hand grenades, sten guns (small automatic guns made in Israel, basically good only for self-defense) and the gut determination of a majority of new citizens who had somehow made it through the Nazi death machine not to give the Third Reich a posthumous victory. We had little else to draw support from on a daily basis. We trained as best we could, relied on military experience mostly from career military men of other nations, volunteering to fight in our army.

I don't, in any way, want to lessen the importance of support and contributions from Jews, and other supporters from around the world. Had it not been for them from the time of the Palestinian Mandate to the early days of the State of Israel, giving us everything from the arms and ammunition to the hats from the hat maker in America, the dream of an independent Israel would certainly have been much harder to achieve.

Still, when you are trying to secure a bit of land with nothing more than a hand grenade and a rifle against the amassed might of an Arab military which includes fighter planes, tanks, heavy arms like machine guns, and millions of soldiers dedicated to your complete extermination, it's difficult not to feel a bit overwhelmed, not to mention very alone in the world.

We tried to prepare ourselves as much as possible for the imminent withdrawal of the British from Palestine. (As a side note, I feel I should mention the Jewish Brigade. It was a British unit made up exclusively of Jewish soldiers which fought bravely in the War. At the end of World War II, they received discharges and stayed in Palestine to fight for the new State of Israel as part of the new Israeli Army. They supplied military knowledge and training which was invaluable.)

One of the things we did before the British left was to steal as much of their equipment as we could. In a way, I rather saw it was a favor for them. Whatever we managed to keep in Israel was that much less they had to transport back to England. Unfortunately, the British did not feel the same way. They gave us nothing, so we captured and stole what we could.

In fact, when the British managed to raid one of our bases or capture some of our soldiers, they confiscated any of our weapons they could find. They then turned many of them over to the Arabs, who then used our own weapons against us.

One of the biggest coups of the underground was the capture of three British tanks. They passed the tanks to another group who hid them within the cover of an orange grove. We had no desire to harm or detain the British soldiers manning the tanks, so we released them. With the three tanks we captured, the Israeli Army had . . . three tanks. We knew we had to have more, but we had to work with what we had. As far as I know, we also had only one airplane in the Israeli Air Force. One plane, with a propeller, in the whole country and we used it only for medical evacuation to get wounded soldiers to hospitals for medical attention as soon as possible. The plane had four beds set up, two on each side. Knowing we had no air power at all, the Arabs sometimes took chances they would not have taken under different circumstances.

The next best thing to having more tanks was to make the Arabs *think* we had more tanks. We accomplished this by creating cardboard fabrications, shaped and painted like tanks which fit over our jeeps, which was one thing we had enough of. Driving the jeeps slowly, like a tank, they appeared to be exactly that. We often observed Egyptian planes flying low to take photographs to estimate our military strength. As far as they could tell, we had a battalion of tanks. I'm certain they must have wondered where we got them all.

We planned to use our three real tanks to capture the Lud Airport, which is now called Ben Gurion International Airport. At the time, it was important, strategically, for us to control the airport. After all, it was on Israeli soil and Israel needed an airport. The Jordanians, who actually had physical control of the airport, felt very differently about the matter.

Jordanian soldiers waited for us at the airport as we arrived in our three tanks. I respected their military skill even as that skill made the battle difficult for us. We lost many fine young men during that battle for the airport. We also lost two of our three tanks. Not wanting to lose the last precious tank, we retreated, hiding it once again in the orange grove.

Despite the losses we sustained in the heavy fighting, we refused to give up. We wouldn't, couldn't allow defeat on our own land. We went back, continuing the fight and, little by little, we gained ground. Finally, we gained control of the airport and set about guarding our prize with the same dedication which the Jordanians had shown earlier—maybe because we wanted it more, or maybe we knew we had more to lose—but we never lost control of that strategic bit of land.

Soon, after we took control of Lud Airport, I was one of the soldiers standing guard on the road. My job was to make certain the perimeter of that particular area remained secure. We saw a group of about twenty Arab women approaching, as though on their way toward Jordan. Though the city of Jaffa, primarily an Arab city, was relatively close by, it still seemed unusual for the women to be so far from home. I became suspicious of them and, along with some of the other soldiers on guard, surrounded them.

It was no surprise to find out the "women" were actually Arab soldiers, hoping the disguise would allow them to pass across the border with no problems. What was a surprise to us was that they easily gave up. We could never have captured them otherwise. I admired their ability and determination on the battlefield, and I wasn't prepared to see them simply give themselves up.

We had very specific orders not to kill any prisoner of war. The moment an Arab soldier gave up, became a prisoner, we could not kill him, and never did so. We treated our prisoners well. We made them work, of course, a little bit, not really much. They ate the same food we ate and slept in conditions similar to ours. We heard stories that the same was not true of our soldiers taken prisoner by the Arabs. They would cut their Israeli prisoners to pieces, killing our soldiers in a cruel, painful fashion. Sometimes, we saw firsthand what happened to Israeli prisoners.

I'll never forget the time we went to capture a little town. Even though the United Nations said the State of Israel encompassed all territory from one specific spot to another on the map, we had to fight for each meter of the land. This town, in Israel, was no different.

I was part of the group of soldiers taken by bus to the town. Naturally, the army didn't have its own buses. We used a civilian bus with a civilian driver. The driver was a nice man, older than any of us, maybe a little over sixty. He felt driving was doing his part for Israel and told us proudly about his only son, who was also in the army.

We got there in time to help a difficult situation. The fighting had been going on for a while and our men took some heavy losses. With the added strength of our group, as well as several others, we finally managed to take control of the town. Even the driver got out of the bus and helped load the machine guns and other weapons we captured. Then the old man saw his son.

His son was lying in the dirt, a casualty from the earlier fighting. The boy's clothing had been ripped, mostly torn from his body. His stomach was slit, one of his shoes wedged inside. His mouth was stuffed with his amputated penis.

The old man went back to the bus and got one of the machine guns. We tried to stop him—not certain what he intended to do. He turned to us, his face damp with his tears, but his voice cold and hard as he spoke: "I'm not a bus driver anymore. I'm going to fight with you. All of us, together."

He'd just lost his son and we didn't want to see him hurt as well. I thought he was too old to be an effective soldier, though I didn't tell him in quite that way.

He had his mind made up and no argument from any of us could change it. His determination made itself known as he leveled the machine gun, at no one in particular, but in our general direction. "If anybody tries to stop me," he said, his tone leaving no room for disagreement, "I'll kill them. He was my only son. I have to settle with them for what they did."

"Nobody's going to stop you," we reassured him. That's how a little old man of over sixty joined the Israeli Army. He turned out to be a very good soldier.

I was assigned to Battalion 88 under Captain Chaim Lipski. We were a division of the 8th Armoured Brigade commanded by Yitzhak Sadeh.

We started from Tel Aviv and, city by city, wrested control from the Arabs occupying that particular city. Many cities in the new country of Israel had large, or even majority, populations of Arabs. The Arabs fought the new State, expecting us to be overwhelmed, pushed into the Mediterranean and oblivion. They wanted to stay for that time when Israel, forced into the sea, became Palestine once again.

The Arab leaders actually helped us in a way. They told their people to leave, make it easier for the soldiers to fight, and once Israel suffered defeat, the civilians could return to their homes. That wound up making our job easier because we didn't have to worry as much about harming the civilians in the population. Most of us had seen too many innocent people die to want to cause the deaths of anyone we didn't have to. That's a big reason why we never killed a prisoner of war. Nothing would have made us happier than not to have to fight and not to kill anyone.

The first city we had to control was Jaffa. Situated close enough to Tel Aviv to shoot from the safety of Jaffa, we had to control it to ensure the safety of Tel Aviv. When my sisters lived in Tel Aviv, Chana worried all the time about her children. Bullets from Jaffa fell into her yard, pocked the side of her house. She often called her children indoors, allowing them to remain outside being potentially fatal. Chana soon moved with her family to Bnei

Barak, a city where her children could play outside without fear of being hit by bullets falling from the sky.

Little by little, city by city, we slowly gained control over our own country. We fought Egyptians, Syrians, Jordanians. For some reason, the Lebanese showed restraint towards us. Some of the Arabs used German officers in the field, hoping the Germans' military expertise would give them a tactical advantage. Unfortunately for them, it didn't work out exactly the way they had hoped.

I remember once in the Negev when the fighting went on into the middle of the night. I could hear the German officers shouting orders to their Arab soldiers. Along with the majority of Israeli soldiers, I understood every word that was said. The same could not be said of the Arabs, who appeared not to speak German at all while the German spoke little or none of the Arab languages. The Germans became increasingly angry as the Arabs ignored their orders. For their part, the Arabs became equally angry at their German officers.

In addition to the German officers, some of the Arab units even had British officers in charge. It was one of the units commanded by British soldiers that we managed to capture without having to fire a single bullet. It's a shame the entire war couldn't have been fought like that, but at least it happened on some occasions.

The unit had entrenched themselves, mining the area around them for a mile or so. At night, we went and pulled out the mines. The work was very dangerous, but worth it in the long run. Little by little, we approached them. They had gotten confident, certain we could not reach their location. Finally, one night we managed to get close enough to overtake them. We encircled them, our bayonets all pointing at the soldiers thinking themselves safe in the trench. Everyone surrendered, but the British officers thought we intended to kill them on the spot.

"I want to speak to your officer," one of them said. Naturally, I didn't understand what he was asking since I didn't speak English then. One of the other soldiers in our unit spoke enough English to tell us what our prisoner was requesting. It certainly seemed a reasonable enough request, so we called the officer in charge of our unit over to talk to the prisoner.

We brought our commander to the British officer, the soldier who spoke some English making the introductions, though our commander spoke pretty good English himself. "Here is our officer," we said to the Englishman.

He didn't believe us. Maybe he thought officers had to be tall and handsome, like in the movies. Maybe he thought we were trying to pull something over on him, presenting the stocky, weathered man as an officer. "He's not an officer," the Briton told us, obviously forgetting just who was the prisoner. "I want to talk with your officer."

By then, our commander had about enough of the game. He said, in his best English, slowly so the Briton could follow what he said, "I *am* the commander. You had better talk with me, or you're going to be in big trouble."

Finally realizing that he was, in fact, talking to the man in charge, he began explaining himself. He told us he was a professional military man, fighting for whatever army was willing to pay him. He told us that he last fought against the Nazis. We treated him the same as we treated any prisoner of war. The fact that he fought the Nazis didn't impress us. After all, the British liberated us from a death camp only to hand our weapons over to the Arabs so they could more easily kill us.

I soon received a promotion to sergeant, putting me in command of about fifteen to twenty soldiers. Not only was I their commander, but I also felt responsible for them, to make sure they went home to their loved ones and families. When I lost someone in my command, I felt as though I had failed in some way—not only failed the Israeli Army and Israel as a whole because we had very few people and soldiers could not easily be replaced, but also failed that person's family. At the time, the entire population of Israel was only about 600,000 people—including children, older people, those who could not fight. Each and every person was valuable and irreplaceable.

With relatively few soldiers, we sometimes relied on the assistance of civilians. Such was the case when we captured an Arab base, giving us trucks, jeeps, all kinds of weapons and the responsibility for about six hundred prisoners. The Egyptians had made themselves a nice little stronghold in what was Israeli territory. We needed to take their base in order to secure the area.

The base was located on a mountain, providing the Egyptians with a strategic military advantage over us. They had a real sense of security there, which was in large part justified. We couldn't get up the mountain in any normal maneuver without our attack being seen and repulsed. Knowing we had no planes, they had no concern about an air attack. The only possible approach was through the desert, which was almost impossible in the best of conditions because the trucks and jeeps quickly mired in the soft sand and any attempt to build a road was quickly negated by the constantly blowing sand. The Egyptians remained in the base, confident of our inability to breach their defenses, both natural and man-made.

What we needed was an army to build and clear a road. What we had was a civilian population, deeply dedicated to the survival of Israel. Early on a Friday night, as people went home to Tel Aviv after work, we stopped all traffic on the road. Most people traveled by bus, so we wound up with a large contingent, ready to help however they could.

We spread a type of wire mesh on the ground in front of the trucks and jeeps, giving them something to drive on. The idea was similar to wearing snowshoes, but for use in the sand. Our problems came with the constant onslaught of the sand covering the mesh, rendering it virtually useless for our purposes. The civilians lined up into two rows, one on either side of our military convoy. Using brooms, they swept away the sand from our makeshift road. Our jeeps and trucks followed directly behind, leaving no chance for the sand to reclaim that small swath of desert.

In one night, we managed to approach close enough to give ourselves a decisive, tactical advantage. We dug in for several hours, allowing ourselves a rest before the actual campaign later that night.

Everything went according to plan. The Egyptians had no idea we found a way to get so close. That night, we moved in, catching them completely by surprise. We caught most of the soldiers sound asleep, while some others finished a leisurely dinner. The biggest coup was the capture of several high officers, even a general or two.

We caught the officers in the middle of a party as they entertained several young women. Many of the Egyptians ran into the mountains; but we followed, capturing them easily in the jeeps. They didn't fight back too much, because most of the ones who ran didn't bother taking the time to grab their rifle. Some didn't even take the time to get dressed, and they ran in their underwear.

Under the circumstances, we had enough forces to surround them and capture everything they had. It was a small, but important, victory in terms both of capturing the officers and commandeering the equipment.

One of the worst incidents was when three of my people and I were heading toward the city of Beersheba, after being on patrol to rejoin the rest of our unit at the temporary base there. We had captured the city only about two days earlier, so at least we knew it was basically friendly territory. I was driving two young men in the back, carrying machine guns and a young woman, in front with me, who was our radio operator. I was driving quickly because the Arabs, specifically Egyptians in this area, knew we had no air force to speak of and felt confident that they could fly in, shooting at anything that moved. A couple of miles out from the city on the main road, the jeep hit a land mine.

One moment, I was driving along, thinking simply of being within a few minutes of Beersheba; and the next moment, the jeep, myself, and my three passengers were in the air, all thrown up and to the side of the road from the force of the explosion. While the others landed near or even under the jeep, as it and they hit the ground, I was thrown clear of it, landing several feet away from the wreckage. That may have saved my life at that moment.

My guess is that the Egyptians laid down the mine at some point since our taking the city, because almost from the moment we hit the ground, their planes came close in, strafing the area, hoping to finish the job the mine had started. Within a couple of minutes, the planes left the area, satisfied they had accomplished their task.

I felt warm, slightly sticky, blood pouring down my face. Knowing, from experience back to my childhood, how much even a superficial head wound bleeds, I wasn't certain for a moment how badly I was injured. As soon as the pain began, I knew it was far worse than I had feared. Touching the top of my head, I could feel blood coming, not from one small wound, but from most of the top and back. My arms, also bleeding, felt as though they had been burned. The pain from my legs, though, kept me from thinking too much about the head wounds.

I tried to stand, then to simply bend my legs to reach a sitting position. Nothing worked. My legs would not respond to any instruction. While my arms hurt, they at least did as I wanted. I pulled myself to the jeep, only to find that the three people under my command had all been killed. Whether by the explosion, the landing or strafing from the planes, I had no idea.

I had already lost a lot of blood, and the flow hadn't stopped or even slowed down substantially. I ripped my clothing into strips of cloth and wrapped them around my head as best I could, hoping it would help. Staying at the jeep would only ensure my own death in a short while. I managed to find my rifle near the mangled remains of people and machine. Though the main road was close by, it appeared almost impossibly far away. No matter the distance to the road, whether actual feet or perceived miles, I knew I had to get there. Still not able to move my legs, I had to find another way to accomplish the task.

Taking my rifle and holding it above my head, I slowly inched my way to the main road, pulling myself forward by stretching out my elbows, firmly planting them on the ground, and dragging the rest of my body up to the new point. I then repeated the process, the strength to continue coming from the fact that I had no other choice.

When I finally reached the road, I felt I had accomplished a task greater than reaching the shores of Palestine. The first thing I did was to put the rifle under my head and rest. I had no strength to do much of anything else. After that, I waited. I didn't think about it, but somehow I knew the wait would not be long. Either I would die shortly, or someone would find me. I had lost too much blood for there to be a third alternative.

I was happy to find the latter option was the one that happened. I was lucky that, after lying by the side of the road for only a few minutes, an Israeli military pickup came along the road. I raised my rifle into the air as high as I could and waved it slowly, trying to catch the attention of someone in the truck.

Again, luck was with me as the driver saw me and pulled up next to me. Two of the soldiers got out and helped lift me into the back of the pickup. They removed the sticky, drenched strips of cloth from around my head to see how badly I was injured and to replace them with clean bandages.

They wasted no more time trying to administer first aid in the field. The moment I was in the truck, the driver was on his way to Beersheba, seemingly determined to travel the few miles in a record breaking time. The clean bandages they wrapped around my head turned red within a few moments. I no longer felt the bumps in the road as I passed in and out of consciousness.

In Beersheba, they gave me what aid and medical attention they could, but it was far from sufficient. At least, they managed to stop the bleeding. That's when they brought in one of the few planes in the Israeli Air Force. The medics in Beersheba stabilized me, as well as they could, and loaded me into the plane, making me as comfortable as possible on one of the four beds.

They took me to a camp near Tel Aviv, which had a barracks that we used as a hospital. The doctors there continued the work done in Beersheba, to the count of hundreds of stitches, and required me to rest in the hospital for many weeks.

During that time, I had two concerns. The first was for my unit and the army in general. I knew the value of each individual serving to fight for the very existence of Israel. I felt I needed to be there, be part of it, helping in any way I could, not sleeping in a comfortable hospital.

The other thing I thought of was the effect that hearing about my injuries would have on my sisters. I decided not to tell them, even though they lived in Bnei Barak at the time, about five miles from the hospital. I didn't want them to worry about me, so I went to great lengths to make certain they thought I was still with my unit.

I wrote to them a couple of times a week, asking about the children, their health, work, and so on. I told them how much I missed them and recounted stories about some of the fighting we engaged in. Some of the stories I made up, but most of it was from what I heard was happening in different skirmishes and some was from what happened in prior fights. I then sent the letters to my unit, which they then mailed for me, making it appear I was with them in the field instead of lying in the hospital.

After being in the hospital for a couple of weeks, I felt better, but still wasn't fully recovered. By then, I thought that I knew better than the doctors how well I was doing, so I left the hospital. I wanted to get back to my unit, give the support of one more soldier to an army where every soldier played a vital role and every loss hurt us. I acted stupidly, without much thought. Severe head wounds have a way of making it difficult to think clearly for quite some time.

I didn't have my uniform, or even civilian clothes, so I wore my pajamas as I climbed over the fence of the hospital grounds and started walking towards Beersheba to rejoin my unit. Within a short time, an MP caught up to me, stopped me, and took me back to the hospital.

The doctor listened patiently as I explained how much I wanted to return to my command. He nodded his head sympathetically as I talked, waiting calmly until I ran out of things to say. He then made a deal with me. I had to promise to stay in the hospital until the doctor, not me, decided I had recovered from the explosion. Then, they would make certain that I returned to my unit. One concession was to release me a week early so that I could visit my sisters.

With only a slight amendment, I accepted the deal. After my release, I went to visit my sisters. I told them we had enough control over Beersheba to allow me to stay with them for close to a week. We all enjoyed the days I spent with them, talking over past times, planning for future times, playing with the children who I felt represented the future of Israel and the Jewish people. They told me it meant a lot for them to receive my letters. I promised that I would continue writing to them.

During my entire visit, I wore a ski cap in order to cover up the injury to my head. I know I didn't fool them, that they knew I had been injured, but no one said anything about it.

When the week ended, I went back to my unit, still based in Beersheba. I felt I had missed so much because controlling the city had not been easy. The men and women who remained there, fighting for the life of a city, were strong, dedicated people. I felt glad to be able to rejoin them, raising their number by one.

Through the efforts of those soldiers, they helped build Beersheba into an Israeli city. Soon after my arrival, we felt it safe and secure enough to leave, continuing our way to secure more of our own country for our people so that no one should live in fear in their own homes in their own city.

In the area of Ujahk Hafeer, we ran into trouble, surrounded by the Egyptian army. We had no way out, no access to help, no food or water. The Egyptians knew they had us and simply decided to wait us out. As the hours and days passed, we rationed everything we had.

We conserved our water only for drinking. No one washed or shaved. It wasn't very long before we ran out food. With our situation growing more and more desperate, we tried to find some way to at least get food, if not military support. Some of the soldiers under my command and I came up with a plan which I took to the senior officer. Generally, we were encouraged to take initiative, think and act for ourselves. We didn't have the luxury of waiting for detailed orders to arrive from above to begin a plan of action. Since our plan entailed great risk, we felt it necessary to, at least, let our higher officers have the chance to comment on it.

The general agreement was that, while our plan was very risky, it also had the possibility of working. We planned on relying on the Egyptians' own sense of security. Part of that came from their assumption that we had no airplanes, except for the little plane we used for medical emergencies. They knew they had nothing to fear from overhead attack or any concern about being discovered by aerial reconnaissance. Because of that, they didn't bother trying to hide themselves. Unlike our efforts to remain hidden, especially at night by keeping lights to a minimum or off completely, the Egyptians traveled openly, headlights on at night, not concerned that we might see them. They knew that if we did see them and wanted to mount an attack, it would necessarily be a ground action; and they would learn of our approach long before we could inflict any damage. Unfortunately, in large part, they were correct.

Like the strategy I used in Dora when I hid the pants I stole by draping them over my arm in plain sight of the Nazis, I intended to travel openly—in plain sight of the Egyptians. We left at night, taking one of our large, enclosed trucks, myself driving, a soldier sitting next to me in the cab, and two soldiers with machine guns in the back. I turned the headlights on and drove, as though I had every right to be there. I didn't try driving slowly or cautiously. That's not how the Egyptians drove, so neither would I. Our truck was British made, like many of the same kinds of trucks used by the Egyptians. I wouldn't be surprised if they drove many of the same models as we did.

As I hoped, they thought my truck was one of theirs. No one stopped me or questioned me. We drove across the Egyptian lines and on into Israeli-held territory. Close to midnight, we came to a house, the first one we saw in what we felt was a safe area. We stopped the truck, got out, and knocked on the door. It was a Jewish house and the woman who answered the door was very scared as she looked at us, immediately taking us for Arabs.

I tried to put her at ease, telling her in Hebrew our story. I'll never forget, it was a Friday night, Shabbat, the day of rest.

"All we want is to wash up a little," I explained to her. "Maybe have a little something to eat. We're very hungry."

Seeing the four of us standing at her door, looking dirty and probably pathetic, she did the only decent thing. She invited us in, made certain we each had a good shower, and made us dinner. She gave us chulint, which I hadn't had since living in Budapest. I ate everything she gave me. I was hungry enough that I would have eaten almost anything on my plate, but the *chulint* she served was very good, which made it enjoyable far beyond the fact that it was warm and filling. The other three ate with every bit as much enthusiasm as I did. For her part, our hostess was glad to be able to help the Israeli Army, even if was just to provide a shower and hot meal for four soldiers.

Early on Saturday morning, we left, fed and washed, and continued on our way to our main base. Naturally, they were surprised to see us, having some idea of the situation at Ujahk Hafeer. We explained how we managed to get through the Egyptian lines and recited a list of the supplies we needed.

We loaded our truck with all the food, water, and other supplies we needed. As soon as we had everything on the truck, we headed back the way we came. Again, we waited for night before crossing the Egyptian lines. With headlights on, we drove right through with not a single challenge or problem.

Supplied with food and water, we waited until reinforcements could arrive. The Egyptians expected us to be weak, or even dead, from thirst and starvation. They did *not* expect us to be healthy, rested, and fighting back. With the help from those joining us, we eventually won that particular engagement.

Many times, a soldier was the only surviving member of a once-large family, the rest killed by the Nazis. Men and women like that had a need to make a home, a strong nation which no one and nothing could deny them. I remember one such incident because I had met the fellow on the way to Auschwitz. How he managed to survive, I don't know. We didn't talk too much about those days. I know he came from a family of six, and only he survived. He was in my group in the army.

One night, our unit was supposed to join a battle, providing backup for another unit. This man was sick with a fever. Our officer told him he could stay and rest. He was sick, and a sick soldier was not as effective as a healthy one.

He shook his head. "I'm not staying," he said. "You need every man there."

The officer allowed him to go, feeling it best not to argue, destroying morale for him and possibly everyone else as well. The poor man got killed that night. He was the last of his family. There were many stories like that—far too many.

When the war officially ended with a cease-fire, I was discharged from the army, anxious to begin making a life for myself. The first job I had was as one of the organizers of a moshav. A moshav is a farming community where each individual works toward the common goal of making the community a success. The Israeli government was interested in seeing the community become successful, so we received not only a loan, but farm animals and equipment to help us start off.

While many of us worked very hard for this goal, some of the others felt that with other people working so hard, they didn't have to work at all. No amount of reasoning or explanation was able to make a difference. It didn't take long before I saw the community have difficulty in making payments on the loans we had. None of that was what I had in mind when I thought of building a new life for myself. I never minded hard work, but I was not interested in working so hard to accomplish nothing.

I scraped together everything I could from the moshav in order to pay back the loan to the government. At that point, I felt I had done everything I could to help the moshav as much as I could. I left the community to find its own way. It may still be there. I never looked back or tried to find out.

From the moshav, I got a job working for Shell Oil, driving a tanker. I made deliveries of gasoline, crude oil, and kerosene to farmers and kibbutzim throughout Israel. They paid well because the job was dangerous. Even though we had made the area within Israel fairly safe, the potential always existed for attack. Plenty of Arabs, from a variety of nations, still lived in and around Israel. Few of them felt very friendly towards us.

In the cab beside me, I always carried a rifle and several hand grenades. Thankfully, I never had to use them; but I felt more confident with them by my side. When I wasn't delivering fuel, I managed a Shell station, located near the moshav Bnei Rem. The moshav was home to about 200 families.

The community was quite Orthodox, and I became the one to help out whenever they needed something on Shabbat. Despite my early schooling and upbringing in Rozavlea, I did not return to Orthodox observance.

For some reason, it seemed that the women of that community tended to choose Friday night to give birth. The farmers didn't have reliable transportation to get to the hospital, and many of them might not have driven on Shabbat even if they did. They came to my station asking for help. I used the large tanker like an ambulance and was able to make certain the women got to the hospital safely in time to give birth. I also had a motorcycle which I used to run errands in emergencies for them.

The community was close to the border with Jordan. The farmers had a lot of problems with Jordanians coming across the border at night, stealing cows from the barns and being safely back in Jordan by the time the farmers discovered the theft. They solved the problem by creating a large, community barn, where each farmer housed his cows at night, rather than each family's individual barn. Armed guards made certain the cows remained in the barn.

My uncle Mordechai was living in that community at the time. After our liberation from Bergen-Belsen, he returned to Rozavlea. He remarried and, in a few years, came to Israel with his wife. He met his sons Abraham, Hertz, and Hanon here. He and his new wife began a family of their own. Uncle Mordechai always wanted to do things on his own, not to have to rely on others. He behaved no differently when the other farmers put their cows together for protection. He didn't want to put his cows in with everyone else's. He felt confident that he could effectively guard his own livestock. In Rumania, before the war, he had his own farm. He felt he knew what to do. He tied up his cows underneath his bedroom window so that if anything happened, he would be certain to hear it and stop any theft before it occurred.

One Friday night, he found out that the Jordanians were smarter than he was. In the middle of the night, they unchained his cows and by the time he discovered it, neither the Arabs nor the cows were within sight.

Naturally, he came to me, wanting me to go to the police. On my motorcycle, I could get there faster than anyone else. The station was located about five miles from the community, so I didn't expect the trip to take very long. I started for the police station, perhaps a little faster than I should have in the middle of the night, but I felt I knew the road well and time was of the essence if we had any chance to catch the Jordanians before they reached the border.

I had only covered about two miles or so when I had a problem with my headlight going out which I tried to fix while I was driving. Not only did I not fix the headlight, but my rifle became caught in the spokes of the wheel, causing me to lose control of the motorcycle, going off the road and down a big ditch. I rolled with the motorcycle three or four times before coming to a stop.

For several moments, I could not move, too stunned to do anything but lie still. I slowly began to realize how badly I was hurt. My entire left side, especially my arm and shoulder, throbbed with pain. I had no choice but to continue the rest of the way. I didn't want to just leave my motorcycle for fear someone might steal it, so I pushed it along as I walked, one hand balancing the bike, my rifle strapped across my back while I held the other hand close to me, trying to at least slow some of the bleeding.

When I finally arrived at the police station, I told them about my uncle and his cows. A couple of the officers went with their jeep to try to find the cows and the Jordanians, but I'm sure they had all crossed the border by then. A couple of other officers took me to the hospital. I wound up in a cast covering my chest and left arm up to my shoulder.

I had dislocated the shoulder, causing it to jut up two or three inches from where it should have been. I was actually surprised how painful something like that could be. After about five weeks, they removed the cast; but I still couldn't move my arm because doing so caused intense pain. It took several months of patient work until I had full use of my arm again.

One night when I was delivering drums of fuel, the axle of the truck broke, due, in part, to my overloading the truck in the hopes of having to make one less trip. Unfortunately, the only town nearby was an Arab town, where I did not feel safe going to ask for help. I got out of the cab and hid in the bushes for the remainder of the night.

Early in the morning, some Israeli trucks came by. I flagged them down, explained what happened, and asked them to relay a message for me. That was the only way anyone knew the truck broke down.

Soon after that, I quit that job, feeling it was far too dangerous for a civilian who wanted nothing more than to start building a life for himself. I became increasingly restless. From the time I was imprisoned on Cyprus, I had been in touch with two of my mother's brothers, Joe living in New Jersey and Lou in New York. I began to seriously consider seeing what hard work could accomplish in the United States. We heard stories, all the time, about how easy it was to earn a living with a little hard work. Hard work never bothered me, especially if I could see I was accomplishing something.

I really believed that I would be gone for a relatively short time and return to Israel. That was the plan I set for myself and explained to my sisters Chana and Frieda. They supported my decision, though it was difficult to think of breaking up our family. By this time, Frieda was married to Benjamin, an accountant. They eventually would have two children, Shmulik and Ruchie, and five grandchildren.

Getting immigration papers to the United States, though, was not as easy a matter as I had thought. Through a relative in Canada, I was able to obtain immigration papers to that country. My plans changed slightly to accommodate that. With the proper paperwork finally in hand, I set out to join my relative in Montreal, Canada.

I had arrived in Palestine, fought to help create a Jewish State, worked to build communities on the rich soil. I left Israel for what I thought was a temporary trip to the New World.

I went to Montreal, putting aside not only physical but emotional ties, leaving behind everything of my old life in Europe and Israel. I was in a New World, ready to begin building a new life for myself.

In 1952, I arrived in Canada.

EPILOGUE

I arrived in Canada with my cousin Moishe, neither of us able to speak English or French, the two predominant languages of the country. We went into business together as peddlers, buying clothing and traveling around to farmers in the area to sell what we had.

From the time I arrived in Canada, I was in touch with Uncle Lou and Aunt Esther in New York. After almost eight months, I finally got the necessary papers to immigrate to the United States. I had picked up a little English, but not enough to really get by. I went to New York to live with Uncle Lou and Aunt Esther. Moishe remained in Canada, where he became a successful contractor.

Uncle Lou and Aunt Esther's children had already left home to establish their own lives, so I became like a son to them. From my earliest memories, the generosity and kindness of my uncle and aunt made an impression upon me. I began to feel that I might finally be able to repay them in some small way. Uncle Lou owned a bakery, and I helped him in the store. I got up each morning at four to prepare the breads for sale when we opened later in the morning. I did whatever I could to help him, learned as much as I could about the bakery line so that I might be useful to him.

To earn a little extra money for myself, I taught Hebrew to the schoolchildren from a local Synagogue. At the same time, I tried my best to pick up the English language. It took me the better part of a year to learn the language well enough to be able to carry on a conversation.

Try as I might, I doubt I will ever be able to repay their kindness. Through them, I found memories of my past, something I thought had been lost forever. They had many pictures of my family which my mother had sent over the years. Because of them, I have pictures of my parents as well as my sisters and other family members who died before or during the war.

I lived with them for close to three years before becoming very tired of the snow. I could speak English fairly well and wanted to see what other opportunities the country had to offer. I had heard from several people in New York that California was a good place to live. I had some cousins living in the Los Angeles area and I came to visit them.

At about that time, I met a man who wanted to go into the restaurant business. It wasn't something I had ever thought about, but it sounded like something that would show results if we worked hard. With the help of a broker, we found a good location and built it into a successful business.

During the time I owned that location, I made a living by also buying other run-down locations, building them up and then selling them. After more than fifteen years of doing business like that, I was tired. I worked seven days a week and had no time for what was really important to me.

Soon after I moved to Los Angeles, I met a wonderful young woman through my aunt Tillie. We started dating and within a few months, I knew this was the woman I wanted to marry. It was my good luck that she felt the same way. We got married and soon started a family of our own, a son and two daughters.

Working the hours I did left me little time to be with my wife and children. I usually left the house before the children woke up and returned at night after they had gone to sleep. I missed being a bigger part of their lives when they were young, but I wanted to make certain they would not have to worry about food or a place to live. I had worked hard all my life and probably didn't know any other way to do things.

I became involved with other businesses throughout the ensuing years, but allowed myself more time with my family. Now, my children are grown up themselves, with children of their own.

I'm very fortunate that they all live close by, giving me the opportunity to see them and the six grandchildren often.

For more than fifty years, I dealt with the time I spent under the Nazis by consciously putting it all to the back of my mind, not thinking about it, but concentrating on the present while trying to build a future

I never again lived in Israel, though over the years I have returned to visit my sisters and their growing families. I am continually impressed by the beauty of the land and the industry of the people.

It's a tradition of East European Jews to name children after a family member who has passed away. It's our way to honor those who are no longer with us. Many members of the new generations of my family carry names inspired by the family I lost. I can look at the child I named for my little sister Gitel Marim or my mother or my father, and see their spirits and memories continue.

May those who are no longer with me rest in peace and may the children carry with them an abiding hope for the future.